NETTING CITIZENS

PUBLIC CONCERNS

Netting Citizens is the third volume in a new series on Public Concerns being published jointly by the University of Edinburgh's Centre for Theology and Public Issues, and Saint Andrew Press. The aim of the Centre and of this series is to offer informed studies of contemporary issues where a theological perspective can make a constructive contribution to matters of public concern. Books in the series are written for church members and concerned citizens, practitioners and policy-makers, and students and teachers in secondary and higher education, as well as academic researchers.

WILLIAM STORRAR and ALISON ELLIOT, *Series Editors*

God in Society: doing social theology in Scotland today
edited by William Storrar and Peter Donald (2003)

Honouring Children: the human rights of the child in Christian perspective
Kathleen Marshall and Paul Parvis (2004)

NETTING CITIZENS

Exploring citizenship in the internet age

Edited by
JOHNSTON R. McKAY

THE BAIRD TRUST

CENTRE FOR THEOLOGY AND PUBLIC ISSUES

NEW COLLEGE

THE UNIVERSITY OF EDINBURGH

SAINT ANDREW PRESS

First published in 2004 by
SAINT ANDREW PRESS
121 George Street
Edinburgh EH2 4YN

Copyright © the Contributors, 2004

ISBN 0 7152 0821 7

British Library Cataloguing in Publication Data
A catalogue record for this book is available from the British Library

Typeset in Sabon by Waverley Typesetters, Galashiels
Printed and bound in the United Kingdom by Bell & Bain Ltd, Glasgow

Contents

Introduction

This book is the result of a conference on 'Netting Citizens' held by the Centre for Theology and Public Issues at the Riccarton campus of Heriot Watt University in November 2001. The idea of the conference arose when the Baird Trust, conscious that the format of the lecture no longer occupied the place it once did, began looking for alternatives to the Baird Lectures which were founded in 1872–3 by James Baird of Auchmedden and Cambusdoon. The lectures were to be given annually by a minister of the Church of Scotland or any other Scottish Presbyterian church on a theme drawn from a broad range of theological and ecclesiastical subjects.

In the course of the Baird Trustees' discussions the point was made that the new Information Communication Technologies (ICTs) were the modern equivalent of the lecture of James Baird's day. In conversation with Professor William Storrar and Dr Alison Elliot of the Centre for Theology and Public Issues at New College in Edinburgh, the conference began to emerge as a way not only of pursuing the Centre's chosen theme of Citizenship but also of enabling the Baird Trust to discover more about the world of ICTs and how, in contemporary fulfilment of James Baird's intention, the Trust might become involved with them. Professor Storrar agreed to chair the conference and, as the statutory Church of Scotland minister on the Baird Trust, I agreed to edit a volume of essays or papers, some of which were delivered at the conference and others that were sought following discussions at it. One of the participants in the conference, and a contributor to this volume, Professor Keith Culver wrote that nowhere had he

> encountered so diverse a group of conference participants as I found at 'Netting Citizens' ... I must admit that I was pleasantly surprised to find under sponsorship of a theological centre the freest discussion I have encountered in examination of e-democracy and the place of cultural difference and other grounds of disagreement in democratic societies.

The Baird Trust's funding for the Conference allowed Neal Ascherson to spend time at New College researching the issues which he dealt with in his keynote address to the Conference. His contribution, along with the paper by Barry Wellman (who spoke at the conference on a different theme) and Bernie Hogan, form the first section of this book.

The second section of the book consists of contributions from Anna Malina and Keith Culver, sought as a result of further issues which the Conference indicated should be addressed

The final section of the book takes the issues raised and places them in a theological, religious or ecclesiastical context. Elaine Graham did this very clearly in the paper which she read at Conference and which is reproduced here. The papers by Heidi Campbell, Alison Elliot, John Flint and Ade Kearns, Brian McGlynn, Marjory MacLean, Andrew Morton and myself all stem from the Conference, though Heidi Campbell and Ade Kearns gave shorter presentations during one of the sessions.

This volume would not have reached publication had I not received the constant help, encouragement and advice of two people. One is Dr Alison Elliot, who organised and participated in the conference and whose election as Moderator of the Church of Scotland's General Assembly in the year of publication not only marks a historic moment for the Kirk but also gives a sense of unalloyed delight to her admiring friends; the other is my wife Evelyn whose computing skills gave the rather disparate form of the various contributions a common shape for the publisher, and whose understanding affection means more to me than it would be appropriate to record.

JOHNSTON R. MCKAY

Contributors

NEAL ASCHERSON is a historian, journalist and political commentator.

HEIDI CAMPBELL is Institute for Advanced Studies in the Humanities Research Fellow at the University of Edinburgh.

KEITH CULVER is Associate Professor of Philosophy and Director of the Centre for Social Innovation in the University of New Brunswick.

ALISON ELLIOT is Moderator of the General Assembly of the Church of Scotland and Associate Director of the Centre for Theology and Public Issues.

JOHN FLINT is a lecturer in the Department of Urban Studies in the University of Glasgow. He led a major research project for the Church of Scotland's Board of Social Responsiblity exploring the role of congregation in Scottish communities.

ELAINE GRAHAM is Samuel Ferguson Professor of Social & Pastoral Theology at the University of Manchester.

BERNIE HOGAN is a doctoral student in the Department of Sociology in the University of Toronto, whose research focuses on how people manage their social support networks through a variety of media including telephone and internet.

ADE KEARNS is Head of the Department of Urban Studies at the University of Glasgow.

ANNA MALINA is a research consultant working independently and collaboratively in the field of ICT and society.

BRIAN MCGLYNN is Director in the Department of Communication of the Church of Scotland.

MARJORY MACLEAN is Depute Clerk to the General Assembly of the Church of Scotland and Secretary to its Email Project Group.

JOHNSTON MCKAY is a former Editor of Religious Broadcasting at BBC Scotland, a writer and broadcaster and in 2004 Clerk to the Presbytery of Ardrossan.

ANDREW MORTON was Associate Director of the Centre for Theology and Public Issues, 1994–2001.

BARRY WELLMAN is Professor of Sociology and NetLab Director at the Centre for Urban and Community Studies at the University of Toronto.

Designing Virtual Citizens

Neal Ascherson

There is a widespread assumption that public participation in social and political affairs is declining, at least in the Western world. This decline is declared to be evident in two main areas. The first is the arena of democratic politics. The second covers the myriad unofficial associations which go to make up civic networks, sometimes defined as 'civil society' and often stated to be the locus of so-called 'social capital' – a society's resources of capacity for solidarity, joint action and mutual support. Two factors – either or both – are usually blamed for this decline. One is the general (but not universal) increase in personal wealth and resources. The other is the growing 'privatisation' of personal life – not least through new techniques of communication – which is supposed to be rendering traditional face-to-face association superfluous.

There are laments for the alleged passing-away of the 'active citizen'. He or she is defined as somebody prepared as a matter. of course to engage with others in public or social activity, intended to defend a community, to fight against perceived injustice or to bring about reform and change. This engagement can happen at any level from that of a housing scheme to the global environment.

The evidence for this decline is not straightforward. There are many cases where civic networks are growing, as in some forms of volunteering or single-issue campaigning, and where new frameworks for physical association are being created. But there can be no doubt that in one area – public readiness to take part in the processes of representative democracy – commitment is dropping away, especially in western Europe and north America. Stephen Coleman has written of a threatening 'crisis of democratic legitimacy and accountability', suggesting that

> there is a pervasive contemporary estrangement between representatives and those they represent, manifested in almost every western country by falling voter turn-out; lower levels of public participation in civic life; public cynicism towards political institutions and parties; and a collapse in once-strong political loyalties and attachments. (Coleman and Gøtze 2001: 3)

The figures bear him out. Turn-out in US Presidential elections fell from 62.8 per cent in 1960 to 51 per cent in 2000. Only 59 per cent of the voters took part in the UK General Election of 2001; for the first time, the 'abstainers' front' became the largest single party in the land. In Scotland, 58 per cent of the electorate voted in the first elections to the Scottish Parliament in May 1999, and the figure in the May 2003 election was 49.4 per cent. Participation in local and council elections in the UK, never high, is dwindling almost into insignificance. In England, figures in October 2002 for turn-out in the direct election of town mayors – an innovation designed to revive public interest and awareness – fell as low as 18 per cent, in one case.

In the last few decades, the network of computer-driven electronic communication has spread across the world with explosive speed. Mobile phone technology is rapidly converging with that of other electronic and computerised media, and will probably be fully integrated within a decade.

Two examples may illustrate the pace of this development. By the spring of 1999, nearly one-third of the adult population of the United States had used the Internet, a proportion increasing at the rate of ten million users every six months. It was reckoned then that the Internet would take only seven years to increase its penetration of the potential market from 1 per cent to 75 per cent. A report by the US Department of Commerce in October 2000 estimated that over 50 per cent of households contained at least one computer, and that over 50 per cent would be accessing the Internet by the summer of 2001.

The picture in Scotland shows very different dimensions but a similar dynamic. A report by the Scottish Consumer Council (SCC) published in January 2002 (*Reaching Out*) suggested that 24 per cent of homes had access to the Internet (the UK average was 37 per cent). The Scottish Executive countered that the SCC figures were obsolete, and that by February 2002 the Scottish on-line percentage was already 30 per cent.

More significantly, the Scottish Executive – in harmony with UK government policy – announced in 2001 that it intended to achieve 'universal access' to the Internet by 2005. Critics pointed out that it was not clear what 'universal access' really meant. The SCC report stated: 'We believe that universal access must mean access in the home', a target highly unlikely to be met in only four years. But an Executive strategy document published in 2001 (*Digital Inclusion: Connecting Scotland's People*) claimed that the figures for on-line households in Scotland were increasing at the rate of 10 per cent a year – a rate comparable to that in the United States.

The arrival of these information and communication technologies (ICTs) provoked apocalyptic claims about their impact and the 'revolution' they were expected to inflict on daily life. But it is worth remembering that we have been here before. Barry Wellman has pointed out that 'large-scale changes associated with the Industrial Revolution' were accompanied by prophecies that they would transform the nature of community. Ever since, and probably long before, 'analysts have kept asking if, in fact, things have fallen apart' (Wellman 1988: 82–3). The telephone, the first device to make possible distant voice-contact in real time, was similarly over-sold and misunderstood.

Alexander Graham Bell himself apparently expected that it would be used as a sort of proto-radio address system, for broadcasting music or speech. Others assumed that the telephone would be primarily reserved for long-range commerce or diplomacy, and that its misuse for private chat should be discouraged. Few people realised that the instrument's function would be overwhelmingly local and personal, as a device to multiply existing human conversation in daily life. As Robert D. Putnam remarked in his celebrated book *Bowling Alone*, the telephone 'somewhat paradoxically ... seems to have had the effect of reinforcing, not transforming or replacing, existing personal networks' (Putnam 2000: 168).

Much the same is proving true about email and the Internet. Spectacular as their possibilities are, their main function so far has been to 'reinforce existing personal networks' of private contact, non-urgent chat and entertainment. In the same way, it might be reasoned that a modern personal computer (PC) is genuinely new only in its chips and circuit boards; functionally, it simply represents the concentration of typewriter, telephone, card index, personal music centre and library into a single tool. But this sort of reductive argument misses the point at which quantitative change becomes qualitative. The reinforcement of existing practices by the new media is so immense and so widespread that all the processes of change already operating in those practices will be thrown into top gear. Reinforcement on this scale inevitably slips over into transformation.

Fifty years ago, as television spread across Europe, there were predictions that habits which involved leaving the home and associating physically with others – for example, political activity, sport, cinema-going, pub drinking – would be destroyed. Some of those habits did lose participants, but none was fatally damaged and all four examples devised ways of exploiting TV for their own benefit and even for recruitment. The spread of the PC and the potential of the Internet at once generated similar speculations. Was there – is there – a connection between the loosening of social and political commitment and the rise of this technology? If so, is that connection causal, and if it is causal, are its results direct or indirect?

Three Views of the Impact of the New Media

The Pessimistic Approach

There is a widespread assumption, more prevalent in the general public than among academics, that on balance the new media function as agents of social disintegration. This view concentrates on the effects of Internet access in the home.

It is argued that home Internet users are encouraged to abandon the public sphere and withdraw into a 'nerdish' isolation. Central to this view is the thought that individuals can now 'customise' their intake of experience and information from the outside. Traditional life in a community exposes its members to a constant browsing diet of the unexpected and often of the unwelcome, as well as to preferred contacts and experiences. But it is precisely this uncontrollable mix, demanding continuous readjustments of outlook and behaviour, which maintains individuals as social beings involved in the lives and needs of other people, encountered singly or as groups.

Professor Cass Sunstein has written that 'unanticipated encounters, involving topics and points of view that people have not sought out and perhaps find irritating, are central to democracy and even to freedom itself' (Sunstein 2001: 3). The capacity offered by the PC and the Internet to filter out unfamiliar or disturbing information and drastically to narrow the range of contact is therefore held to dilute the content of citizenship or 'social capital'.

Pessimists often assert that human social activity requires actual physical presence in order to function and develop. The phrase 'virtual community' is therefore a contradiction in terms, above all when applied to political activity. Less sweeping criticisms suggest that deliberation between remote ICT users may be impoverished because it lacks some essential dynamics of face-to-face discussion. For example, the recent study *What Sort of Scotland Do We Want to Live In?*, produced by the International Teledemocracy Centre at Napier University, strongly favoured the extension of 'e-consultation' in the political process but admitted that 'there is some evidence that reduced social cues (e.g. lack of facial expressions) hinder respect for other contributors, which in turn impedes useful discussion' (Smith and Macintosh 2001: 5). This point can be expanded. In a group where members are physically present, much of the pressure to move towards agreement or consensus is exerted through adaptation to the views of other group members. This adaptation is substantially prompted by complex emotional cues conveyed by a variety of physical means: by voice, by general appearance and its associations with authority or marginality, by the smile which promises approval or the scowl which registers disapproval or impatience. Time constraint ('We have to be out of this room in ten minutes; we really must agree on our recommendations!') is at once a weakness and a strength of traditional 'committee work'. Lacking these cues and disciplines, 'e-consultation' can be loose and inconclusive.

The Optimistic Approach (Political)

There are common factors between all politically optimistic views of the new media. Most observers would agree that political apathy in Western democracies is alarming in itself. But many would go on to argue that the crisis is not so much public apathy as institutional fossilisation. According to this view, the spread of the PC/Internet culture has accelerated the transformation of the members of contemporary societies into more mature and self-sufficient individuals. Such individuals have outgrown the apparatus of traditional representative democracy and the party system, which they find increasingly unconvincing – and inconvenient. In other words, politicians who complain of a 'disease' in the public's commitment to politics are echoing Brecht's ironic advice to the East German leaders – that they should dismiss the people and elect another one. It is for the institutions to find where the people have gone, and to catch up with them.

What sort of democratic structure is suitable for an on-line citizenry? Ideas range from the utopian to the gradualist or pragmatic. At the extreme, it is possible to argue that ICTs and 'universal access' allow the whole pyramid of representative structures and intermediate bodies to be scrapped. As Renan said about nationhood, democracy would become a 'daily plebiscite' – even an hourly one. Politics would be composed of constant direct choices and instant referenda, as the public – at its PCs or gathered in 'electronic village halls' – issued a ceaseless stream of instructions and amendments to lawmakers.

Representatives, losing most of their decision-making power, would act as little more than executants of the popular will as delivered to them on-line. The central difficulty about 'direct democracy' is that nobody seems to want it. More accurately, most people do not want to fill the horizon of their lives with twenty-four-hour political choice. As Stephen Coleman and John Gøtze memorably wrote in *Bowling Together*, their critical commentary on Robert Putnam's work: 'it is undoubtedly true that most people are not interested in most policy issues. But it is equally true that all are interested in some ...' (Coleman and Gøtze 2001: 15).

In its extreme form, on-line direct democracy relies on something like total participation. Without it, the continuous decisions 'by majority' will only represent the opinions of the few with enough time and commitment to take those decisions: the 'nerdocracy'. There are of course various theoretical ways round this problem. The most convincing is radical anarchism: the break-up of the nation-state into small self-managing units in which continuous and direct participation would become practical. The more localised direct democracy becomes, the less vulnerable it is to manipulation.

But there are much less radical suggestions for updating democracy into the computer age. The Scottish Parliament is clearly in the 'moderate optimism' category. Its vision for the future is not direct democracy, but the use of a panoply of ICT techniques to render existing representative democracy more popular, more comprehensible and far more accessible to citizen participation.

There is an invisible frontier here, beyond which reform becomes revolution and on-line lawmaking by referendum or citizen choice begins to subvert decision by elected representatives. The Scottish Parliament does not want to cross that frontier. None the less, it is extending on-line participation in directions which would ultimately allow people to take a real-time part in – for instance – the drafting and debate of bills.

Such moderate programmes of 'interactive law-making' do not entirely escape the problems of direct democracy. The probability is that only a small minority will take part in such debates – those who are involved in the particular issue, those with access to and mastery of the right digital equipment, those with loud voices and large egos. Inevitably, the views of participants will lack traditional 'democratic accountability'. In the worst case, the 'citizen voice' could become a shared monopoly between highly professional lobby groups and the little corps of individuals with an opinion on everything who dominate the letter-columns in Scottish newspapers. Against that, the hope is that the participating minority will at least revolve, changing composition issue by issue. 'All [people] are interested in some [policy issues], particularly when they affect them or when they have specific expertise or experience' (Coleman and Gøtze 2001: 15). The techniques of 'e-consultation' or 'e-democracy' ought to create an ever-widening reserve of individual citizens or local groups confident that they can participate. At the same, ICTs help to tip the scales in favour of the distant individual and against the practised eloquence of centrally-based pressure groups.

The Optimistic Approach (Social)

Robert Putnam's *Bowling Alone* is often loosely cited as a book about how computers and the Internet have undermined 'social capital' and active citizenship. In fact he makes the opposite point. If there is an electronic device he blames for killing civic engagement, it is television. But, although he is sceptical about 'virtual democracy', Putnam finds no evidence to connect Internet users with a deficit of civic activity. Studies show that they are no more or less 'active' than non-users. Putnam observes:

The absence of any correlation between Internet usage and civic engagement could mean that the Internet attracts reclusive nerds and energises them, but it could also mean that the Net disproportionately attracts civic dynamos and sedates them … (Putnam 2000: 171)

It has been often noticed that the most effective 'virtual' networks tend to exist where there is already a high degree of face-to-face community. The first is complementary to the second. But could the reverse also be true? Can cyber-community actually create or revive face-to-face community? This is a decisive question for the whole optimist/pessimist controversy. Might not the establishment of a vigorous website or email community – especially a locality-based network – help to bring people together into face-to-face communities? Will those who grow to trust other members of a group in cyberspace become more inclined to commit themselves to off-line structures of reciprocity, mutual support and obligation?

There are grounds to think that this can happen. Most of the evidence is anecdotal and scanty. Nevertheless, this assumption is the foundation on which many hopeful strategies are built. In this country, the Church of Scotland is one organisation which encourages its congregations to develop lively websites, partly in the hope that 'virtual' church activity will eventually become physical attendance and membership. How far this encouragement has been fruitful is another matter. A study carried out in 2002 by Dr Heidi Campbell of the Centre for Theology and Public Issues suggested that the use of on-line communication by Church of Scotland congregations, though sometimes vigorous, was rather inward-looking. She commented that

many of the websites did not appear to encourage inter-activity or involvement … Few had links to community-, cultural-, or politics-related sites. Overall most sites

appeared to be hi-tech international bulletins or on-line
store fronts highlighting what was happening inside their
congregations but not encouraging others to look in other
directions or beyond their congregation's programmes. (See
Appendix 2)

The Scottish Parliament is a second example. Using 'e-
technologies' to persuade people to follow and participate
in its proceedings, the Parliament hopes to accumulate a
sort of democratic humus in which traditional political
involvement can revive.

Two final points about technology apply to pessimist
and optimist alike. The first is that 'technology is never
neutral in any process, least of all the democratic process'
(Coleman and Gøtze 2001: 6). The toys of e-democracy
need to be closely inspected to recognise the immanent
ends built into their means, and not everyone would agree
with the words of the Napier electronic consultation study
that 'the web, in itself, is a passive medium' (Smith and
Macintosh 2001: 80).

The second, related point is that the technology's false air
of impartiality deceives its customers into imagining that
they are choosing solutions to problems. But – as Professor
Klaus Lenk of the University of Oldenburg has pointed out
– in reality it is often the problems which are selected by
the solutions. A new technical solution is about to enter the
market; a problem must therefore be found and re-designed
in order to fit it. Lenk's warning, against the whole tide of
the market, is that political and social needs must be defined
first. Only then should a system be designed to meet those
needs (Lenk 2002).

Experiments with 'Governance'

In the broad field of 'governance', three main branches can
be defined.

E-Government

This is the use of the Internet principally as a public notice-board. It means basically one-way communication from authority to subjects, conveying information on a multitude of topics. In themselves, e-government methods are no guarantee of democratic government.

The nature of the Net, however, means that it cannot easily be used as a mere Tannoy system. Public information can of course be sent out by the authorities through email. Most of it, however, has to be sought out by those who wish to look for it on an official website.

The one-way nature of e-government is also qualified by the spread of 'consultation' in many forms. The simplest and most common form is providing answers to questions about government. The questions are lodged on a particular section of the official website and may be answered personally. More complex, but sometimes more manipulative in its effect, is the use of 'consultation' with the public by questionnaires and polling conducted through the website. At its best, this is fulfilling a promise to take the opinions of voters seriously. At its worst, it is opinion testing disguised as public participation.

E-Community

This is the provision by a public authority of a network of Internet access points in public places, through which community members are encouraged to follow their own interests and form lasting links with others. Beyond this 'civil society' or 'social capital' function, e-communities usually have a political dimension, encouraging local inhabitants to explore on-line access to authority and express their opinions on what should or should not be done.

A well-known example of e-community in the United Kingdom is the Sunderland 'Pathfinding Through Partner-ship' scheme. Beginning in 1994 as an electronic notice-board concerned with economic development and local information, it has proliferated strikingly. Among its functions and aims are:

> training citizens to use the equipment and to master the process for expressing opinions on council services, or for contacting councillors or MPs
>
> sponsoring opinion polls on sample clusters of issues (housing strategy, the Sunderland development plan, etc.)
>
> running a 'Community Consultation Framework'
>
> offering e-government services which permit people to access and operate council services on-line (including financial business with the council),
>
> providing at least one PC-equipped 'Community Access Point' in every ward, bringing 100,000 Sunderland people into the 'local democratic process' by 2005, allowing them to follow policy debates and see pre-decision information,
>
> Electronic Village Halls (EVH). The Sunderland definition for an EVH is 'a community facility in which local people can have free access to ICT kit and get help to use it'. In other words, it has two immediate aims: to train and empower the public as New Media users, and to encourage the growth of private on-line common-interest groups (slimming clubs, chess groups, recipe exchanges, short training courses etc.). In practice, 'Community Access Points' will probably be found within Electronic Village Halls. EVHs in Sunderland are basically physical sites: the plan is to have one in all twenty-four wards. But there is access to the EVHs and their groups in pubs, youth clubs and private homes.[1]

E-Democracy

This family of projects shares the aim of using the new media to enhance democracy. By this, its proponents generally mean (a) opening the whole structure of government to much closer scrutiny, and (b) enabling the public to take some active part in shaping policies – something more than the right to be consulted after legislation has taken shape.

The most radical form of e-democracy would be direct democracy (see above) by continuous referendum. Short of that extreme, it is possible to imagine citizens within a framework of representative democracy with a right to initiate legislation or a referendum – as in some countries they do.

No forms of e-democracy, whether already practised or merely projected, are new to the dictionary of political ideas. All have ancestries, in utopian literature, in traditional rights or in the self-management experiments of small communities. But all, without exception, become easier and faster to instal and run with the use of ICTs.

Forms of e-democracy intended to make governance more transparent include websites, webcasting and the use of ICTs to exploit Freedom of Information legislation.

Forms intended to allow wider and more immediate expression of opinion – without conceding control – include all the numerous forms of consultation: 'non-binding' referenda, polling, citizens' juries, focus groups, on-line 'national debates' about particular issues and sites where citizens can make suggestions and exchange views on current policy projects.

Forms which go beyond rights of consultation and offer the public a positive share in decision-making are rarer. One form, obvious enough, is the introduction of distant voting, whether by email or from a mobile phone. Another is the public petition, which lies across the borderline between the mere expression of opinion and the exercise of the wish or right to participate in policy-making. In some parliaments (Westminster, for example), governments have no duty even to read petitions. In others (Scotland and Germany, for example), the public petition has specified rights to be studied, assessed and answered – and may, if the appropriate parliamentary committee agrees, become the embryo of new legislation.

In this category, the most exciting and contentious area is conceding to the public a formal right to participate directly in policy deliberation – for example, the right to take part in the drafting and amending of legislation at the parliamentary committee stage.

Two points should be stressed here. One is that ICTs are peculiarly suited to handle this complex process of 'interactive government'. The second, a local difficulty, is the obstacle presented by the archaic British constitutional doctrine of parliamentary sovereignty (or parliamentary absolutism). The United Kingdom structure has no place for the generally recognised doctrine of popular sovereignty, and in theory cannot share policy-making rights with any extra-parliamentary body. If a referendum is promoted as 'binding', for example, then this is only because the Westminster Parliament in the particular instance has agreed to respect its outcome.

The Scottish Parliament

The Scottish Parliament, suspended or abolished at the 1707 Union, was revived in 1999 as a devolved legislature within the United Kingdom.

This followed twenty-five years of agitation, debate and unsuccessful attempts at legislation. But all through those years there was a consensus among the supporters of devolution that a new Scottish Assembly or Parliament must not be a colonial repetition of the Westminster model. It should be modern, open and democratic, diverging sharply from many of the obsolete institutions and practices of Westminster.

Among the main divergences were the introduction of proportional representation for elections, fixed-term parliaments and a system of powerful parliamentary committees which took over the main business of drafting legislation from plenary sessions. 'Normal' working hours were introduced, and – mostly through new candidate selection procedures in the Scottish Labour Party – 37 per cent of the 129 MSPs elected in May 1999 were women (only the Swedish and Danish parliaments have more). To the Parliament's planners, openness and accessibility were values with supreme priority. Scotland has no written Constitution, but certain texts are treated as unofficial 'constitutional documents'. One is the 1997 Scotland Act. Another text which has acquired formidable constitutional authority in the last few years is the 'Four Principles' of the Consultative Steering Group on the Scottish Parliament (CSG).

Drab as their title was, the CSG were to become the main source of innovation. Set up after Labour's 1997 decision to legislate for a Scottish Parliament, the CSG's task was to plan the Parliament's institutions. Many CSG members had already been involved in the unofficial or semi-official bodies and campaigns which had prepared plans for devolution, such as the Scottish Constitutional Convention, and the CSG borrowed liberally from this pre-existing resource of democratic proposals.

In their report, completed in 1998, the CSG cited Four Principles which had guided their work, and invited the future Parliament to endorse them. They are important enough to be quoted in full:-

The Scottish Parliament should embody and reflect the sharing of power between the people of Scotland, the legislators and the Scottish executive;

The Scottish Executive should be accountable to the Scottish Parliament and the Parliament and Executive should be accountable to the people of Scotland;

The Scottish Parliament should be accessible, open, responsive, and develop procedures which make possible a participative approach to the development, consideration and scrutiny of policy and legislation;

The Scottish Parliament in its operation and its appointments should recognise the need to promote equal opportunities for all.

The language is not inspiring, and the Principles have been shortened in daily use to a few words: 'power-sharing, accountability, accessibility and equal opportunities'. But three striking points stand out in the principles. The first is the nervous, repetitive emphasis on something like a doctrine of popular sovereignty: in this power-sharing, 'the people of Scotland' are to be the senior partners. The second is the instruction to the Parliament to 'develop procedures' which will allow the people of Scotland to participate in the 'development, consideration and scrutiny' of policies. The third is the absence (apart from Principle 4) of any hint about what sort of general programme the Parliament should adopt.

This absence was inevitable. Policy suggestions were, naturally enough, outwith the CSG remit. But the silence on policy had a skewing effebct on their report. The Four Principles are venerated today in a way which their framers probably never anticipated. But as they stand, they imply that the primary mission of a Scottish legislature is not so much to pass laws as to build a new quality of democracy.

How was this to be achieved? By May 1997, when the advent of the Blair government set the devolution process in motion once more, there had already been many years of discussion about modern parliamentary procedures. But the debates on methods for the Parliament's 'participation mission' only began in the weeks and months after Labour's electoral victory.

From the start, there was almost universal agreement that the Parliament must rely on a large-scale and adventurous experiment with electronic communications in order to become 'accessible, open, responsive, and ... participative'.

A large conference on the application of ICTs to politics, sponsored by British Telecommunications, was held in 1997 in the old Royal High School at Edinburgh. Jim Wallace, leader of the Scottish Liberal Democrats and at that time MP for Orkney and Shetland, declared at Heriot-Watt University in Edinburgh that the coming Parliament should be 'the engine of an IT revolution and the blueprint for a new style of computerised democracy, by harnessing digital power and the Internet to put voters and MSPs in permanent instant contact ...'

Technological optimism reached its peak in this interval between 1997 and the first session of the Scottish Parliament in 1999. As Coleman, Taylor and van de Donk comment in their *Parliament in the Age of the Internet*, there was a sense in which 'ICTs became part of the rhetoric of democracy in this period' (Coleman, Taylor and van de Donk 1999: 70).

The CSG report, presented in December 1998, was cooler. Most of the report consisted of proposals for the Parliament's structure and procedures. But the CSG had commissioned an 'expert panel on information and communication technologies', whose conclusions were published as 'Annex J' of the report. The panel's Sub-Group on Democratic Participation made various essentially 'e-government' recommendations about the Parliament's information services, and were at pains not to overlook the electronic have-nots. However, the Sub-Group also suggested the development of 'Community media centres across Scotland where assistance is available to local communities to develop submissions to the Scottish Parliament' (Annex J to 'Report of the Consultative Steering Group on the Scottish Parliament; Expert Panel on Information and Communications Technologies: Sub Group on Democratic Participation', Recommendation 16, p. 2). Vaguely phrased, this at least acknowledged the existence of visions of participative e-democracy.

The conclusions of the main CSG report were strikingly cautious about new-media possibilities. Section 3.6 ('Access and Information'), in its paragraphs about ICTs, is almost exclusively about servicing MSPs, increasing parliamentary efficiency and distributing information to the public. Indeed, paragraph 20 defines the usefulness of ICTs as 'promoting openness, accountability and democratic participation ... by using technology to make information about the Parliament and its work available to everyone'.

In other words, the commitment to 'power-sharing' would be fulfilled by simply providing official information, accessible to the public by computer. This minimalist, bureaucratic approach was a long way from Jim Wallace's ambitious dreams. As it turned out, it was also a long way behind the future staff of the new Parliament, who were to interpret the Four Principles and their realisation through ICTs in a very different spirit.

The 'Shaky Start'

After five years of work, the Scottish Parliament's impact on public opinion is ambiguous. There can be no doubt at all that the Parliament is constructing a huge *potential* extension of citizenship, mostly through imaginative use of new electronic media. So far, however, this opportunity has only been taken up by a very small minority. Most people remain unaware that they can follow webcast debates in real time, or that they can submit 'e-petitions' or join 'forums' on some categories of bill.

This is not the place to evaluate the legislation or debates of the first Parliament. It has passed through a number of convulsions and crises: the unexpected death of Donald Dewar, the 'Clause 2a' uproar over the ban on promoting homosexuality in schools, the resignation of Dewar's successor as First Minister, Henry McLeish, the uncontrolled cost escalation of the new building at Holyrood, to name a few. But ministers and MSPs alike have been unnerved by what they regard as the unfair and aggressive treatment of the Parliament in the Scottish media, not only in the tabloid press.

Bad journalism overshadows good. There is serious and positive comment and reporting, but much media energy has been devoted to the feeding-frenzy 'monstering' of individuals and the presentation of MSPs as greedy and ambitious politicians indifferent to the 'real' opinions of the public. Correspondingly, much of the work of the Parliament and its committees goes unreported. Much of this carnivorous journalism is both competitive and imitative, a Scottish version of new styles of political journalism at Westminster which in turn are an adapted import from the United States.

Steven Barnett, writing in *The Political Quarterly*, describes this as a new and most destructive phase of political journalism which he names 'the age of contempt. It can be seen in reporting by both press and broadcasters, but is at its most lethal in the hands of print journalists under no statutory obligation to be impartial' (Barnett 2002). A few years ago, Andrew Marr, the Scottish journalist who is now the BBC's political editor, defined an acid 'culture of abuse' which was 'eating away at the thoughtful culture of public discourse, burning out nuance, gobbling up detail, dissolving mere facts. And that, in turn, cannot help a struggling democracy' (Marr 2002). He was writing about Westminster, but the young Edinburgh democracy is even more vulnerable.

But politicians always over-estimate the power of the media to change and shape public opinion. Surveys of Scottish opinion suggest that media contempt for the Parliament and its politicians does not accurately reflect the opinion of readers, listeners or viewers. There is disappointment and a degree of mistrust, but nothing like fundamental rejection (see The Public View: A Paradox? at p. 23, below). More damaging, probably, is omission. The public are offered only a highly selective and abbreviated version of what really goes on in the Parliament, whether in main-chamber debates or in committees. This negative image is taken extremely seriously by MSPs and the parliamentary staff, mindful of the Four Principles. One positive effect, over the last three years, has been to give the information and participation operations of the Parliament a new urgency and to accelerate experiments in webcasting, e-consultation and e-democracy.

'Informed' Criticisms

Far from the media sharkpool, the performance of the Parliament has been criticised by some of those involved in the long campaigns for a Scottish parliament, in the Constitutional Convention and in the CSG itself. I have selected two instances in which the new institutions have been held to have fallen behind the promises of 'power-sharing' and 'participation'.

One of the most important criticisms concerns **the initiation of legislation.** The CSG report anticipated that not only the Scottish Executive but the parliamentary committees would have the right to introduce bills, although the report remarked that 'there appears to be little doubt that … the majority of legislation will originate from the Executive' (3.5.5). Among the committees is the Public Petitions Committee, which can adopt a petition and pass it forward to the appropriate subject committee which might, in turn, decide to make it the basis of a parliamentary bill.

In this way, the three-way 'power-sharing' demanded by CSG Principle 1 could be said to function. The Executive, the Parliament (through its committees or through individual MSPs) and the 'people of Scotland' using the petition procedure would share the right to initiate legislation.

In practice, though, the overwhelming majority of legislation since May 1999 has originated from the Executive.

By March 2002, the Parliament had passed some thirty new items of legislation, of which only one – on the rights of battered or abused spouses or partners – originated in a committee. Two more committee bills, on a Standards Commissioner and on a Children's Commissioner, reached their final stages by the end of 2002.

By early 2002, public petitions through the Public Petitions Committee had provided material for six debates and had led to the incorporation of three minor amendments to legislation being drafted by subject committees. No complete bill had originated from a petition.

The explanation lies partly in the control of the Executive over the parliamentary timetable, but also in the dire and seldom-mentioned shortage of qualified parliamentary drafters – a serious bottleneck impeding the Parliament's work. Whatever the causes, the Executive's near-monopoly of legislation runs against the underlying 'power-sharing' aspiration of the Parliament.

Another focus of anxiety has been **the Scottish Civic Forum**. The Forum originated in the pre-devolution period as an unofficial debating chamber, in which representatives from Scotland's main interest groups could exchange views and prepare a reform agenda for a future Scottish Parliament. For a time there was an idea that it might perform some of the functions of a second chamber when a Parliament was set up, and it was briefly referred to as a 'Senate'. This notion was discarded in 1999, when the Civic Forum was redefined as a body intended (in its own words) 'to push forward the boundaries of consultation, moving beyond the present system of limited consultation exercises to real engagement of civic society in a participatory, dialogic democracy' (*Building Participation in the New Scotland*, Scottish Civic Forum, 2001). Its membership consists of some 700 civic organisations, and it has regularly provided the Scottish Executive with partners for a variety of consultations.

But although the Civic Forum has officially recognised status, and receives funding from the Executive, there is a feeling that it has not played the prominent role expected of it. Many organisations bypass the Forum and make their own direct contact with the Executive. Moreover, the Parliament has grown restless with the practice of consultation through spokespeople for structured groups. As a member of the Parliament staff put it,

> we don't want aggregated opinion, Civic Forum style. We want to get at people who are disgruntled and discontented. The Civic Forum thought they would have a monopoly of presenting public opinion to us, but they have yet to prove that they can deliver something we want.

That is a harsh judgement. In fact the Civic Forum (for instance in its 2001 campaign to gather opinions about sustainable development) has recently made great efforts to bring in 'local people who haven't spoken' as well as practised group representatives. But it is true that some of the Civic Forum's possible functions have already been pre-empted by the Parliament.

In 2001, the Procedures Committee began a lengthy audit, based on public hearings, of the Parliament's progress towards fulfilling the Four Principles. This was a job for which the Civic Forum might well have tendered. And the move towards 'real engagement of civic society', a stated Forum ambition, is in practice being driven by the participation and information services of the parliamentary staff. The Forum remains an interesting and often helpful collection-box for extra-parliamentary views. But hopes that it would act as the main engine of 'participation' seem unlikely to be fulfilled.

The Public View: A Paradox?

At a briefing in January 2002, held to measure the Parliament's achievements in its first two years, the Institute of

Governance at the University of Edinburgh produced a
selection of opinion poll results. The questions concerned
constitutional preferences and the performance of the
Parliament. The answers, mostly taken over several years,
were sometimes puzzling and at times seemed contradictory.

Three results were especially striking. The first (from
Scottish Social Attitudes) measured replies to the question:
'Which institution has most influence over the way Scotland
is run?' In 1999, the first year of devolution, 41 per cent
thought it was the Scottish Parliament. Only a year later,
this had collapsed to 13 per cent, while 66 per cent said
that Westminster had most influence. But asked (in 2000)
which institution ought to have most influence, no less than
72 per cent preferred the Scottish Parliament.

Another poll, from the same source, asked if respondents
thought that the Parliament would 'give ordinary people
more say in how Scotland is governed'. In 1997, the year
of the Scotland Act, no less than 79 per cent agreed that
it would. In 1999, the Parliament's birth-year, that had
slipped to 64 per cent. But in 2000, it had slumped down
to 44 per cent, little more than half the figure for that
confident year of the devolution Referendum.

A third poll (ICM for *The Scotsman*) asked: 'From
what you have seen and heard, do you think that the
Scottish Parliament has achieved a lot, a little or nothing
at all?' This sounding was taken in September 2000 and
again in February 2001. Its outcome was curious. The
figure for those who thought 'a little' remained absolutely
unchanged at 56 per cent – far the largest group. But the
extremes of approval and disapproval changed sharply.
Those who thought the Parliament had achieved 'a lot'
more than doubled, to 25 per cent. Those who thought it
had achieved nothing whatever were halved, down to 14
per cent. (For comparison, the percentages of No voters to
the two questions in the 1997 Referendum were around

25 and 35 per cent respectively, on a 60.4 per cent turn-out).

What is to be made of these results? Political opinion polling can be inaccurate and misleading, not least in Scotland. But a rough diagram does emerge. It has three main features:

> Those who thought that this version of self-government would be something close to independence have found out their mistake. But they are not so much alienated as dissatisfied. Their way ahead is more power for Scotland, not less.

> A widespread expectation that this would be a quite new sort of Parliament, offering 'ordinary people' an effective share of power, has deflated. But this disillusion has not produced disaffection. It seems to have led to a sober estimate that this Scottish Parliament, for all its excited promises about unprecedented democracy, is a normal legislature not much worse or better than the average.

> The prevailing popular view of the Parliament seems to be tepid, even sceptical acceptance. But the movement of opinion, if at all accurately reflected, is a drift towards definite approval by a growing minority.

It is worth noting how little impact seems to have been made by the hostility of part of the media to the Parliament. Scotland shares the mood of cynicism about politics and politicians which affects most of the Western world. But this Scottish version of *politische Verdrossenheit* does not apparently extend to democratic institutions as such, or to the Scottish Parliament in particular. The way ahead is not perceived as less politics but as better, more responsive politics.

The Parliament in Search of a Public

THE SEARCHERS

In the campaign to involve the public more directly and intimately with the Parliament, the main source of energy is the parliamentary staff itself. This covers the 'Corporate Body' responsible for managing and running the Parliament and its employees, including the Research and Information Services, the Participation Services, the Education Service and the Clerks of the parliamentary committees. Members of the staff are not civil servants, although many used to work in the old Scottish Office. They are free from the intrigues and constraints of a large bureaucracy, and from its career pressures to conform. They answer only to the Presiding Officer and the Corporate Body.[2]

Unexpectedly, the parliamentary staff have emerged as a distinct force with a strong sense of identity and mission, and something like an agenda of their own. This is an unusual development. In most legislatures, the permanent staff confine themselves to servicing the needs of representatives discreetly and take little or no part in broad projects of democratisation. In Scotland, the formal responsibility for opening up the Parliament's structures to wider public participation belongs to the MSPs, working through their committees. But in practice almost all the new ideas for expanding accessibility and public involvement originate with the staff. This 'corps d'élite' has its own radical vision of what the Parliament might become, and in its routine contacts with the elected MSPs it identifies those who have the capacity to grasp this vision and work towards it.

The workload of MSPs and ministers in the Executive is heavier than anybody anticipated, and leaves little time for broad reflections on the extension of democracy. But that is only part of the explanation. The permanent staff are sharply aware that the Scottish Parliament is not an immemorial, deep-rooted institution like the Houses of Parliament at Westminster, but an experiment for which many of them feel personal, almost parental responsibility.

In private, some will express the fear that if this young Parliament does not manage to root itself securely in the confidence of the Scottish people, it could fail. That does not mean that Westminster might revoke devolution. It means that the electorate might come to regard the Scottish Parliament as hopelessly remote and ineffectual; public interest and participation would drop away until the Parliament simply lost all claims to democratic authenticity.

In the course of 2001, anxiety about the Parliament's apparent failure to connect with the public grew more acute. The concern of the staff converged with unease and impatience among MSPs and some ex-ministers who had experience of government in the Executive.

The 'real world' outside politics had been using digital 'encounter' techniques – forums, chatrooms, on-line polling – for years. There was no excuse for the reluctance of democratic parliaments to adopt these techniques. The Parliament staff's development of new channels of interactive debate through ICTs, which had been steadily driven ahead since 1997, now gained more impetus.

'THE USUAL SUSPECTS'

At the time of writing, the last eighteen months have seen increasing discontent, public and parliamentary, with traditional methods of consultation. One line of complaint focused on the Executive's alleged practice of issuing 'a glossy brochure' (the Cultural Strategy document, for instance) and giving the public a few months to comment. Could this be described as a genuine consultation?

A second complaint concerned the 'usual suspects' phenomenon. Whether it was a consultation arranged for a department of the Executive, or a parliamentary committee hearing witnesses as it prepared legislation, familiar faces – representing the familiar list of established interest groups and professional networks – tended to reappear. As one ex-minister told me, 'the civil servants' idea of consultation is to put up the same old faces every time. Their philosophy is simply predictability. If it worked smoothly before, then repeat it.' Over one proposal for changes, she had been reduced to sending out her own private emissaries to tour the country and collect impressions of what people really thought of her idea. 'What I wanted was the Unusual Suspects'.[3]

In short, there is growing impatience with 'aggregated opinion', perceived to be a barrier screening legislators from the silent mass of people with something to contribute but no habit of being heard. This is an admirably democratic impulse. But, if taken to extremes, it could lead to new problems which might be described as 'civic Bonapartism'. A regime may wish to go straight over the heads of civil society, with its web of associations, and draw its authenticity directly from the people 'out there'. History suggests that this seldom leads to more democratic control, but often to a licence for a government to do as it pleases.

Consultation through 'the usual suspects' is becoming discredited in Scotland, for convincing reasons. But the fact is that for many years those associations – from trade unions to community health projects – were almost the only channels through which public demands could reach government in the form of the old Scottish Office. They have their own roots and legitimacy, and they cannot be evicted from the consultation process altogether.

With electronic means, consultation becomes temptingly easy. But the use of ICTs does not efface the essential distinction between *confirmatory consultation* – often little more than opinion-testing or generating the illusion of public involvement – and *creative consultation* which offers a genuine share of power to participants. One may be called 'e-government' and the other 'e-democracy'. But the difference between them is political rather than technological.

A Parliament Out In Front

Most new political projects set out with high aims which are gradually moderated by experience. The Scottish Parliament has, on the whole, moved in the opposite direction. The plans of the parliamentary staff to make possible genuine and effective public involvement, principally through the imaginative use of ICTs, are more ambitious now than they were in 1999. Many of the devices today being used to open the Parliament's work to public participation were not contemplated four years ago, and the appetite for innovation is still growing. This steady deepening of the will to create a 'new model of parliament' also explains the ascent of the CSG Four Principles, originally mere guidelines, to something like the status of constitutional commandments.

The result is a small national triumph unknown to most Scots, and probably to many MSPs. The Scottish Parliament has become the world leader in the application of digital technology to democracy. As a report by the Bertelsmann Foundation remarked in April 2002: 'There is no doubt about it. As regards participation, Scotland is out in front' (*Balanced E-Governance* 2002).

There are many examples where particular applications have gone further. The German Bundestag's use of ICTs in the office work of its petitions committee is far more extensive (although less original) than the 'e-petitioning' work of the Scottish Parliament. Edinburgh cannot compete with the United States Senate's twenty-four-hour dedicated cable TV channel, financed by a tax on cable companies, or with the American wealth of digital resources servicing members of Congress. The 'Minnesota Project', driven by a private individual rather than by government, offers a range of e-participatory devices in that small state. There are 'e-government' schemes, some highly elaborate and responsive, working in almost all European countries. And yet a senior member of the Scottish parliamentary staff, returning from a visit to the United States, commented: 'I thought they would be light-years ahead of us. But I found that we were light-years ahead of them.'

The uniqueness of the Scottish operation is its sheer range of 'e-experiments' in participatory democracy. No other legislature, it would appear, has such an extensive and varied panoply of digital communications available to its citizens.

Is Anyone Out There Listening?

The spectacular array of technology is, unfortunately, only half the story. It takes two or more to communicate. As mentioned above, the downside of the Scottish situation at present is the enormous disproportion between the offer and the take-up.

Only a tiny minority of the public is prepared to use any of these technologies and opportunities in order to access parliamentary information, to follow the work of the Parliament on-line or to influence and shape policy. There are grounds to believe that this indifference is beginning to dissolve. But it may well be that most Scots are still unaware of the range of these opportunities, or even that they exist at all. Some of the reasons for this lack of response will be examined later.

The Parliament's e-Equipment

This chapter has already cited some of the basic figures (or guesses) about Scotland's connection to cyberspace. By November 2002, the last month for which figures are available, it was estimated that between 30 and 40 per cent of Scottish households had access to the Internet. That figure is growing at the rate of at least 10 per cent per year, although at some point – somewhere around 70 per cent household penetration? – the rate may decline steeply.

Broadband Thinking

Government policy throughout the UK is to achieve 'universal access' to the Internet by 2005. But high-speed broadband technology is spreading only very slowly (in 2000, less than 11 per cent of American on-line households used broadband, while the British figure was about 3 per cent). The Scottish Executive is committed to 'make affordable and pervasive broadband connections available to citizens and businesses across Scotland' ('Digital Inclusion', The Scottish Executive, 2001). The problem here is partly geographical. Especially in the Highlands, the great distances and small population which make regions of rural Scotland unattractive for the heavy infrastructure investment required for broadband. Moreover the privatised British Telecomunications plc, the only potential investor, enjoys a virtual monopoly in remote areas. As the SCC *Reaching Out* report points out, 'broadband provision will mean little or nothing to consumers who can't take advantage of a competitive market in basic telephony'. Although broadband will eventually become essential for local prosperity and development in the Highlands, European Union regulations make it difficult for government to fund this investment gap without raising taxation.

'Digital Exclusion'

There is much anxiety about 'digital exclusion' in Scotland, perceived as a gap which can only widen general social exclusion. The Executive's document *Digital Inclusion: Connecting Scotland's People* emphasises that only a minority of households have access to the Internet, and goes on: 'The digital divide is not related to a lack of telecommunications structure, but to poverty, lack of awareness and low skill levels. The groups most affected by the digital divide are those which are already most excluded within society.' The document also recognises that the ability to use the new communications technology, in or out of the home, is one of the most effective escalators out of powerlessness and isolation. But if government does not intervene, 'the level of comparative social disadvantage experienced by the digitally excluded can be expected to worsen'.

In the strict sense, that is true. The general empowerment of those on-line will increase much faster than that of the digitally excluded. But the rate of household Internet penetration is so fast that within a few years the percentage of the digitally excluded will be a mere fraction of what it is today. None the less, this penetration can be expected to slow up dramatically as it reaches the boundaries of chronically disadvantaged social groups. The danger is that a small minority, perhaps less than 10 per cent, will come to be abandoned as an impenetrable, unreachable 'underclass'.

The causes of digital exclusion are rather more complex than the Executive's 'poverty, lack of awareness and low skill levels' suggests. Simple lack of cash to rent or buy a PC or computer games is not a big factor, while the motivation to join the world of cyber-entertainment and cyber-contact is almost universal.

'Low skills' may be nearer the mark. The basic skills required to enter the on-line universe are reading and accurate writing and, to a far lesser degree, numeracy. Like most European countries, Scotland harbours an unknown but substantial number of people who are functionally illiterate. Most of them resourcefully navigate their way through daily life without letting their difficulty show. But with computers, their bluff is called.

There is a compensation here, though. Britain is seeing a rapid expansion of public schemes to give people free access to on-line computers and simultaneously to train them in their use (in Sunderland, e.g., or in the two 'Pilot Digital Communities' launched by the Scottish Executive in March 2002 in northern Argyll and West Dunbartonshire). Training applicants to use a computer and keyboard can in effect be training them – and motivating them – to achieve 'normal' proficiency and accuracy at reading and writing. And computer courses, carrying none of the old stigma of 'adult literacy courses', offer a discreet way to overcome a personal problem without embarrassment.

The Website

The Scottish Parliament's main channel of direct communication with the public is its website. The facilities offered by the website in late October 2002 included: general information, contact details and biographies of MSPs, instructions on how to petition, details of the Parliament's educational and school-visit programmes, 'Your Online Library' (documents, reports of proceedings etc.), the agenda of upcoming business and a block of links to other on-line services, including webcasting and 'Interactive Discussion Boards' or forums.

The site opened up in May 1999, at the time of the first elections to the Parliament, and has been drastically upgraded and improved since then. The design is attractive, and users now generally find it accessible, informative and efficient. The official report of plenary proceedings in the Chamber has to be published on the website early in the morning of the following day. Committee reports are usually published within two or three days. Where possible, data and documents and agendas for committee sessions are posted in advance. A Gaelic version of this information is provided.

What do we know about the users? Not as much as the Webmaster would like. In a sample month, November 2001, there was an average of 4,272 visits to the site each day, and 26,063 page views. Only 4 per cent of the users were in the Parliament's own system. Where the rest came from is not clear. But charts of the time of using the website were suggestive: about a third to a quarter of the usage occurred at weekend or out of normal working hours. This might be read to mean that over a quarter of the website's visitors were non-institutional users – 'private citizens'. Nevertheless, it is fairly clear that most users are business people, lawyers and lobbyists.

Webcasting

Webcasting, the streaming of live parliamentary events, began as a permanent institution in September 2000. There had already been a series of preliminary experiments, including the webcasting of the Opening Ceremony on 1 July 1999, and the streaming of parliamentary sessions held in Glasgow in May 2000. The webcasts at first covered only the main-chamber plenary sessions. In November 2000, they extended to cover three committee sites, and today all parliamentary committee sessions are webcast live.

The quality of webcasting is high, with the main-chamber streaming done on broadband (used in no other parliamentary webcasting in the world). While the webcasting has its own address, its site is increasingly integrated into the main Parliament website. It now includes a searchable on-line archive.

But take-up of this 'virtual public gallery' has been slow to develop. Between January and June 2001, the weekly average of viewers was 856. Almost all of these (over 85 per cent) watched main-chamber proceedings, with peak interest for First Minister's Question Time. A viewing record was set by the main-chamber debate on banning fox-hunting, in early 2002, which attracted 1,500 webcast watchers.

Interest in watching committee sessions has been very low, on the whole. Members of the parliamentary staff have noticed occasions on which people in the 'real' public gallery outnumbered those following a committee session by webcast – a virtual attendance often in single figures. There is a point here which applies to all e-democracy operations, however brilliant their technology. Advance publicity, on-line or conventional, is immensely important. People have to be made aware that something worth watching is going to happen. The arguments leading up to the fox-hunting debate, although considered irrelevant by many people, had attracted huge coverage from the media in the preceding months. And when the Parliament itself puts special effort into pre-publicity (as with the visit of President Thabo Mbeki of South Africa to the Parliament), webcast viewing figures jump upwards.

The decisive influence of effective pre-publicity has been known to television producers for many years. The providers of e-democracy have had to learn the hard way. But the Broadcasting Service of the Scottish Parliament has recently launched an ambitious campaign to promote and advertise its webcast products.

Interactive Discussion Boards/Forum Features
The Scottish Parliament's Broadcasting Service, responsible for webcasting among other operations, has been moving into more interactive experiments with ICTs. Forums, or 'Interactive Discussion Boards', began to function in late 2001. Essentially these are bulletin boards: the site managers introduce the topic briefly and invite the public to post comments and to debate the proposition. In October 2002, there were eight such forum features open on the website. Their titles ranged from the future of local post offices or the choice of an appropriate memorial to the poet Hamish Henderson to the Middle East crisis.

All the forums dealt with matters recently or currently discussed in the Parliament. Much the most significant element is the move to involve the public in debates on legislation, by commenting or suggesting in the early stages before a bill has taken final shape. At present, this involvement is limited to Members' Business: debates on motions put forward by MSPs acting as individuals. These debates are usually easy and sometimes entertaining to follow, and are not usually discussed along party lines. Far the most popular of these forums concerned 'the plight of chronic pain patients', on a motion introduced by Dorothy-Grace Elder MSP. Although the debate took place many months ago, postings are still coming in from all over the world; at the time of writing, there have been 188 messages on fifty-one pain-related topics.

This was a limited experiment, which formally ended in June 2002. Its purpose was to educate MSPs in the potential of e-democracy, to assess the likely public uptake of forums, and to recommend future steps towards a wider-based and permanent forum service (Smart 2002).

But the opening of Members' Business debates to 'virtual' participation is one matter. Letting the public voice be heard during mainstream Parliament legislation is another. This is a decisive threshold, and the Broadcasting Service is determined to cross it. A proposal was made early in 2002 to open a Discussion Board on the bill to ban hunting with dogs – a bill which had aroused violent feelings in the Parliament and in a few sectors of public opinion. This idea was apparently turned down by the Corporate Body, as too hot to handle. However, in a report on the forum experiment (Smart 2002), the Head of the Broadcasting Services, Alan Smart, recommended that it should be extended to all legislation, and that the 'bulletin board' format should be supplemented by chatrooms (in which citizens could discuss directly with individual MSPs) and by on-line voting on selected issues. (Smart also proposed, in order to strengthen the scheme's credentials, that responsibility for promoting and moderating these features should be transferred from the Parliament to an independent board of 'Untouchables', preferably located outside Edinburgh.)

In the Parliament's management and among some MSPs, proposals to extend the scope of these devices are sometimes treated warily. There are two interconnected reasons for this. The first is the fear that the intervention of strident public comment in the real-time process of lawmaking could deter MSPs from speaking their minds and voting according to their own judgement. This is the old Burkean argument that a representative is not subject to mandate by his or her constituents.

The second reason is that somewhere here, close and yet invisible in the fog, runs the unmarked frontier between 'consultation' and 'participation'. That frontier separates two concepts: allowing the public a right to criticise and suggest, and – in contrast – conceding the public a right to impose its will during the drafting of legislation. When Dorothy-Grace Elder decided to adopt a bright amendment from one of her forum contributors, then we were still doing traditional representative democracy. But when public opinion can veto a clause in real time, through on-line polling or referenda, then we are in the realm of direct democracy.

It can be well argued that a new, choosing, e-proficient society cannot be confined in a political system which gives voters only a single chance to influence it every four years. A democracy of continuous choice must be the future. Possibly so; there are many such voices around Holyrood. Alternatively, there is also the voice of Professor Klaus Lenk, with his warning that a new technology goes round looking for a problem which it can solve. The fact that ICTs are the perfect toolbox for constructing direct democracy does not by itself mean that direct democracy is urgently needed.

Much more urgent, for the Participation or Broadcasting Services of the Scottish Parliament, is the need to be noticed and used by the Scottish public. One member of the Parliament's staff complained privately of 'our complete lack of a communications strategy'. Alan Smart's report estimated that 'less than 10 per cent of those with Internet access *and* with a direct interest in the forum we have hosted even knew about the existence of the forum' (Smart 2002: 11).

E-Petitions

The petition is among the oldest of all channels leading from subject to ruler. At Westminster, it has fallen into low esteem. Only MPs can submit petitions, which are dropped into a large green bag behind the Speaker's Chair where they often remain. But the planners of the Scottish Parliament, on their mission to overcome the remoteness of power, built a formal petitioning procedure into the new structure.

The Public Petitions Committee (PPC), composed of seven MSPs, has considered 747 petitions since opening for business in June 1999 – 137 of them in the parliamentary year 2000/01, when forty-five petitions were referred to subject committees for further consideration, and many of these persuaded a subject committee to open a formal enquiry. Petitions do not have to originate in Scotland, but to qualify for consideration by the Committee, they must ask for some action which is within the powers devolved to the Scottish Parliament and Executive.

In a contribution to the journal *Scottish Affairs*, Peter Lynch and Steven Birrell tried to work out roughly who the petitioners were. 'Was [petitioning] actually effective as a mechanism to link individuals to the political process, or were the 'usual suspects' of Scottish politics – the pressure groups ... – using petitions as an additional mechanism for lobbying and activity?' The figures for the first year were skewed by Mr Frank Harvey, an indefatigable Glasgow pensioner who contributed nearly a third of all individual petitions himself. But even allowing for the 'Harvey Effect', it turned out that individuals were the largest single block of appealers, responsible for 42.5 per cent of all petitions received, while pressure groups contributed only 28 per cent. The third largest block comprised what Lynch and Birrell termed 'community groups' – community councils, residents' associations or church and school groups. This was much the balance which the planners of the petitions system had hoped for (Lynch and Birrell, 2001: 1–18).

In September 2001, the PPC visited the German Bundestag's petitions committee. This is a vast and well-established operation, with a staff of twenty-nine handling some 20,000 petitions a year. Why is the Scottish petition intake so slight in comparison? In giving evidence two months later to the Procedures Committee, the PPC convener, John McAllion MSP, explained that the PPC had avoided any 'large-scale publicity campaign to increase public awareness of the petitions system' because its existing resources were too small to handle any significant increase in petitions submitted. If he was satisfied that the Parliament and its committees would expand their capacity to deal with more petitions, then the PPC could prepare a publicity strategy to promote petitioning more effectively.

In late 1999, it was decided to open the PPC to on-line petitioning. The experiment was designed and is still being run by the International Teledemocracy Centre at Napier University. This is not just a facility to email petitions to the Parliament, but an elaborate 'e-petitioning tool' which allows the sponsor to add background information and encourages others to express opinions about the petition on an integrated discussion forum. Most importantly, signatures can be added on-line. Here a small boundary was crossed; there have been security reservations about cyber-signatures, for example, in the European Parliament, but the PPC and the Teledemocracy Centre decided that the additional risk of fraudulent support was negligible. After all, how checkable are handwritten names and addresses on a petition? The e-petitioner system is content to give each name and address a 'confidence rating', based on various factors including the recurrence of the same address (Beddie, Macintosh and Malina 2002: 702).

The Bundestag petitions committee uses ICTs to cope with its enormous workload, but the Scottish Parliament appears to be the only legislature to run an e-petitioner system. So far, however, use of the Scottish e-petitioner tool has not been heavy. The scheme is still regarded as experimental, and – as with conventional petitioning – has not been strongly promoted or advertised. At present, the Napier ITC e-petition website holds about nine items, seven of them originating from established interest groups, and one each from a community group and an individual.

The move to the new Parliament building at Holyrood in 2004 may be the occasion for e-petitioning to leave the experimental stage and promote itself into a much bigger operation. Critics might suggest that the adoption of e-petitioning is another case of 'Lex Lenk', given that the use of the whole petitioning facility has been so light. The answer must be that the expansion of conventional and on-line petitioning, and the committing of serious new resources to them by the Parliament, is necessary and inevitable. When a determined effort is made to encourage the public to use petitioning more widely, then the existence of the e-petitioner and the experience already gained in running it will become invaluable.

Partner Libraries

A pilot scheme to provide local out-stations for information about the Scottish Parliament was launched by the Scottish Council for Voluntary Organisations (SCVO) in the summer of 1999. About 280 computers were provided by BT, with funding shared between BT and the Millennium

Commission, and placed in village halls and other community centres. They were intended to provide a link for local communities to the Parliament website, to access MSPs and parliamentary reports and to enable on-line discussion between citizens and prominent politicians. This 'Holyrood Project' project was not meant to be permanent and has now ended. SCVO did not attempt to quantify its impact, but a member of the Council suggested that 'maybe its legacy was that it got people thinking about engaging'. Many of the PCs are still 'out there', although it is not known how they are being used.

Subsequently, the Parliament's own Information Services launched the Partner Library scheme. Scotland has 702 public libraries, not counting 103 mobile libraries. The scheme designated eighty public libraries as Partner Libraries – 1 for each constituency, plus an additional eight in geographically larger constituencies.

Each PL is provided with a selection of paper documentation from the Parliament, and is allowed to choose from a range between 'Complete Collection' (CC), (the full hard-copy output) and 'WHISP' ('What's Happening in the Scottish Parliament': the Parliament's' in-house magazine or digest). In February 2002, the Complete Collection was taken by eighteen Partner Libraries; most preferred to take a 'Key' or 'Key Plus' collection of core documents.

In addition, each PL was to be equipped with a free-access computer, allowing library users to make their own contact with the electronic services of the Parliament from documentation and general information to webcasting and e-petitioning.

Management of the PL project is a condominium. Libraries and their expenditure are controlled by local authorities, who take the decisions about the level of parliamentary information they require and how it will be offered to the public. At the same time, the supply of paperwork and PCs, and the provision of training for library staff in

PL work, is run by the Parliament through the energetic figure of Paul Anderson, the Library Liaison Officer, who is in charge of the Partner Library scheme.

In 2002, the Partner Libraries' on-line service was over-shadowed by the coming of the 'People's Network', the UK Government's plan to equip every public library in Britain with enough PCs to offer free and universal access to the Internet. This plan is linked to the 2005 target for a fully on-line Britain.

The People's Network PCs will be used for every kind of training or activity, but the PN website does not include political activity among them. There was some anxiety in Scotland that this inrush of public-access terminals (Angus alone has received fifty-seven PCs) might swamp the dedicated Scottish Parliament PC in each Partner Library. But both the Partner Libraries management and the librarians themselves regard this worry as baseless. On the contrary, most of them think that this powerful boost to general e-proficiency will persuade more people to investigate and use the on-line services of the Parliament.

On its own, the Partner Libraries plan has not been an unqualified success. In the spring of 2002, Ailsa Macintosh was commissioned by the Centre for Theology and Public Issues and the Baird Trust to carry out a telephone survey of all the Partner Libraries, in order to study the take-up of hard-copy or on-line parliamentary materials and the use made of the dedicated PC by library visitors. Her general conclusions are included in this paper as Appendix 1. But some broad points, from her evidence and from other sources, can be made at once.

Almost all libraries suffer from shortage of space and staff. Most of them would like to reduce their intake of paper, and welcome both the offer of parliamentary proceedings on CDs and the increasing use of on-line access. But only up to a point: a significant minority of library users lack ICT skills and require paperwork.

At the outset, the match between the PC terminals and the Parliament website was shaky. The terminals were often too old and slow; the website – before its redesign – was sometimes puzzling or impassable. These problems are being rapidly sorted out, but in early 2002 a fair number of librarians either could not receive webcasts or had not been trained to deal with them.

MSPs seldom work closely with the Partner Libraries. The PL managers have invited them to use the libraries as constituency offices or for surgeries. Where they have done so, public awareness of the e-government and e-democracy opportunities has increased. But few have taken up the offer.

There is still widespread confusion about the difference between the Parliament and the Scottish Executive. Many people have no clear idea of what are local government matters, what is a Parliament responsibility and which powers remain with Westminster.

No assessment has been made of how many people have used either the paper or electronic services, or why. Librarians lack the time and the inclination to count and interrogate users. But their intelligent guesstimates cannot be far from the truth.

The take-up of parliamentary information or contacts through Partner Libraries has ranged from the slight to the imperceptible. Five or six enquiries a month, often to discover the name of the MSP, is a generous guess at an average. Local issues under debate or dramatic episodes widely publicised in the media (such as the Clause 2a uproar over the supposed promotion of homosexuality in schools, or the ban on hunting with dogs) can make a temporary difference. Many – perhaps most – users are researching background information on personal problems such as pensions. Live webcasts of debates are seldom followed.

In spite of this lack of interest, librarians appear to remain firmly and sometimes enthusiastically committed to the Partner Library idea. Only one of Ailsa Macintosh's respondents confessed to total despair: 'It is simply not being used for anything at all, never mind for forums, etc. … Having more computers will help if people want the information, but I think the phrase is "flogging a dead horse".' But this was untypical. Most respondents felt that they were offering a vital service, and that the tide would eventually turn when there were more computers available (under the People's Network plans) and when people became aware of what was on offer. Some librarians actively fight public indifference, for example by switching on the webcasts of interesting debates and letting library visitors collect around the screen.

To sum up, the Partner Libraries are an admirable and indispensable device for enriching citizenship and distributing e-democracy, which has had less success than it deserves. The next few years look more promising. Meanwhile, the main difficulties faced by the PL scheme appear to be these:

Lack of publicity. As with so many other items in the Parliament's array of democratic technology, few people in Scotland know that the PLs exist.

Lack of resources at the delivery end. Libraries lack space, time, staff and money to expand – or advertise – their connection to the Parliament. Scotland's output of trained librarians is inadequate, and graduate starting salaries (£14,000) are miserably low.

Divided command. The Library Liaison Officer in Edinburgh can only recommend what should be done. Power over libraries rest with the councils. Some are indifferent to the purposes of Partner Libraries. A very few are hostile to any Parliament 'colonisation' of local government.

Duplication of networks. In addition to the Parliament's library 'portals', the Scottish Executive runs its own chain of local computer access points. So does the European Union. The citizen can be forgiven for losing his or her way.

The current ill-repute of party politics and politicians. It would be absurd to ignore this. But it is not the same as indifference to politics. Scottish public opinion has shown several times in recent years that it can be rapidly and powerfully mobilised on particular issues. Politics of that kind are bound to adopt participative ICTs, sooner or later, to gather support and focus it on the centres of power.

Appendix 1   Partner Libraries Survey

Between March and June 2002, Ailsa Macintosh carried out a telephone survey of Partner Libraries, on behalf of the Centre for Theology and Public Issues at New College, University of Edinburgh, and the Baird Trust.

The survey took the form of seven questions:

Which of the four categories of paper parliamentary documentation, ranging in completeness from 'Complete Collection' to the WHISP digest, does your library take? Do you intend to stay with your choice?

Do you have a public computer with Internet access?

Do you have a public computer dedicated to the Scottish Parliament? Is it equipped to receive live webcast debates with sound, to access e-petitioner and/or to let the user participate in parliamentary discussion boards and forums?

How much do the public use the computer access to the Scottish Parliament?

As far as you can tell, what are they using this access for? Can you give a rough percentage of users who are seeking general information/live debates/forums/the e-petitioner site?

How much do the public use the paper documentation from the Parliament?

Do you think there is a danger that the current UK 'People's Network' scheme will swamp the Partner Library programme, by offering far more public computer terminals for all kinds of purposes? Or will the PN scheme be complementary?

With the detailed results of her research, Ailsa Macintosh returned the following summary.

On the whole, librarians are extremely supportive of the Partner Library scheme, despite the low use of the Parliamentary material. There is a commitment to providing this service, and a belief that the information should be widely available even if people are not that interested in the Scottish Parliament.

Most libraries, however, have acknowledged that they should reduce the quantity of paper material they take due to problems of storage. The vast majority of libraries have public PCs with Internet access, but there is a recognition that not all their customers are IT-literate. Problems with Internet access (either due to local difficulties or to the complexities of the SP site) have made quite a few librarians reluctant to rely on the Internet as the only source of Parliamentary material.

It is extremely rare for members of the public to be interested in accessing the debates, forums or e-petition facilities on the SP website. A few of the libraries have used the site to listen to webcasts, but this has tended to happen as a result of proactive staff rather than through customer demand.

Very few librarians felt able to make anything more than an educated guess at the numbers who were using the SP site on a monthly basis. Most thought that the use was very low, and where it existed it was to search for background information rather than to lobby Parliamentarians or contribute to consultations, etc. The same applies to the use of the paper material. Quite a few librarians thought the paper material worked well as a support to the SP site, because it was easier to read and easier to check on several sources of information at the same time.

The PN [People's Network] computers are warmly welcomed by the majority of libraries as complementary to the Partner Library scheme. They are not seen as replacing the PL connection. Some librarians mentioned the hope of dedicating one PC to the SP site for webcast debates and research. This was something which would not be possible before getting the PN computers. Most librarians welcomed taking less SP material, but were not keen to become paper-free.

Geographical location is a factor in terms of a library's role in providing access to SP material. The libraries that take the 'Complete Collection' of papers tend to be (or see themselves as) the key libraries for the area – either because they are main city libraries or because they serve Highland or Island areas. Given that the Scottish Parliament is based in Edinburgh, some librarians from the smaller libraries in the capital thought that their role was not as crucial – in that the SP itself was more accessible.

Where librarians were proactive in promoting the SP connection, interest in and use of the materials was higher but this tended to last only as long as the promotion continued. A large number of librarians thought that the SP or MSPs or SPICe [the Scottish Parliament Information Centre] could help local libraries more with their promotion work. Posters could be updated, local issues flagged-up and advance warning could be given of forthcoming debates or contentious topics. Tapping into local issues is a possible way of increasing political interests, for example, boundary changes or wind-farms. If success of the Partner Library scheme is to be measured in terms of the numbers of people using the material, then ongoing promotional work is required. Currently, the PL scheme appears to be a passive resource – available to those who are active themselves in seeking out information, but not engaging the interest of those more distant from politics.

There was a general consensus that, on the whole, people are fairly apathetic about politics. A couple of people mentioned that politically active people probably have their own sources of information (private PCs or through political groups) and would not necessarily use the library as a regular resource. There is a question whether libraries themselves require more promotion.

Many people mentioned the benefits to staff of the PL connection in terms of training and confidence. Librarians often used the SP material or website to provide information for customers, even if the customers had not thought to look at the SP site themselves.

There seems to be widespread confusion about the different roles of the Scottish Executive and the Scottish Parliament, as well over which powers have been devolved to Scotland from Westminster. Those people using the library for information (in more depth than 'Who is my MSP?') tended to be following Bills in their later stages. Information on issues needs to be publicised much earlier, to encourage participation at a phase when lobbying can be most effective.

Printing material from the Internet is a cost consideration for financially stretched library services. Given this restraint, if e-democracy is to be socially inclusive then the Scottish Parliament should provide the paper material rather than laying the cost on individuals or libraries.

Appendix 2   Church of Scotland Websites – Summary of Findings

(Details taken from a survey carried out by Dr Heidi Campbell, Centre for Theology and Public Issues, Edinburgh, in 2002.)

Website Design

Number of websites reviewed: 37, 5 being 'dead hits'. (This amounted to 15 per cent of the 245 possible Church of Scotland sites.)

Average number of pages: 8.

None had search functions.

Updating: number indicating dates: 15 (= 40 per cent)
within last 6 months: 4
within last 3 months: 5
within last month: 6.

Webmasters listed: 20 (+ 54 per cent).

Organisation and Presentation.

Contact information listed: 28 (= 76 per cent).

Contact email: 22.

Service information listed: 31 (= 84 per cent).

Community information listed: 4 (= 11 per cent).

Interactivity

Number with Guestbooks: 11 (= 28 per cent).

Number with BBSs: 1 (= 3 per cent).

Links

Church of Scotland web link listed: 23 (= 62 per cent).

Other Church of Scotland web links listed: 17 (= 46 per cent) (local/regional Presbytery most common link listed).

Other Denominations' or Religious Organisations' web links listed: (= 38 per cent).

Community groups web links listed: 14 (= 38 per cent).

Cultural web links listed: 7 (+ 19 per cent).

Scottish Churches' Parliamentary Office web link listed: 1
(= 3 per cent). International web links listed; 12 (= 32 per
cent) (Christian Aid most common link cited)

Number of sites without any links: 7 (= 19 per cent).

Notes

1. The UK Government's 'People's Network' programme, currently
   distributing free public access PCs and training facilities in an
   effort to achieve 'universal access' to the Internet by 2005, is in
   some ways the extension of Sunderland structures to the whole
   of Britain.
2. The Corporate Body consists of six members, headed by the
   Presiding Officer, George Reid. The Parliament contains 129
   MSPs and 400 parliamentary staff. In addition, MSPs or
   parliamentary parties have 333 employees of their own.
3. A good illustration of this spreading discontent was the consultation in early 2002 over educational reform. The Executive's
   Department of Education, whose minister was Cathy Jamieson,
   launched an on-line 'National Debate on Education'. At the
   same time, the parliamentary Committee for Education,
   Culture and Sport set up a 'wide debate' on 'The Purposes of
   Scottish Education', and established a special on-line bulletin
   board which invited public comment on six chosen themes.
   While the two operations were officially in 'partnership', there
   was evidence of rivalry between Parliament and Executive as
   they competed to be seen to be reaching beyond the 'familiar
   faces'.

   The Executive invited some 200 organisations to consider
   how to 'reach people who do not usually participate in this kind
   of exercise' (in other words, the usual suspects were asked to
   produce unusual suspects). 'This is the start of a genuine and
   inclusive dialogue ... Instead of the traditional method of a
   consultation paper from Ministers, we are seeking the public's
   views on "the big questions"'. The Committee responded that
   its own operation aimed to build on the Executive's efforts and
   provoke 'debate in more depth on key issues'.

References

Balanced E-Governance (2002) (Berlin: The Bertelsmann Foundation).

Barnett, S. (2002), 'Will a Crisis in Journalism Provoke a Crisis in Democracy?', *Political Quarterly*, 73(4) (October–December).

Beddie, L., A. Macintosh and A. Malina (2002), 'E-Democracy and the Scottish Parliament', in Beat Schmid, Katarina Staneovska-Slabeva and Volker Tschammer (eds) (2002), *Towards the E-Society: E-Commerce, E-Business and E-Government* (Boston/Dordrecht: Kluwer Academic Publishers).

Coleman, S. and J. Gøtze (2001), *Bowling Together: Online Public Engagement in Policy Deliberation* (Hansard Society).

Coleman, Stephen, John Taylor and Wim van de Donk (eds) (1999), *Parliament in the Age of the Internet* (Oxford: Oxford University Press in association with the Hansard Society for Parliamentary Government).

Digital Inclusion: Connecting Scotland's People (2001) (Edinburgh: The Scottish Executive).

Lenk, K. (2002), 'Electronic Government: a Cooperative Perspective', lecture at University of Edinburgh, 27 February.

Lynch, P. and S. Birrell (2001), 'Linking Parliament to the People: the Public Petitions Process of the Scottish Parliament', in *Scottish Affairs*, 37 (Autumn).

Marr, A. (1999), 'The Lying Game', *The Observer*, 24 October.

Putnam, R. (2000), *Bowling Alone: the Collapse and Revival of American Community* (New York: Simon & Schuster).

Reaching Out: The Consumer Perspective on Communications in Scotland (2002) (Edinburgh: The Scottish Consumer Council).

Report of the Consultative Steering Group on the Scottish Parliament (1998) (Edinburgh: The Scottish Office).

Smart, Alan (2002), *Interactive Parliament: Report on Member's Business Pilot Project* (Edinburgh: The Scottish Parliament), June.

Smith, E. and A. Macintosh (2002), *What Sort of Scotland Do We Want to Live In? Assessment of the E-Consultation Process* (Edinburgh: International Teledemocracy Centre, Napier University).

Sunstein, C. (2001), *Republic.com* (Princeton: Princeton University Press). Also http://bostonreview.mit.edu/BR26.3/sunstein.html.

Wellman, B. (1988), 'The Community Question Re-evaluated', in M. P. Smith (ed.), *Power, Community and the City* (New Brunswick, NJ).

Acknowledgements

I am grateful to many members of the staff of the Scottish Parliament and MSPs for their patient and friendly responses to my questions, and for sparing the time to assemble dossiers and papers for me. In particular, I would like to thank Paul Anderson, Rosemary Everett, Steve Farrell, Eric MacLeod, Hazel Martin, John Patterson, Janet Seaton, Alan Smart, Jeannie Speirs, Andrew Wilson and, among MSPs: George Reid, Deputy Presiding Officer, Susan Deacon, Kenneth Macintosh and Mike Russell. The Revd Graham Blount counselled my research in the early stages and provided me with the outstanding bulletin service of the Scottish Churches Parliamentary Office.

In the university and research world, I was assisted by the ideas of Professor David McCrone of the Institute for the Study of Governance, Edinburgh University; Dr Keith Culver of the University of New Brunswick in Canada; Professor Klaus Lenk of the University of Oldenburg in Germany; Dan Lerner; Professor Ann Macintosh at the International Teledemocracy Centre at Napier University, Edinburgh; Professor Helen Petrie of the School of

Informatics, City University, London; and Professor Charles Raab of the Department of Politics, University of Edinburgh. Among librarians, I had especially useful advice from Elaine Fulton of the Scottish Libraries Association, Pauline Flynn at Dunoon Library, Andrew Ewan, chief librarian of Argyll and Bute, and Cathy Gormal at Paisley Central Library. Wise advice and information came also from Debbie Wilkie of the Scottish Civic Forum, Hope Johnstone of the Education Department of the Scottish Executive, and Alistair Dutton of the Scottish Council for Voluntary Organisations.

Ailsa Macintosh came vigorously and efficiently to my aid, carrying out the survey of Partner Libraries for this paper. But nothing could have been begun without the friendship and sponsorship of Professor Will Storrar, Alison Elliot and Alistair Hulbert of the Centre for Theology and Public Issues, at New College, University of Edinburgh, with whom I was privileged to enjoy months as a Temporary Fellow at New College while undertaking this project. And I will never forget the generosity of the Baird Trust, whose members seemed to draw real personal satisfaction from providing the financial support for my work.

More than any other individual, I want to thank Marion Ralls, whose New Town apartment became my home for many comfortable and happy months through an Edinburgh winter.

The Immanent Internet

Barry Wellman and Bernie Hogan

The Descent of the Internet

The Internet has descended from an awesome part of the ethereal firmament to become immanent in everyday life. As it descended, the Internet developed, mutated and proliferated, providing a multitude of computer-mediated options for people to communicate. The stand-alone capital-I 'Internet' became the more widespread and complex small-i 'internet'.

Although the technological nature of the immanent internet does not determine social behaviour, it provides both opportunities and constraints for social relationships. The internet has become intertwined with a larger paradigm shift in how people are connected: from relatively homogenous, broadly embracing, densely knit and tightly bounded groups to more heterogeneous, specialised, sparsely knit and loosely bounded social networks. Although the transformation began in the pre-internet 1960s, the proliferation of the internet both reflects and further facilitates this shift in social organisation to networked individualism.

The internet was originally viewed as a dazzling light shining above everyday concerns. In the 1990s, when the internet moved from the arcane scholarly world to homes and offices, it was heralded as the gateway to a new illuminating Enlightenment. The very term 'Internet' became used for any snazzy new electronic activity. Early adopters congratulated themselves on being progressive elites, and techno-nerds rejoiced in newfound respect and fame. Bespectacled, nerdy Microsoft founder Bill Gates was as much a superstar as rock singers and professional athletes. Special newspaper internet sections were created in the boom to capture dot.com ads and reader interest. All things seemed possible. The internet had astounded and mesmerised the world. The cover of the millennial December 1999 issue of *Wired* magazine (the *Vogue* of the internet world) graphically represents the optimism of the times. It shows an Icarian cyberangel leaping from a cliff to reach for the ethereal sun. The angel's graceful posture points upward, placing boundless faith in an unfettered cyber-future

In the euphoria, much early writing of the impact of the internet was unsullied by data and informed only by conjecture and anecdotal evidence. Travellers' tales from *internet incognita* abounded. The analyses were often Utopian: extolling the internet as egalitarian and globe-spanning and ignoring how differences in power and status might affect interactions on- and off-line. The internet was seen as an ethereal manifestation of Teilhard de Chardin's noösphere (1964), providing the technological means for the collective consciousness of the world. Philosopher Eric Raymond makes this transcendent connection clear in his *Homesteading in the Noosphere* (2000), showing how open source hackers stake their claims on the frontier of programming ideas and approach their projects as a simultaneous combination of property and gift.

Communication was the internet's main use during these early years. The predominant use was asynchronous, person-to-person email, but there was some use of asynchronous discussion lists and synchronous chat groups, multi-user simulations (MUDs, MOOs), and after 1997 instant messaging.[1] Some seers felt that it would not be long before all would be connected to all, transcending the boundaries of time and space. As John Perry Barlow, a leader of the Electric Frontier Foundation (and songwriter for the Grateful Dead), wrote in 1995:

> With the development of the Internet, and with the increasing pervasiveness of communication between networked computers, we are in the middle of the most transforming technological event since the capture of fire. I used to think that it was just the biggest thing since Gutenberg, but now I think you have to go back farther (p. 36)

> In order to feel the greatest sense of communication, to realize the most experience ... I want to be able to completely interact with the consciousness that's trying to communicate with mine. Rapidly ... We are now creating a space in which the people of the planet can have that kind of communication relationship (p. 40)

Some cyber theorists started to consider the body as essentially a host for the superhighway cruising mind. Early writers of cyberpunk set the terms through with characters who 'jacked-in' to a separate and more engaging reality. The novels *Neuromancer* (Gibson 1984) and *Snow Crash* (Stephenson 1992) played a substantial part in shaping this cultural fantasy, with Gibson's 'cyberspace' term becoming a metaphor for life on the internet. Sherry Turkle's non-fiction *Life on the Screen* (1995) portrayed the internet as fracturing a person's unified sense of identity. As one of her respondents says: 'RL [Real-Life] is just one more window ... and it's not usually my best one' (p. 13).

Yet Turkle's close observations led some pundits to mistake the leaves for the trees and forests. Extrapolations from her tiny sample of early adopters to the population at large popularised the perception of a transcendental life-consuming internet.[2] Rather than seeing denizens of virtual communities as a special minority, pundits often pointed to them as precursors of the future, linked in a Borgian meta-mind (Berman and Pillar 1995) as 'connected intelligence' (De Kerckhove 1997) and 'collective intelligence' (Levy 1997).

Many people lost their perspective in their euphoria and became parochial and presentist. In their *presentism*, they forgot that long-distance ties had been flourishing for generations, using automobiles, telephones, airplanes and even postal (snail) mail. Others had no perspective to begin with, and just jumped on the internet bandwagon to find fame and fortune. Like Barlow, they thought that the world had started anew with the internet (see the review in Wellman and Gulia 1999).

Parochially, many pundits and computer scientists assumed that only on-line phenomena are relevant to understanding the internet. They realised that computer-mediated communication – in the guise of the internet – fostered widespread connectivity, but they insisted on looking at on-line phenomena in isolation. They committed the fallacy of *particularism*, thinking of the internet as a lived experience distinct from the rest of life. This approach often shaded into *elitism*, as only the small percentage of the technologically adept had the equipment, knowledge, time and desire to plunge so fully into cyberspace.

To be sure, there was scholarly research, much of it good, but it was mainly laboratory experiments, well summarised in Sproull and Kiesler's *Connections* (1991) or ethnographic accounts such as Turkle's. The media were permeated with traveller's tales of journeys to the exotic internet, much like early travellers to sixteenth-century America wrote. For example, the tagline on the cover of Mary Dery's cultural study of the internet suggests the book is 'an unforgettable journey into the dark heart of the information age' (1997: book cover). Enthusiastic computer scientists filled meetings of 'CSCW' (computer-supported cooperative work) and 'CHI' (computer–human interaction) conferences with reports of their amazing new applications. All of these accounts provided rich detail and a sense of process, but their particularity created the danger of inaccurate generalisation. While it was true that some people were immersed on-line, most were not.

The dystopians had their say too. They similarly assumed the future would find humanity engulfed by the internet but found the proposition distressing. They worried that ephemeral on-line identities would trump their off-line counterparts. Anecdotes of gender deception were told and retold (Van Gelder 1985; Turkle 1995; Dery 1997; selections from Bell and Kennedy 2000) They continue, with a 2004 *New Yorker* cartoon portraying a little old lady sitting at her PC and typing 'Oh baby ... oh baby ... oh baby ...' (Duffy 2004).

A mini-industry developed to deal with internet patholo-gies. Several psychologists claimed to treat people with 'Internet addiction' (e.g., Young 1998). One psychologist's diagnostic tool was adapted from a gambling addiction questionnaire, with 'Internet' substituted for gambling (Greenfield 1999). Such approaches ignore the positive benefits of being involved with the internet. Compare a statement such as 'I am gambling too much' with one such as 'I am communicating too much'. Such concerns continue. In February 2004, a Toronto reporter asked one author (Wellman) to comment on the deaths of four 'cyber-addicts' who spent much time on-line in virtual reality milieus. When Wellman pointed out that other causes might be involved and that 'addicts' were probably a low percentage of users, the reporter lost interest. Nor are such pathologies necessarily the result of internet use. As one dishevelled man points out to a bar mate in another *New Yorker* cartoon, 'I was addicted to porn before there was an internet' (Vey 2004).

A more pervasive concern has been that the internet would suck time out of in-person connectivity, fostering alienation and real-world disconnection. Thus, Texas broadcaster Jim Hightower worried that 'while all this razzle-dazzle connects us electronically, it disconnects us from each other, having us "interfacing" more with computers and TV screens than looking in the face of our fellow human beings' (quoted in Fox 1995: 12).

Fuelling this fear, one scholarly report showed that heavy adolescent users were more alienated than other teens from their households (Kraut et al. 1998). This was trumpeted in newspaper headlines that neglected to report that the differences were only a few percentage points and occurred only among a small minority of internet users. Despite its limitations, at least this research was a pioneer of field-based systematic research with a representative sample. It was a marked improvement on the 1990s' attempts of pundits and computer scientists alike to get a handle on what was happening without taking account of social science knowledge.

Frustrated with the prevalence of presentism and paro-chialism, one of the authors wrote an article arguing that the internet was not the coming of the new millennium (Wellman and Gulia 1999). Rather, it was a new computer-mediated technology following the path of other promoters of transportation and communication connectivity, such as the telegraph, railroad, telephone, automobile and aeroplane. The article showed how community dynamics continued to operate on the internet. There was no disconnection between the 'virtual world' and the 'real world'. Rather, on-line communications have become – and probably always were – immanent parts of the real world of flesh and computers.

The dot.com stock market bust of 2000 curbed media enthusiasm and tempered the polarised rhetoric of utopian hope and dystopian fear. Special newspaper sections shrank in the wake of instantly vanishing dot.com vanity ads. The pages of *Wired* magazine, the internet's greatest cultural champion, shrank 25 per cent from 240 pages in September 1996 to 180 pages in September 2001, and another 22 percent to 140 pages in September 2003. Revenue and subscription rates followed suit (Figure 1), with *Wired* editors noting ruefully that their magazine 'used to be as thick as a phone book' (*Wired*, 2004, p. 23).

FIGURE 1   *The* Wired *Magazine Trajectory*

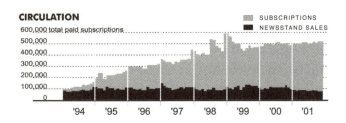

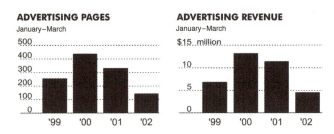

Data: Audit Bureau of Circulations: Publishers Information Bureau

Chart Source: Sheldon Ungar, Dept. of Social Science, Scarborough College, University of Toronto, May 2002

The dot.com bust brought expectations down to earth just as the internet achieved its most important sociological milestone – indifference. The internet has become so widely used in developed countries that its use is becoming a matter of routine. Familiarity breeds cognitive neglect. Many pundits have shifted their gaze from the internet to the other technologies amenable to their utopian rhetoric, such as nanotechnology. Like the telephone and the automobile before it, exotic stories diminished just as the widespread diffusion of the internet increased its true social importance (see the discussions in Wellman and Haythornthwaite 2002; Jankowski et al. 2004).

The Immanent Internet

Despite the dot.com meltdown, both the number of internet users and their frequency of use have increased. The internet's growth meant it no longer stood apart from the rest of life, if it ever had. The internet has become embedded in everyday life, a routine appliance for communicating, and being informed. Indeed, reports emailed to the discussion list of the Association of Internet Researchers in late 2003 suggest that many people do not even think they are on the internet when they are instant messaging or chatting. It is just something they do, and not a privileged form of communication to get excited about. As Susan Herring puts it, the internet is now 'slouching toward the ordinary' (2004: 26).

The story after the death of internet hype continues to be interesting, if less fashionable. The internet plugs into existing social structures: it reproduces class, race and gender inequalities; brings some new cultural forms into the foray; and maps onto everyday life in both novel and conventional ways. Attention now focuses on the broader questions of the 'internet in society' rather than on 'Internet societies'. Where the first age of the internet was a period of exploration, hope and uncertainty, the second age of the internet has been one of routinisation, diffusion and development.

This is reminiscent of the transformation in the use of the telephone. Where our great-grandparents used to shout at the telephone receiver during a local call and our grandparents were reluctant to make expensive long-distance calls, almost all residents of the developed world use the telephone routinely, without any consciousness of the technological marvels that sustain it. Moreover, young people apparently feel undressed without their mobile phones – so much so that it can become their 'third skin' after biological skin and clothing (Fortunati, Katz and Riccini 2003). In cafés in Europe, automobiles in North America and railroads in Japan, mobile phones come out as soon as people sit down. The use of mobile phones is so habitual that people often talk into them without any apparent awareness that their conversations impinge on the comfort of nearby listeners (Ling 2004).

The ethereal internet light that previously dazzled has now dimmed to a soft glow permeating everyday concerns. We have moved from a world of internet wizards to a world of ordinary people routinely using the internet. The internet has become an important part of people's lives, but not a special part. It is has become the utility of the masses rather than the plaything of computer scientists. It has become the infrastructure for a variety of computer-supported communications media, and not just the specialised conveyor of email.

In retrospect, its easy to see how early diffusion patterns had fostered the emergence of the ideology of the internet as transcendent force. When the internet connected few members of society it was likely that disproportionate time on-line would be spent connecting with people living far away. Something as prosaic as a neighbourhood message board is unthinkable when only three people on the street are on-line. As the network effect of this technology took hold, people adopted it because others they already knew were on-line. Communication was not primarily with far-flung mysterious others in virtual worlds, but with the people whom users already cared about most: family, friends and workmates (Quan-Hasse et al. 2002; Boneva and Kraut 2002).

As the internet has become immanent in everyday life, its uses have kept multiplying and democratising. The initial killer application of email is now routinely accompanied by interactions via chat rooms, instant messaging and webphones. Pictures, streaming video, music and data files of all sorts now accompany text. The World Wide Web is now comprehensive, usable and often aesthetically pleasing. Search engines, such as Alta Vista and later Google, have developed clever algorithms to shift web surfing from a cognoscenti's game of memorising arcane URLs and IP addresses to successful surfing through a few well-suggested words. Blogs have moved web creation beyond institutional designers' expertise to everyperson's soapbox (Nolan 2003). Desktop computers have been joined by much smaller laptops (which now represent about 40 per cent of the personal computer market in North America and probably more in East Asia) and PDAs (personal digital assistants such as the Palm). Smart phones are converging with PDAs as the quest for a universal, portable personal appliance continues.

Although a majority of people in developed countries has access to the internet, the digital divide persists. For one thing, access does not necessarily mean use, as people have real or imagined reasons and fears about why they do not use the internet. They are more apt to use mobile phones. In most countries it is the economically privileged or educated (typically men) who are the early adopters. Racial minorities, the economically disadvantaged, and those who do not read English use the internet less than others. This has serious social consequences as companies and government agencies place more services exclusively on-line (Chen and Wellman 2004).

Once the issue of access is resolved, the issue of cultural barriers emerge as the dominant concern. The quality of the Internet experience is a key concern for reducing social inequality (Servon 2003). First, the ability to perform a complex and efficient search is not a skill learned by osmosis, but through experience and openness to the potential of the technology (Hargittai 2003). Second, bloated software that inundates users with ambiguous options and icons can intimidate novices (Baecker et al. 2000). Third, there are time lags in informed use between experienced early adopters, late adopters and newbies. These populations can have significantly different expectations about what to do on-line, and how to do it. Fourth, many sites are only available in English, a language not read by most of the world. Fifth, there are network effects: if one's network members are not on-line, there is less need to use the internet (see Rogers 1995).

The digital divide is narrowing in most developed countries, so that old as well as young, rich as well as poor, are frequently on-line. As time wears on, both women and the less privileged typically turn on, often for the perceived benefit of their children. The gender gap is disappearing in developed countries, with women coming to use the internet as much as men, with the notable exception of Italy. However, the socioeconomic gap persists in most countries even with increasing use, because poorer folks are not increasing their rate of use as much as wealthier, better-educated ones. And the global digital divide is getting even wider, as internet use in developed countries increases much faster than in developing countries (Chen and Wellman 2004).

Although the demographic trends show that internet use is converging within countries, the character of internet use can differ widely between countries. For example, Catalans mostly use the internet for acquiring information and shopping – train schedules, theatre tickets – and less for communicating by email. Catalonia is a local society in a salubrious climate where people gather in cafés to chat face-to-face (Castells et al. 2003). To take another example, teens in developed countries communicate more by mobile phone and instant messages than by email (Ling 2004). In Japan, the proliferation of web-enabled phones means that two hitherto separate communication media are becoming linked: Japanese teens and young adults frequently exchange emails on their mobile phones, or use their PCs to send short text messages to mobile friends (Miyata et al. 2004; Ito et al. 2004). The extent to which such media as email or instant messaging are used depends on the complex interplay of people's tastes, financial resources, culture, geographic location, location in the social structure and national infrastructure.

Pundits have often claimed that the internet is yet another way in which the world is being recast as a 'global village' (McLuhan 1962: 31). The metaphor implies that the role of place is deprecated due to the speed of electronic communication. Yet, the internet is a social phenomenon, and for many reasons one's social network remains at least partially rooted in locality. In Catalonia, when email is used, it is usually to contact someone nearby. In the wired Toronto suburb of 'Netville', those residents with always-on, super-fast internet access knew the names of three times as many neighbours as their unwired counterparts, spoke with twice as many, and visited in the homes of 1.5 times as many (Hampton and Wellman 2003). A Toronto and a Chicago study each found that co-workers were more likely to use the internet when they worked in the same building, in part because they had more tasks and concerns in common (Koku, Nazer and Wellman 2001; Quan-Haase and Wellman 2004). People often use the internet to communicate quickly with nearby others without the disturbance of a phone call or in-person visit. Even many long-distance ties have a local component, as when former neighbours or officemates use the internet to remain in touch, or distant ties arrange a get-together in 'meatspace'.

Nevertheless, the globe-spanning properties of the internet are real, as in the electronic diasporas that connect émigrés to their homeland. The internet enables diasporas to aggregate and transmit reliable, informal news back to often-censored countries (Miller and Slater 2000; Mitra 2003). With physical co-presence also continuing to be important, the internet supports *glocalisation* – both long-distance and local connectivity (Wellman and Hampton 1999) – rather than the imagined 'global village'. In the community and at work, the internet facilitates physically close local ties as well as physically distant ties.

Interestingly, glocalisation has not led to a reduction in levels of communication for the internet actively supports all forms of contact: interpersonally, within organisations, and between organisations. Far from pulling people apart, the internet often brings them closer together. Internet users are more likely than non-users to read newspapers, discuss important matters with their spouses and close friends, form neighbourhood associations, vote and participate in sociable off-line activities, controlling for demographic factors. The more they meet in-person or by telephone, the more they use the internet to communicate. This 'media multiplexity' suggests that the more people communicate by one medium, the more they communicate overall. For example, people might phone to arrange a social or work meeting, alter arrangements over the internet, and then get together in person. Rather than only connecting on-line, in-person or by telephone, many relationships are complex dances of serendipitous face-to-face encounters, scheduled meetings, telephone chats, email exchanges with one person or several others, and broader on-line discussions among those sharing interests.

However, the extensive use of the internet as communications media is not fully pervasive. Gregarious, extroverted people seize on all media available to communicate. They embrace the ways in which the internet gives them an extra and efficient means of community. By contrast, introverts can feel overloaded and alienated (Kraut et al. 2002).

In addition to the workgroup and Netville studies mentioned above, our NetLab research group has observed the presence of media multiplexity in two separate worldwide studies of the internet. The National Geographic Survey 2000 found that overall contact with far away friends is 255 per cent more frequent[3] for heavy email users than for those who never use email, and 149 percent more frequent for far away kin (see Figure 2; Chen, Boase and Wellman 2002; Quan-Haase et al. 2002). The

FIGURE 2   *Frequency of Contact with Far-away Kin (Days/Year)*

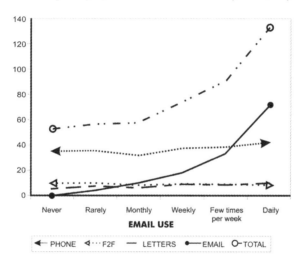

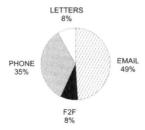

Percentage of Media Used For Contact
With Far-Away Kin (>50 km)

Source: National Geographic Society Survey 2000, North American Data
(*Wired* magazine trajectory).

later National Geographic Survey 2001 showed that email users had 43 percent more days in the run of a month where they would discuss important matters with their spouse via telephone and 7 per cent more days discussing important matters in person[4] (Table 1; see also Hogan 2003). One curious fact emerging from these studies is that people are being more selective of whom they communicate with. Despite the fact that internet users communicate more often with their close friends and spouses, they communicate in person less with those kin who do not communicate online.

TABLE I   *Mean Days of Contact per Month by Type of Relationship*

	Total	On-line = Never	On-line >1/month	Percentage difference
Spouse				
On-line	4.4	0.0	11.5	n/a
Telephone	15.1	15.0	21.4	44
In Person	37.1	36.0	38.7	7
Family in House				
On-line	2.8	0.0	8.0	n/a
Telephone	8.0	4.9	13.8	184
In Person	26.9	28.6	24.3	-15
Family Away				
On-line	5.0	0.0	7.4	n/a
Telephone	10.0	8.1	10.9	34
In Person	5.6	6.1	5.3	-13
Close Friends				
On-line	10.9	0.0	14.3	n/a
Telephone	10.6	7.8	11.5	48
In Person	14.8	11.9	15.6	32

The question matrix was: 'in the past thirty days, how often did you discuss important matters with [relationship type] by [internet, telephone or in person]?'
n/a = not applicable

Neither the utopian hopes of Barlow nor the dystopian fears of Hightower have been borne out. Despite Barlow's hopes, the internet has not brought a utopia of widespread global communication and democracy. Despite Hightower's fears, high levels of internet use have not lured people away from in-person contact. On the contrary, the more people use the internet, the more they see each other in person (distance permitting) and talk on the telephone (Wellman and Haythornthwaite 2002). This may be because the internet helps arrange in-person meetings and helps maintain relationships in between meetings (Haythornthwaite and Wellman 1998). Mobile phones have become a key to arranging get togethers among people who frequently move between social roles and physical sites. Although it is too early to provide a definitive interpretation of such findings, they suggest that internet users are supplementing contact with people with whom they share characteristics (kinship, same ethnic group, same neighborhood) with increased contact with people with whom they share common interests.

The Social Affordances of the Internet

Social scientists have repeatedly shown that technological changes do not determine social behaviour (e.g., Oudshoorn and Pinch 2004). For example, communication scientists mistakenly thought in the 1980s and early 1990s that the lower 'media richness' of the internet would preclude emotional and social conversations. It would be good only for narrow, instrumental matters, such as exchanging information or making arrangements (see the review in Haythornthwaite and Wellman 1998). Yet we daresay that every reader of this chapter has used the internet to exchange emotional support and experience sheer sociability.

Although technology creates certain opportunities and constraints for interaction, 'social affordances' (Norman

1990; Bradner and Kellogg 1999), the actual use of technology is affected by both social structures and social conventions. Technological constraints, be they bandwidth or software capability, prevent people from engaging the internet in a particular way. For example, people cannot stream webcam video on a modem that transmits 28 bits per second, and no amount of textual virtual community will eliminate this constraint. And the switch from the textual DOS interface to the graphical Windows (or Mac) interface afforded the spatial organisation of files and programs. Yet this shift constrained blind people who preferred the sequentially organised command prompt over a mouse-driven interace.

The use of technology is socially malleable. Different cultures use the internet in a wide variety of ways that map on to their existing social patterns. For example, Catalans have a convivial culture that is not amenable to on-line interaction (Castells et al. 2003). As such, they use it most often for coordination and information retrieval. The Japanese send many more short text messages by mobile phones than do Americans, but they use PCs less (Miyata et al. 2004).

Globalised ubiquitous connectivity is another affordance. Inexpensive, rapid internet communication helps immigrants with many long distance ties to maintain their connections back home. At the same time, the digital divide between and within countries means that only the technologically well-connected can be socially well-connected to loved ones abroad.

Personalisation is an emerging affordance. Users can have their own settings, email accounts and desktop aesthetics. Accounts, such as email, are for the person rather than for the household. Coupled with ubiquitous computing, personalisation could soon mean that whenever people log on to communications devices, the device will soon know who they are, where they are, and what settings they prefer. Such personalisation, even at its early stages, is fostering societal shifts from place-to-place connectivity – a particular telephone or computer wired in place – to person-to-person connectivity – a particular user's mobile phone or internet account, wherever located (Wellman 2001a, 2001b)

Although some affordances, such as increased bandwidth, are the result of recent technological developments, others are the result of software innovation (asynchronous email, downloading music). Some affordances combine hardware and software innovation with ideological and cultural shifts to promote personalisation and ubiquitous connectivity. Communication tools such as email, instant messaging and chat rooms are now widely taken for granted in the developed world. If people are not on the internet itself, their family, workmates or friends are.

Rather than a special world, the internet has extended real-world communication. Consider how discourse has shifted in the past fifteen years:

1. 'Have you heard about the Internet?'

2. 'Do you have an email address?'

3. 'What is your email address?'

4. 'Which of your email addresses shall I use?' (reflecting multiple roles).

5. 'Send me an IM [instant message: North American]. Text me a message on your mobile phone [Japan, Europe].'

6. 'I've attached [to this email] pictures of my baby/ boudoir/trip.'

7. 'Do you have a website?'

8. 'What is your web address?'

9. 'Do you have a blog?'

10. 'I've missed seeing you. Let's get webcams.'

11. 'Let's get internet phones and talk to each other all night.'

12. And soon we are going to have buildings, objects and people talking to our personal digital assistants as location becomes salient again for communication and information: 'My PDA says you're in the area. Let's go for a coffee.'

Towards Networked Individualism

A funny thing happened on the way to the embedding of the internet in everyday life. The nature of everyday life changed for many people, from group-centric to network-centric. Much social organisation no longer fits the group model. Work, community and domesticity have moved from hierarchically arranged, densely knit, bounded groups to social networks. In networked societies boundaries are more permeable, interactions are with diverse others, linkages switch between multiple networks, and hierarchies are flatter and more recursive.

The shift to a ubiquitous, personalised, wireless world fosters personal social networks that supply sociability, support and information, and a sense of belonging. Individuals are each becoming a switchboard between their unique sets of ties and networks. Rather than membership in a few broadly supportive groups, people are operating their specialised ties separately to obtain resources. Although people remain connected and supportive, individuals in unique networks have supplanted the traditional organising units of the household, neighbourhood, kin group and work group.

The technological development of computer networks and the societal flourishing of social networks are allowing the rise of networked individualism in a positive feedback loop. Just as the flexibility of less-bounded and spatially dispersed social networks creates demand for collaborative communication and information sharing, the rapid development of computer-communications networks nourishes societal transitions from group-oriented societies to a society of networks.

Rather than fitting into the same group as those around him or her, each person has her own personal network. Household members keep separate schedules, with family get-togethers – even common meals – on the decline in North America (Putnam 2000). Instead of belonging to two stable kinship groups, people are just as likely to have complex household relations, with stepchildren, ex-marital partners (and their progeny) and multiple sets of in-laws. Communities – both in the flesh and the ether – are far-flung, loosely bounded, sparsely knit and fragmentary. Most people operate in multiple, partial communities as they deal with shifting, amorphous networks of kin, neighbours, friends, workmates and organisational ties. Their activities and relationships are informal rather than organisationally structured. Only a minority of network members are directly connected with each other. Most friends and relatives live in different neighbourhoods; many live in different metropolitan areas. At work, people often work *with* distant others and not those sitting near them (Wellman 1999).

The internet has been fostering this transformation by giving people the possibility of communicating and obtaining information when they want, with whom, wherever, whenever, and have their experiences person-alised. This is the societal turn away from groups and toward networked individualism: people connected to each other as individuals rather than as members of households, communities, kinship groups, workgroups and organisations. Yet the internet did not start or predetermine the shift to a network-centric society: the transformation began earlier. Even before the advent of telephones and aeroplanes, some ties with friends and relatives stretched long distances. In the developed world, the flourishing of person-to-person connectivity has been fostered since at least the 1960s by social changes such as dual-career (and dual-schedule families) and liberalised divorce laws reducing household size, and by technological changes that have increased personal mobility and communication. Low-cost flights and motorway trips have enabled in-person get-togethers at distances. Low-cost local and long-distance telephone – and now internet – communication enable rapid connectivity, constrained more by time zone differences than by space (Wellman 1999).

As a result, people probably maintain more long-distance ties with friends, kin and workmates than ever before. It is easy for internet users to search for and be actively involved in far-flung communities of shared interests that are thinly represented on the ground. Groups may have declined (Putnam 2000), but connectivity has not (Wellman 2001b).

Networked individualism is having profound effects on *social cohesion*. Rather than people being a part of a hierarchy of encompassing groups like nesting Russian dolls, they belong to multiple, partial communities. It is not a matter of moving from place to place, but from person to person. People are not so much concerned to gain the support of the group, but to please each network member, one-by-one.

Even as social networks have become less dense, *social linkages* have increased. Internet connectivity adds on to in-person and telephone contact; almost all people had stopped writing letters long before (Wellman and Haythornthwaite 2002). As email can be stored until accessed, it increases contact with long-distance relationships. Moreover, the velocity of internet contact approaches the speed of light, meaning that the only significant delay in email interaction is the time lag set by the user's attention. Additionally, email is seen as less intrusive than telephone calls or in-person meetings. It is often the medium of choice for practical, socially considerate reasons. In short, there is probably more interpersonal contact among more people than ever before.

Although increasing *specialisation* of tastes and combination of roles is not a product of the internet, the culturally rooted design of the internet in a specific brand of individualism considers the person regardless of place and regardless of a socially imposed structure such as a kinship network. Consider how email messages and mobile phone calls arrive sequentially, without inherent regard to the place of reception or to their relationship to the preceding or the following messages. Work messages are followed by postings from interest group lists and communication among family members.

Even as more people go on-line, the uneven distribution of the internet in the individualised networked society creates situations of *social exclusion*. Not only are fewer poor people, less-educated, rural people and non-English-speaking people on-line, their disconnection increasingly excludes them from the opportunities that the internet provides: information, social connection and access to instrumental resources. This disparity is growing between countries as much or more than within countries.

The nature of *citizenship* is changing as part of the turn towards networked individualism. The change began before the coming of the internet, but the immanent internet has accelerated this change and helped shape its nature. Connectivity is up; cohesion is down. Journalists often ask us: 'Is this a good thing or a bad thing?' Our answer is, 'It is just a thing'. It will have good and bad outcomes. However, while the internet is immanent, its effects are not technologically predetermined nor sociologically predestined. They are evolving and their use can be shaped by human decisions.

Notes

1. Search engines to find information had not reached their Netscapian ease of use, and producing web content still required knowledge of computer code. Most businesses did not think that a web presence was crucial until the late 1990s.
2. Howard Rheingold's *The Virtual Community* (1993) is a classic statement, although he markedly tempers his outlook in the second edition (2000). For other recent and more balanced ethnographies, see Kendall (2002) and Chayko (2002).
3. Measured in terms of days per year with contact via any medium.
4. Measured in terms of days per month.

References

Baecker, R. M., K. S. Booth, S. Jovic, J. McGrenere and G. Moore (2000), 'Reducing the Gap between What Users Know and What They Need to Know'. *Proceedings of ACM Conference on Universal Usability 2000*, pp. 17–23.

Barlow, J. P. (1995), 'Property and Speech: Who Owns What You Say in Cyberspace?', *Communications of the ACM*, 38(12), pp. 19–22.

Bell, D. and B. M. Kennedy (2000), *The Cybercultures Reader* (London: Routledge).

Berman, R. and M. Piller (1995), *Star Trek Voyager* (Syndicated television series).

Boneva, B. and R. Kraut (2002), 'Email, Gender, and Personal Relationships', in B. Wellman and C. Haythornthwaite (eds), *The Internet in Everyday Life* (Oxford: Blackwell), pp. 372–403.

Bradner, E. and W. Kellogg (1999), 'Social Affordances of BABBLE', presented to the CHI Conference, Pittsburgh, PA, May.

Castells, M., I. Tubella, T. Sancho, I. Diaz de Isla and B. Wellman (2003), *The Network Society in Catalonia: An Empirical Analysis* (Barcelona: Universitat Oberta Catalunya). http://www.uoc.edu/in3/pic/esp/icl.html

Chayko, M. (2002), *Connecting: How We Form Social Bonds and Communities in the Internet Age* (Albany, NY: State University of New York Press).

Chen, W., J. Boase and B. Wellman (2002), 'The Global Villagers: Comparing Internet Users and Uses around the World', in B. Wellman and C. Haythornthwaite (eds), *The Internet in Everyday Life* (Oxford: Blackwell), pp. 74–113.

Chen, W. and B. Wellman (2004), 'Charting Digital Divides within and between Countries', in W. Dutton, B. Kahin, R. O'Callaghan and A. Wyckoff (eds), *Transforming Enterprise* (Cambridge, MA: MIT Press), forthcoming.

de Chardin, T. (1964), 'The Formation of the Noosphere,' *The Future of Man* (New York: Harper & Row).

De Kerckhove, D. (1997), *Connected Intelligence: The Arrival of the Web Society* (Toronto: Somerville House).

Dery, M. (1997), *Escape Velocity: Cyberculture at the End of the Century* (New York: Grove Press).

Duffy, J. C. (2004), 'Oh baby ... oh baby ... oh baby ...' [cartoon]. *New Yorker*, 16 February.

Fortunati, L., J. Katz and R. Riccini (2003), *Mediating the Human Body: Technology, Communication, and Fashion* (Mahwah, NJ: Lawrence Erlbaum).

Fox, R. (1995), 'Newstrack', *Communications of the ACM*, 38(8), pp. 11–12.

Gibson, W. (1984), *Neuromancer* (New York: Ace Science Fiction).

Greenfield, D. N. (1999), 'The Nature of Internet Addiction: Psychological Factors in Compulsive Internet Use', presented to the American Psychological Association, Boston, August.

Hampton, K. and B. Wellman (2003), 'Neighboring in Netville: How the Internet Supports Community and Social Capital in a Wired Suburb', *City and Community*, 2(3), 277–311.

Hargittai, E. (2003), *How Wide a Web? Inequalities in Accessing Information* (Dissertation, Department of Sociology, Princeton University).

Haythornthwaite, C. and B. Wellman (1998), 'Work, Friendship and Media Use for Information Exchange in a Networked Organization', *Journal of the American Society for Information Science*, 49(12), pp. 1,101–14.

Herring, S. (2004), Slouching toward the Ordinary: Current Trends in Computer Mediated Communication. *New Media & Society*, 6(1), pp. 26–36.

Hogan, B. (2003), 'Media Multiplexity: An Examination of Differential Communication Usage', presented to the Association of Internet Researchers, October.

Ito, M., M. Matsuda and D. Okabe (eds) (2004), *Portable, Personal, Intimate: Mobile Phones in Japanese Life* (Cambridge, MA: MIT Press).

Jankowski, N., S. Jones, L. Lievrouw and K. Hampton (eds) (2004), *What's Changed About the Internet?*, special issue of *New Media & Society*, 6(1).

Kendall, L. (2002), *Hanging out in the Virtual Pub: Masculinities and Relationships Online* (Berkeley: University of California Press).

Koku, E., N. Nazer and B. Wellman (2001), 'Netting Scholars: Online and Offline', *American Behavioral Scientist*, 44(10), 1,750–72.

Kraut, R., S. Kiesler, B. Boneva, J. Cummings, V. Helgeson and A. Crawford (2002), 'Internet Paradox Revisited', *Journal of Social Issues*, 58(1), pp. 49–74.

Kraut, R., M. Patterson, V. Lundmark, S. Kiesler, T. Mukhopadhyay and W. Scherlis (1998), 'Internet paradox: A Social Technology That Reduces Social Involvement and Psychological Well-being?', *American Psychologist*, 53(9), 1,017–31.

Levy, P. (1997), *Collective Intelligence* (Cambridge: Perseus Books).

Ling, R. (2004), *The Mobile Connection: The Cell Phone's Impact on Society* (San Mateo, CA: Morgan Kaufman).

McLuhan, M. (1962), *The Gutenberg Galaxy: The Making of Typographic Man* (Toronto: University of Toronto Press).

Miller, D. and D. Slater (2000), *The Internet: An Ethnographic Approach*, Oxford: Berg.

Mitra, A. (2003), Online Communities, Diasporic, in K. Christensen and D. Levinson (eds), *Encyclopedia of Community* (Thousand Oaks, CA: Sage), vol. 3, pp. 1,019–20.

Miyata, K., J. Boase, B. Wellman and K. Ikeda (2004), 'The Mobile-izing Japanese: Connecting to the Internet by PC and Webphone in Yamanashi', in M. Ito, M. Matsuda and D. Okabe (eds) *Portable, Personal, Intimate: Mobile Phones in Japanese Life* (Cambridge, MA: MIT Press).

Nolan, J. (2003), 'Blogs', in K. Christensen and D. Levinson (eds), *Encyclopedia of Community* (Thousand Oaks, CA: Sage), vol. 1, pp. 96–7.

Norman, D. (1990), *The Design of Everyday Things* (New York: Doubleday).

Oudshoorn, Nelly and Trevor Pinch (2004), *How Users Matter: The Co-Construction of Users and Technology* (Cambridge, MA: MIT Press).

Putnam, R. (2000), *Bowling Alone: The Collapse and Revival of American Community* (New York: Simon & Schuster).

Quan-Haase, A. and B. Wellman (2004), 'Local Virtuality in a High-tech Networked Organization', *Analyses und Kritik*, 16 (Summer), forthcoming.

Quan-Haase, A. and B. Wellman with J. Witte and K. Hampton (2002), 'Capitalizing on the Internet: Network Capital, Participatory Capital, and Sense of Community', in B. Wellman and C. Haythornthwaite (eds), *The Internet in Everyday Life* (Oxford: Blackwell), pp. 291–324.

Raymond, E. (2000), *Homesteading the Noosphere*, accessed 28 January 2004, from http://www.catb.org/-esr/writings/homesteading/homesteading/.

Rheingold, H. (1993), *The Virtual Community: Homesteading on the Electronic Frontier* (Reading, MA: Addison-Wesley).

Rheingold, H. (2000), *The Virtual Community*, rev. edn (Cambridge, MA: MIT Press).

Rogers, E. (1995), *Diffusion of Innovations*, 3rd edn (New York: The Free Press).

Servon, L. (2003), *Bridging the Digital Divide: Technology, Community and Public Policy* (Oxford: Blackwell).

Sproull, L. and S. Kiesler (1991), *Connections* (Cambridge, MA: MIT Press).

Stephenson, N. (1992), *Snow Crash* (New York: Bantam).

Turkle, S. (1995), *Life on the Screen: Identity in the Age of the Internet* (New York: Simon & Schuster).

Van Gelder, L. (1985), 'The Strange Case of the Electronic Lover', *Ms.* (October), 94–104, 117–23.

Vey, P. C. (2004), 'I was addicted to porn before there was an internet' [cartoon], *New Yorker*, 2 February.

Wellman, B. (ed.) (1999), *Networks in the Global Village* (Boulder, CO: Westview Press).

Wellman, B. (2001a), 'Designing the Internet for a Networked Society: Little Boxes, Glocalization, and Networked Individualism. *Communications of the ACM*.

Wellman, B. (2001b), 'Physical Place and Cyberspace: The Rise of Personalized Networks', *International Urban and Regional Research*, 25(2), pp. 227–52.

Wellman, B. and M. Gulia (1999), 'Net Surfers Don't Ride Alone: Virtual Communities as Communities', in B. Wellman (ed.), *Networks in the Global Village* (Boulder, CO: Westview), pp. 331–66.

Wellman, B. and K. Hampton (1999), 'Living networked On and Offline'. *Contemporary Sociology* 28(6), 648–54.

Wellman, B. and C. Haythornthwaite (eds) (2002), *The Internet in Everyday Life* (Oxford: Blackwell).

Wired (2004), 'Hypelist', February 2004, p. 23.

Young, K. S. (1998), *Caught in the Net: How to Recognize the Signs of Internet Addiction – and a Winning Strategy for Recovery* (New York: Wiley).

Acknowledgements

Our research has been supported by the Social Sciences and Humanities Research Council of Canada. We appreciate the help of Julie Wang.

Public Concerns:
E-networking Transformation
and Civil Literacy in Scotland;
Consideration of E-citizenship
and Ethical Dimensions of Strong
Democracy Supported by ICTs

Anna Malina

This chapter considers the development of contemporary information and communication technologies (ICTs), now in process of transforming societal formations and public life in Scotland. The concept of e-citizenship, elements of e-participation, stronger forms of democracy central to the notion of electronic democracy (e-democracy), ethical dimensions associated with this ideal, and the case for tailored programmes in ICT and civic literacies are examined.

Different claims about new digital media have led to public uncertainty about their societal significance, civic worth and consequences for public life. As the opening chapter by Neal Ascherson shows, views on ICTs can be traced to at least three different camps. First are the early pioneers of cyberspace, who believed new technologies could provide the foundation for a new utopia. Second are the negative thinkers, who have seen the embryonic form of a new dystopia. Third are those who visualise a neutral though inherently democratic space, openly available and wholly malleable. The outmoded but still dangerous suggestion in all three viewpoints is that technology somehow develops autonomously, in a space apart from routine contexts and power constructs in society. However, this chapter is based firmly on the premise that ICTs are both social and technical. The use of ICTs influence and are influenced by changing technological developments, historical and geographic environments and a range of societal and human circumstances. The framework of change is subject to different routine contexts, power constructs and a variety of other shaping forces. While the ways in which ICTs are used can never be wholly predicted, certain sets of relations and hegemonies over others inspire, constrain and otherwise guide their development and use (Thompson 1995).

The chapter begins by outlining some of the different explanations of ICT and society. Forces at different geographic levels affecting technology development in the UK are reviewed, and ICT policy development, social inclusion and community development plans in Scotland are briefly outlined. Here, reference is made to how uneven access to ICTs has been seen as a challenge by the UK government and the Scottish Executive. Consideration is given to closer correlations between ICTs, community development planning and social inclusion strategies in Scotland. Ethical dimensions and the moral obligations generated by increasing political interaction on-line are considered, and thought is given to how civic values, aspects of e-citizenship and the features of strong democracy might be incorporated into the design of ICTs. The chapter also examines the features of public participation as they are reflected in concepts of e-government, e-democracy and electronic community networking. Public understanding of the different relationships developing between ICTs and society is considered, and ICT and civic literacy programmes tailored to meet specific needs are suggested. Finally, the chapter offers suggestions for further research.

Some Explanations of Technology and Society and Design of New Roles for Contemporary ICTs

Social explanations of technology and society tend to adhere to one or two general approaches. Arguments stemming from 'functionalism and structuralism propose an imperialism of the social object' (Cassell 1993: 89). In other words, these positions often focus on constraints or even the absence of human agency altogether. Prominent among explanations of the power constructs that drive technology are Marxist perspectives. These include the suggestion that socio-economic forces are the primary influence on the development of new ICTs. Major importance is attached to private concerns – powerful stateless corporations to small and medium-sized enterprises – which seek to increase profit through the commercialisation of new computer-based technologies and the information content they process.

The power contexts in which decisions about the accumulation and distribution of wealth are made are central in the political economy approach to understanding society. Marxist political economists (e.g., Mosco and Wasko 1988; Schiller 1996), for example, attach paramount importance to the social, cultural, political, economic and environmental contexts where technical change actually takes place. Here, structural properties, that is, broader society and its institutions are considered the primary shaping forces on ICTs. In contrast, in human studies, action and human agency are the primary explanation of human behaviour, and interpretative paradigms and discourses focus on the sovereign importance of the subject (Cassell 1993; Taylor et al. 1997).

Structuration theory (Giddens 1993) provides a useful framework to examine the relationship between structure and agency, and resolve the dichotomies between agency and structure; subject and object; process and structure; and interpretivism and functionalism (Giddens 1993). Taking an interactionist perspective, Anthony Giddens argues that structures influence people but are themselves not inevitable since, at least to some extent, they are influenced by the actions of human beings for their own reasons. In this way of thinking, everyone is capable of agency to some degree (Giddens 1993; Cassell 1993). The argument here is that the power and capabilities of technology are guided by human use, established out of the dynamic and constantly changing nature of routine interaction and the interplay of power between human agency and structure (Giddens 1993).

In the 1950s, Harold Innes highlighted the ability of different communication devices to introduce bias into societal processes. The focus here is on the different ways communication devices can be designed. Drawing from work developed under the auspices of the Programme on Information and Communication Technologies (PICT), Mansell and Silverstone (1997), in their publication *Communication by Design*, investigate the history of technological innovations, outlining the characteristics of human agency and engaging with the politics, economics and sociology of modern ICTs. The authors place emphasis on the importance of people, societal organisation, adoption of new ICTs and control, and focus on the 'unpredictable' and 'contradictory' ways that ICTs influence everyday activities (p. 1).

Importantly, the authors also dwell on the meaning of the term design, 'because it embodies the traits of intentionality and purpose, and, therefore, the capability to initiate, as well as constrain, action' (p. 23). A key argument is that particular choices are shown in rational social, economic and political actions, which always reflect the meanings and interests of the dominant groups involved.

Several other commentators have referred to quite distinct descriptions of design, development and use of ICTs for different communities and groups of people in society. Sclove (1995) and Schuler (1996), for example, argue that ICTs can be designed for democratic purposes. New roles for ICTs underpin developments in e-government, e-governance and e-democracy. According to Winner (1996), technologies can promote political change. MacKenzie and Wajcman (1996) illustrate how economic interests can be the primary force involved in the design of technology. We also see new roles developing for ICTs in the community and voluntary sectors to increase organisational efficiency and save money (Osborne 1996). In addition, many community and voluntary sector organisations support public access to ICTs and help to motivate low-income communities to become more active on-line. The aim here is to make communities more democratic and increase entrepreneurial potential, broaden educational capabilities and foster community development (Schon, Sanyal and Mitchell 1999).

Shaping Forces: Global to Local Influences

Information resources supporting use of ICT have grown exponentially over the past few years. Many provide web-links to global information, government projects, trans-national, national, sub-national and local sites, and non-government projects concerned with e-government and e-democracy.[1] The wide-ranging nature of these resources emphasises the interrelationships between global, international, national, regional and local levels. Recognising the growing interdependence between different nations and geographic locations, the heads of state or government representing the world's leading industrialised nations have for a number years met annually to address the major economic and political issues facing their nations and the international community as a whole. Participating countries have shared goals to tackle unemployment, create more jobs and deal with social exclusion.

Collaborative means have been sought to improve the quality of life in cities and towns. Devising directives for sustainable growth in the global economy, growth in individual economies and ability to create jobs and tackle social exclusion in cities and towns were key objectives throughout the 1990s. A major focus fell on the dispossessed and socially excluded and it was agreed that much greater attention should be directed at ways to develop community and address social and cultural problems thought to threaten quality of life in deprived areas. If nothing was done, residents in these marginalised localities were considered most in danger of being excluded even further by the arrival of an information-based society.

Since 1995, the G8 Government On-Line Project, which brings together the heads of governments of twenty developed nations, has outlined strategies for the information society, e-government and e-democracy.[2] Countries in the developing world are being informed by so-called developed countries,[3] for example, in a *Roadmap for e-Government in the Developing World*, issues and problems common to e-government efforts are highlighted and questions are posed that are 'crucial to successfully conceiving, planning, managing and measuring e-government' (Pacific Council on International policy).[4] In 2001, the OECD (Organisation for Economic Co-operation and Development)[5] report titled *Citizens as Partners: Information, Consultation and Public Participation in Policy-making,*[6] suggested that OECD countries must spend time and effort in building the legal, policy and institutional frameworks to ensure citizen access to information and greater involvement in consultation and active participation in public policy-making. It was indicated that governments should also evaluate their performance in achieving these goals.

Rapid policy innovation at the European Union level since the 1980s established the European Commission (EC) as a key actor in the ICT field (Gram 1997). Several land-mark documents have shaped development of ICTs in Europe spreading the belief that new technologies would transform the economies of member states, increase jobs and promote sustainable development. The preamble to the EC's White Paper, *Growth, Competitiveness and Employment* (1993) (also known as the Delors Report), suggested the need to foster debate and to assist decision-making – at decentralised, national or Community level – so as to lay the foundations for sustainable development of the European economies, thereby enabling them to withstand international competition while creating the millions of jobs that are needed.

The White Paper (1993) pointed to the need to exploit 'assets' such as 'abundant non-physical capital (education, skills, capacity for innovation, traditions)' (from *Growth, Competitiveness and Employment*) and to exploit fully the economic and social opportunities seen to be on offer in a newly emerging Information Society. Following on from the White Paper, a report to the European Community (EC), entitled *Europe and the Global Information Society: Recommendations to the European Council* (1994), also known as the Bangemann Report,[7] predicated widespread panic in announcing that ICTs were generating a new industrial revolution throughout the world, already as significant and far-reaching as those of the past. While there was little empirical evidence to back up such massive claims, the Bangeman Report suggested that new working patterns and new jobs must be created and new skills learned to suit a new information era. The fear emerged that all those unable to adapt would be left behind.

Shaping a focus on critical mass, the Bangemann Report recommended that public awareness should be promoted about the power of ICT and that 'particular attention should be paid to the small and medium-sized enterprise (SME) business sector, public administrations and the younger generation'. The Bangemann Report also highlighted the need for new interrelationships and promoted the idea of partnership between individuals, employers, unions and governments. Much as European policy had endorsed development of enterprise capitalism, however, directives post-Bangemann also highlighted social inclusion and the need to support European citizens likely to be further marginalised by rapid ICT developments. The Green Paper, *Living and Working in the Information Society: People First* (1996), developed many of the directives around employment, skills and social cohesion and also ensured a continuing focus on the importance of SMEs and uptake of IT in Europe.

The fear was that the emergence of an Information Society might exacerbate existing problems or lead to new forms of social exclusion. In appraising the circumstances where some groups exist on the margins of society, the European Union applied the term social exclusion. Duffy (1995) in Oppenheim (1998: 13) later defines social exclusion as 'alienation' and 'inability to participate effectively in economic, social, political and cultural life'. The INSINC Report (1997: 15) suggests social exclusion is 'fundamentally an economic phenomenon which has important social and political consequences'. In Oppenheim's (1998) view, however, those suffering poverty are not necessarily socially excluded, although poverty often is a contributory factor. One answer has been to find innovative ways to prevent social exclusion and also to bring excluded groups on the periphery of society back into the mainstream. Policy initiatives in the UK and its regions have attempted to address the problem and much EU funding has found its way into small-scale deprived communities to promote social inclusion.

In addition to the promotion of projects to increase social capital and address issues of poverty, joblessness and social exclusion, the EU has also encouraged the idea of partnership between the public, private and third sectors.

Partnership has also been encouraged between different tiers of government and at European and local geographic levels. The potential of the community and voluntary sectors to build trust in user groups and increase civic participation was also identified.

The EU promoted a central institutional framework which became the dynamic driving force behind policies for the elaboration of ICT throughout Europe (Gram 1997). DGXIII was responsible for the development of a broad research programme for ICT, and in the 1990s ICT policy was seen 'as a central aspect of the transformation of the European economy' (Gram 1997: 79). Initially devised as a medium-term planning device, a series of Research and Development Framework Programmes was initiated. A number of Framework Programmes has now run, and the UK along with other member states has had to negotiate for a share of what became loosely known as structural funding.[8] Such funding was allocated to specific projects and locally organised pilot schemes often organised by voluntary groups and community organisations. It could be argued that voluntary groups and community organisations have been obliged to adopt the ideals established at a central European level and support the notion of digital inclusion. Key elements of digital inclusion are contained in *e-Europe 2002* and *e-Europe 2005*. A trend towards social change management suggested greater efforts would heighten local community identity and increase democratic participation. Over time, EU funding has continued to be available for bottom-up projects in local communities which involve the development and use of ICT to support inclusion and broader and deeper forms of public participation.

Setting off a chain of new policy guidelines, the UK Government White Paper *Modernising Government* (1999)[9] put forward the view that good policy must be 'strategic, holistic and focused specifically on outcomes and delivery, evidence based, and inclusive'. The focus on being inclusive refers to the need to take account of the impact of policy on different groups. From 2000, decision-making in the UK was strongly influenced by the concept of joined-up government, devised by central government to 'wire the British State together again' (Richards and Smith 2002: 21) At the Prime Minister's request, a report titled *Wiring it Up* (2000) was produced by the Performance and Innovation Unit (PIU), primarily to identify what tensions and weaknesses within the UK's Whitehall government needed to be reformed and modernised. The report indicates that more cross-cutting action would guard against 'purely departmental objectives', and a vision and strategy is outlined here for improving cross-cutting policy and service delivery for the twenty-first century. The UK government also established a Cabinet Committee to oversee e-democracy in the UK, and to develop a strategy for its development and roll out.

A development and action plan for e-democracy was produced for public consultation during the period between July and October 2002. In this document, which set out the UK government's aim of using new technologies to strengthen democracy, the government highlights the need for broader society to help define e-democracy, and to engage directly with those that e-democracy policy concerns. Action is proposed in two main areas: e-participation and e-voting. The document suggests that public participation is essential to effective policy making. The document proposes that e-democracy policy should illustrate the importance of ICTs in helping to facilitate, broaden and deepen participation in the democratic process. Facilitation involves easy access to public information, ability to follow the political process, discuss and form groups, to get engaged in policy formation, scrutinise government and vote in elections. ICTs were also seen as potentially useful in helping people interact directly with their elected representatives, and with government and political parties.

Broadening participation relates to using ICT to include more people in the democratic process, particularly those who are already excluded. It also refers to using ICT to encourage and motivate those who are unable or unwilling to participate. Deepening participation is about developing and sustaining civic interaction in the long term to promote stronger forms of participatory democracy.

Striving to achieve universal access to the Internet by 2005, the Scottish Executive indicated commitment to closing the digital divide (for more information, see Malina and MacIntosh 2004). Considerable emphasis has been placed on expanding the communications infrastructure (see *Connecting Scotland: Our Broadband Future* 2001), also to addressing poverty, lack of awareness, and low skill levels, which may be seen as benchmarks to analyse digital exclusion/inclusion (see *Digital Inclusion, Connecting Scotland's People* 2001). Well-funded initiatives support the idea of socially inclusive information society development. A network of Internet access points has been established to make provision in poor areas of Scotland, using sites such as bus stations, hairdressers, pubs, shops and doctors' surgeries.

The Scottish Executive is working under the twenty-first-century government banner to ensure technology is used innovatively to support modern, high-quality, efficient and effective public services. As the report *Information Age Government in Scotland: A Common Approach*[10] indicates, joined-up services are necessary to ensure that organisations work in partnership and focus on the citizen/customer. A common framework is being developed to bring savings from economies of scale. The hope is that problems in relation to access, authentication and data protection will be cheaper to deal with using a common approach. It is also hoped that exchanging information will help to support good practice in areas such as data-sharing, management and skills development.

The UK's e-government interoperability framework provides policies and standards to ensure that the internet and world wide web and common usable standards are adopted for all UK government systems. There is a commitment to removing pre-existing policy barriers that might unintentionally create problems: for example, under old legislation, local council meetings cannot be held electronically. As the report points out, it will be possible to remove some legislation using the UK Electronic Communications Act (2000). However, to support electronic service delivery by 2005, primary legislation will be required to remove other barriers in Scotland.

Scottish technical standards for the operation of websites, call centre and digital TV will be in line with the rest of the UK. With a key focus on the citizen, government portals across the UK are offering services they feel are relevant to life episodes. Closely linked to the UK Government Portal,[11] the aim is to bring the Scottish Government Portal under the brand of Open Scotland,[12] to promote choice and public take-up of services. Important web-based information sites and web-enabled services that already exist will also be brought together. Authentication is an important issue, and implementation of effective security procedures adheres to a common framework set out by the UK Cabinet Office working group, comprising representatives from the devolved regions. Working groups have been set up to assess potential and ensure technical standardisation.

The development of technology supported identity cards (ID cards) has been contentious. While over a hundred countries already have compulsory ID cards, including Germany, Belgium and Spain, citizens and civic liberty organisations resist their implementation in other countries. The use of these cards is seen by many as an infringement of the citizen's right to remain anonymous if they so choose. Moreover, while ID cards give the state powers it has only ever had before in wartime, no hard evidence is available to show that they actually do provide additional security for citizens. As yet, there is no empirical evidence that ID cards will reduce crime or terrorism. Many members of the public opposed the use of ID cards during a public consultation organised by the UK government.

The problem of civil liberties has often been cited in relation to ID cards. However, the government has tended to dismiss these objections, highlighting instead unresolved issues to do with cost and effectiveness. More recently, the Prime Minister argued that ID cards could potentially protect civic liberty. On the face of it, the government appears to be more cautious in regard to the development of an ID card system. However, there are plans to test the potential of 'biometrics' in relation to the use of ID cards. This involves storage of face, hand or finger features such that they can be read by a computer. There are plans also by the UK Passport Service to test technology that checks the identity of passport holders using automated face recognition. Ten thousand volunteers will receive a smartcard and help test the use of face, iris and fingerprint recordings. This would pave the way for UK passport procedures to be harmonised with those in the USA. A biometric ID card is also likely to be phased in over a period of several years to deal with issues such as illegal working, immigration abuse, fraud, terrorism and organised crime. In addition, an ID database will form the basis of child protection reforms. Each child in England will have a unique identity number linked to a local authority database. It seems very likely that the path towards a comprehensive ID card system in the UK will be carved out in incremental steps over the coming years. The Queen's speech in November 2003 indicated a compulsory system could be in operation by 2010. Such a system would only be possible after a decision by the Cabinet and a vote in Parliament.

In Scotland, *Information Age Government in Scotland: A Common Approach* suggests that privacy, protection of the rights of citizens, and processing of personal data is safeguarded by the Data Protection Act (1998). The argument is being made that 'smartcards' are potentially useful to businesses and citizens, in that they can provide access or proof of entitlement to services. Plans are being made to introduce a trial 'entitlement card' scheme in different areas of Scotland. The cards are being tested in service areas such as library loans, the paying of rent, and the provision of health information. Security for government data and systems are supported by the accepted international standard for information security. The expectation is for public bodies to comply with these standards.

The notion of networking is central to joining up service delivery at different levels. The Information Age Government in Scotland report shows that the Scottish Executive's computer network and a range of UK government bodies are connected to one another through the Government Secure Intranet (GSI), providing information services such as government information, travel, news, business and procurement. The eventual goal is to join up GSI content and services with community intranets to support further the UK government's goal of joined-up government. Scottish Local Authorities may also join the GSI extranet since it provides a network infrastructure supportive of electronic service delivery. Taking a common approach and ensuring common standards will help support information sharing and will also help with joining up services.

Geographic Information Systems (GIS) provide spatial information and comparative information about local neighbourhoods in Scotland. It is expected GIS will support the Executive's Neighbourhood Statistics Initiative. An Electronic Record Management system records individual transactions that will be retained and maintained in a controlled manner over medium to long terms. Again UK-wide standards are considered key aspects. Public sector skills are highlighted as necessary in delivering goods, and the Cabinet Office is in process of identifying and analysing what skills are necessary. Effective leadership is needed to see the big picture, according to the report, to assess how things can be improved and also to identify key priorities. In developing new systems, the Scottish Office keeps in close contact with the central UK Government's Office of the e-Envoy and the Cabinet Office in Whitehall. Links to local government have been established through appointment of a local councillor and senior official as authorised twenty-first century government advocates.

A Central/Local Government forum oversees developments. Planning for service delivery is being built into the business plans of public sector organisations. These plans shape delivery targets and overall business strategies. Services that could be on-line or that could provide great benefit are to be identified and prioritised. While Scottish Executive plans are in place to monitor developments across the whole Scottish Public Sector, local government procedures are to be monitored by the Central/Local Government Forum. Sharing best practice across the spectrum of e-government development and e-public service delivery is of central importance.

According to Denhardt (1993), public administration in the past has been limited by business values and the quest for efficiency, and also by adherence to hierarchy and bureaucracy. In his view, efficiency and control have long taken precedence over democratic principles such as freedom, justice, equality and participation in public sector organisation. However, he argues, democratic principles such as liberty, justice, equity and responsiveness should guide management in public sector organisations. A high level of participation and the involvement of all members of public sector organisations would improve quality and productivity; and values such as participation, involvement and a sense of community would better serve public service delivery to the citizen/consumer.

Local government throughout the UK is primarily based on a model of representative democracy. In practice this has meant that involvement in democracy has become quite passive for citizens. However, with the arrival of interactive technology and the growing focus on the ideals of governance, increased participation at community level is now gaining momentum. Supporting arguments for a new democratic polity, Pratchett (2000) suggests drawing on elements of direct, consultative, deliberative and representative democracy to enhance a new democratic governance order that is better suited to the modern world.

The modernising vision for local government in Scotland underlines the intention to move beyond the politics of consumer satisfaction towards a more inclusive, deliberative and participatory democratic politics supported by ICTs. The Local Government in Scotland Act (2003)[13] supports development of the Scottish Executive's modernisation agenda for local government, and gives councils in Scotland more responsibility to act in partnership with other bodies and communities, and to build a framework that will enable delivery of more effective and responsive public services. Increasingly, local councils in Scotland have adopted an 'enabling' role to support partnership processes, community planning and a range of new ways to involve citizens and communities. Enabling community leadership and supporting community and voluntary sector organisations in interacting with citizens is increasingly vital to the model of local governance now being adopted in Scotland.

The Local Government in Scotland Act (2003) provides a statutory basis for Community Planning in Scotland. This is primarily a framework for making modern public services responsive to, and organised around, the needs of communities. The *Evaluation of the Working for Communities Programme* (DTZ Pieda 2003 – Research

Findings No. 163/2003), indicates that two main aims are to:

- ensure people and communities are generally engaged in the decisions made on public services which affect them; allied to:
- a commitment from organisations to work together, not apart, in providing better public services.

Two principles are associated with this:

- community planning is to be the key over-arching partnership framework helping to co-ordinate other initiatives and partnerships and where necessary acting to rationalise and simplify a cluttered landscape.
- community planning is to improve the connection between national priorities and those at a regional, local and neighbourhood level.

Community planning has been developed to ensure that the needs of individuals and communities are addressed cohesively and in joined-up fashion by all local organisations. According to *Communities Scotland: Integrating Social Inclusion partnerships and Community Planning Partnership* (August 2003: 2),[14] community planning is about 'the structures, processes and behaviours necessary to ensure organisations work together with communities to improve the quality of people's lives, through more effective, joined-up and appropriate delivery of services'. It is also recognised that cultural changes are needed and existing partnerships and networks need to be improved where they are lacking, and built upon where they are seen to be working well.

Communities Scotland,[15] a Scottish Executive Agency, has been set up to deal with housing and to improve regeneration action. This organisation is working in partnership with a broad range of national, regional, local and community organisations and with local authorities to renew the social economy, ensure social justice and tackle disadvantage in Scotland. A variety of partnerships is to come under this umbrella. Social Inclusion Partnerships (SIPs), whose remit since the mid-1990s has been to tackle poverty and disadvantage in communities across Scotland, will be integrated into the Community Planning Framework. SIPs and Community Planning Partnerships (CPPs) that already exist are also being integrated and are expected to play a key role in helping communities in Scotland take control of community regeneration.

A key aspiration, according to *Integrating Social Inclusion Partnerships and Community Planning Partnerships* (August 2003), is to ensure 'local regeneration takes place within the wider strategic context of community planning so that core services and core budgets of public bodies are working together to close the opportunity gap for disadvantaged communities' (p. 3). Another aim, according to the same report, is to 'allow decision-making on regeneration to be taken at the neighbourhood level within a national framework' (p. 3).

Other goals are to link up physical, social and economic regeneration more effectively, build on previous strengths, support disadvantaged geographic and interest communities, and maintain a clear focus on the needs of communities and how agencies involved in community planning are meeting those needs (p. 3). ICTs and electronic networks are to provide key supports.

The government target of delivering services on-line by 2005 will be the main driver in preparing and implementing an e-business strategy for Communities Scotland. Information and communications technology infrastructure and systems are being upgraded to make them compatible with the rest of the Scottish Executive.

Recognising the importance of the community and voluntary sectors in supporting a socially inclusive information society, the National Grid for Learning (NGfL) Scotland Communities Channel[16] offers on-line advice, support and content for community and voluntary sector organisations working to bridge the digital divide in local communities. The channel aims to provide learning support to all those promoting the use of information and communications technologies (ICTs) in the community. Working in partnership with others at the community level, the Communities Channel is designed to serve community development practitioners throughout Scotland. Their strategy document outlines the vision to ensure that 'every member of all communities has the access, capability and motivation to exploit the information and learning environment facilitated by the National Grid for Learning'.

A toolkit is available to provide help with practical issues surrounding the use of ICT in a community project. The case studies section of the communities channel website provides information about existing projects in Scotland and many others internationally, and also offers insight into partnerships, funding sources, lessons learned and useful contact details.

The Communities Channel works closely with Scotland's Digital Inclusion Champions team.[17] This three-year programme is managed by Scottish Enterprise to help all late adopter groups in the most disadvantaged communities in Scotland gain access to and use ICTs and the Internet. Champions are based in Local Enterprise Companies (LECs) and work in partnership with others in their SIP area to improve ICT provision and use of ICT. The goal is to provide expert advice, guidance and practical help to local community and voluntary organisations who want to fund new and innovative ICT initiatives in their own community.

Incorporating Ethical Values to Advance Democracy and Civic Participation On-line

A minimalist Schumpeterian view of democracy suggests a system in which rulers are selected by competitive elections rather than by unscrupulous or violent means (Przeworski, in Shapiro and Hacker-Gordon 1999). However, voting periodically to elect representatives is sometimes considered a 'thin' form of democracy in which people have little direct influence on important public decisions. Support for stronger forms of participation, drawing on the ethical principles of what Barber (1992) and Sclove (1995) have termed 'strong democracy', has gathered momentum. This moral ideal envisages better opportunities for citizens to develop responsibility and participate in important decisions that affect themselves and other members of the public. More direct public participation, however, need not totally replace representative democracy. Instead, deeper and wider forms of participation associated with the ideals of strong democracy can be harmonised with interactive technologies to complement representative democracy and form a new composite model.

Sclove (1995) perceives technology as a form of social structure, and he argues that technological design needs to be democratised. In this approach the public should become more involved in designing the technology they will use for democratic purposes. This is in marked contrast to processes of technological development that are guided primarily by market forces and most often allied to the self-interested intentions of large corporate organisations.

According to Fotopoulos (1997), 'inclusive democracy' requires activity in all realms of life. It requires public participation 'in any area of human activity where decisions can be taken collectively and democratically' (p. 206). These include political, economic and social realms.

Fotopoulos defines the political realm as the sphere of political decision-making. The economic realm relates to economic choices and economic decision-making, and the social realm includes decision-making in the workplace, education, and any other economic or cultural institution which is part of a democratic society.

Citizen Participation: E-government, E-democracy, M-communications and Electronic Community Networking

As tax payers in a democracy, citizens in democracies increasingly feel they have a right to government information. In addition people increasingly want ethical and responsible use of funds for quality, high-standard multi-channel service delivery, managed by transparent and accountable governmental institutions and officials. E-government is about the different ways in which a modern government and its institutions design and use ICTs, both internally and externally, to conduct the business of government and improve the organisation of service delivery. Promoting better and more efficient public services, incorporating citizen needs and collective interests, and increasing transparency, public accountability and trust in government initiatives are central. A continuum model in four stages to develop e-government is described by Backus (2002). The first stage is for government to disseminate information. The second is to increase two-way interaction between government and citizens. The third is to establish a system of 'transaction' in order to handle administration for different processes, for example, using e-forms to complete tax returns or conduct registration payments. The fourth stage is to support democratic transformation by increasing democratic participation.

Government portals[18] are being designed to support cheaper, more effective and more efficient electronic government administrations, better associations with business and closer electronic relationships between governments, their representatives and citizens. The UK Government provides a government gateway to transactional services. The hope is also to ensure that those members of the public with disabilities are able to use assistive technologies to access services. Listening to feedback from the public is important to make the changes that will provide the kind of on-line services that meet citizen expectations of good service delivery. Simplified language is important and effective search capabilities and site navigation is also helpful. The hope is that improving public service delivery will be more convenient, and will also enhance procurement procedures and lower cost.

Mobile communications, m-communications, are also providing important channels of interaction between governments and citizens. Throughout different areas of the world, citizens may now choose to receive information relating to public services using their mobile communication systems. In Singapore, for example, citizens are able to receive alerts when they need reminders about road tax or passport renewal. In London, the police are sending text message alerts to businesses about security threats. In the Philippines, SMS-based services provide new opportunities for citizens to request information and/or comment on the performance of government services and/or government officials. SMS-based services are also being developed to facilitate mobile transactions and payments.

The concepts of e-democracy and electronic citizenship highlight new opportunities for closer associations between ICTs and the Internet, the organisation and practice of democracy, and the nature of citizenship in modern democracies. In particular, these concepts signify new possibilities for citizens who are supported by ICTs to assume the rights and duties associated with democratic citizenship and become involved in on-line political discussions and decision-making, interacting openly with governments, state institutions, political representatives and with one another.

In 2001, an OECD report *Citizens as Partners: Information, Consultation and Public Participation in Policy-making* suggested that OECD countries must spend time and effort in building the legal, policy and institutional frameworks to ensure citizen access to information and greater involvement in consultation and active participation in public policy-making. By 2003, the European Commission had created a new web portal with information available in all eleven EU languages to make it easier for all European citizens to make their voices heard in EU policy-making.[19]

Governments within many countries are using the internet to provide citizens with access to policy information and opportunity to respond and influence decision-making. Some countries have placed emphasis on developing electronic consultations (e-consultations), electronic deliberation (e-deliberation) forums and/or electronic petitioning (e-petitioning).

E-consultations are organised to input public views to decision-making at pre-policy and draft policy stages. The Cabinet Office of the UK government has outlined a code of practice for both written and electronic consultations.[20] E-deliberation illustrates how people can use ICTs to exchange information and conduct open rational debate about a range of issues, Citizens are enabled to go on-line to talk openly about a particular issue, and are able to access a range of electronic information on the subject area, perhaps listening to a range of opinions and alternative points of view on-line and adding their own opinions to the debate. Citizens are able to use on-line platforms to express their views and persuade others. The organisation of deliberative forums does not demand face-to-face synchronous interaction and allows a great many more people to be involved in decision-making processes at times suited to their own busy schedules.

A petition traditionally is a submission to a governing body requesting that an action be taken or a view considered. Some electronic petitions (e-petitions) take the form of a simple chain email while others are hosted on websites designed by pressure groups, third party organisations or legislative authorities. Depending on design, an e-petitioning system can offer potential to extend citizen participation. E-petitioning can, for example, provide electronic information on the petition issue and opportunities to submit views on-line about the issue and petition text itself. Signatories may add their names electronically in asynchronous time from remote locations anywhere in the world. It is also possible to submit the petition electronically and provide on-going feedback to indicate progress and any actions taken after the e-petition has been submitted to an authority. Several parliaments accept e-petitions, for example, the German Bundestag and the Scottish and UK Parliaments.

Democratic entitlements encompass rights and responsibilities for both state and citizenship, including the right to vote. Increasing attention is centred now on developing e-voting. After a great many flaws came to light in the Florida e-voting trials during the 2000 presidential elections, scepticism increased. However, many liberal democratic countries are continuing to experiment at small-scale and community levels in attempts to overcome problems. Attention has been given to poll site voting, kiosk voting and remote Internet voting. At poll sites, people could vote using the Internet under the control of election officials. It is possible for e-voting kiosks to be placed in local communities in the places people use frequently. Election officials could still monitor voting procedures, perhaps using remote cameras to ensure proper procedures are followed. Remote voting can be organised from any location where it is possible to access the Internet. Citizens could, for example, vote from open-access community centres, home, work and play and from anywhere outside the country, even when on holiday.

M-voting and use of SMS and mobile devices are also being developed to enhance participation. In the UK, experiments in voting via mobile phones are being conducted. Proponents of electronic voting believe it could help increase voter participation. There are many problems still to overcome, for example, security and validity, and the jury is still out as to the eventual form of e-voting/m-voting. But what is absolutely clear is that while the arrival of electronic technology mobile communications offers many new possibilities for modernisation, merely introducing technology to streamline the way people vote is unlikely on its own to address the root problems of public distrust of government. With increasing access to alternative news services provided via new ICTs, many people are going in search of independent, accurate, spin-free news and information to supplement mainstream news.

Digital inclusion strategies have high priority in many modernising countries in the world. Concerns have been expressed over the so-called 'digital divide', the gap between populations that are computer literate and have widespread access to the Internet and those populations that have no familiarity with computers and no Internet access. Digital inclusion policies are designed to prepare everyone, including previously excluded groups and individuals, for on-line interaction. A torrent of state funding has been produced to support a range of developments and local community projects. Much work has centred on extending universal access and promoting widespread acquisition of skills that will make it possible to participate in all aspects of the on-line world.

Civic associations and organisations are thought to be the basis of democracy, and Putnam argues that citizens in less civic regions tend to feel oppressed, estranged, and helpless. Civic participation, as conceived by communitarians, is about enhancing community feeling. In parts of the USA, Canada and Europe in the mid-1980s, community activists and volunteers began to join up with computer enthusiasts, hobbyists, the voluntary sector, universities, local authorities and private Internet Service Providers to design low-cost public access to a range of local community networks and on-line information and communication resources that could help build community. The focus was primarily on civic participation to enhance social, cultural, political and/or economic life in local communities. Electronic community networks were designed to address community and public interest issues. People began to interact in on-line public spheres that were largely separate from government and the market.

Community media, primarily driven by social rather than profit-making motives, provide a conduit for developing equitable public interaction at local levels. The goal of community media is primarily to empower people, nurture local knowledge (rather than replace it with standard solutions) and support civic participation. The concept of participation at the local level has a long history supported by civic networks. These networks exist off-line as well as on-line. Pinkett (2000) and Turner and Pinkett (2000) suggest that local people resident in a geographic neighbourhood can be encouraged to use ICTs to express aspects of their cultural heritage, to interact broadly in technology supported community forums, building community assets and recognising themselves as active change agents. In relation to community network content, the fundamental premise of this paradigm is that local residents are the active producers of community information.

To be socially inclusive technology infrastructure needs to be built from the bottom-up. Locality is extremely important, in particular because people living in local communities provide the vital foundation for ICTs and local networks of relations to develop.

ICT Literacies to Broaden and Deepen E-participation and Democratic Practice

However, not everyone wants to use new technology. A study by the Oxford Internet Institute (Rose 2003) suggests that 'while the battle for digital access is being won, we now face a struggle to convince everyone the net is worth using ... people who don't use the internet don't see how it will help them in their everyday affairs'. It seems people generally find it difficult to see why they should use the Internet and what it will offer them.

While much attention has been placed on increasing the public's ability to use technology, there are arguments also for more meaningful use and for development of ICT literacy strategies[21] to increase understanding and sharpen critical thinking skills. A report of the International ICT Literacy Panel, *Digital Transformation: A Framework for ICT Literacy* (2002), posits that 'IT literacy cannot be defined primarily as the mastery of technical skills ... the concept of ICT literacy should be broadened to include both critical cognitive skills as well as the application of technical skills and knowledge' (p. 1). ICT literacy is viewed by the panel as a continuum of skills and abilities. Truly informed action can only come from knowledgeable, reasoned insights.

According to the 21st Century Literacy Summit, held in 2002 in Berlin, literacy levels need to be built in three key areas: education, workplace skills and civic engagement. The 21st Century Literacy Summit White Paper (2002: 4–5)[22] argues that to enhance knowledge and critical thinking skills in these areas, attention needs to be given to build:

- technology literacy – ability to use new media such as the internet to access and communicate information effectively.
- information literacy – ability to gather, organise, filter and evaluate information, and to form valid opinions based on the results
- media creativity – growing capacity of individuals everywhere to produce and distribute content to audiences of all sizes
- social competence and responsibility – competence to consider the social consequences of an on-line publication and the responsibility vis-à-vis children.

Several international examples of initiatives in education, the workplace and public policy are described in this White Paper. The suggestion is made that governments must involve diverse communities in developing on-line services. In addition, there is need for mechanisms to listen to feedback from users. Tools should be easy to use, convenient and reliable. According to the White Paper, government employees could also be involved in developing public services. Benefits of using technology should be very obvious to users, for example, through broader opportunities to influence events via e-petitioning or shorter times in completing and filing tax forms. Provision of services that are of value to people is crucial, as is information about how public input is considered and processed by government.

Additional recommendations in this White Paper (p. 11) include:

- Democracy, even in electronic form, is not something that can simply be delivered to the doorstep. It takes commitment from all parties involved and requires the willingness to test new ideas and challenge old assumptions'.

- e-government programmes must not simply provide electronic delivery of services. They must also ensure that diverse ideas and opinion are fully integrated into public decision-making processes.

- Public sector web offerings must operate in a client-operated manner, continually recognising and evaluating people's preferences, and providing appropriate solutions.

- Sufficient resources must be provided to train the public in twenty-first-century literacy skills and ensure equitable access to the necessary tools.

- The broad range of e-democracy tools available today should be bundled and made available to those organisations that have not been among the first generation of non-government organisations (NGOs) to use the Internet. The establishment of an e-democracy competence centre can co-ordinate these efforts efficiently.

- More commitment is needed to strengthen non-government interest and action groups. The value of e-democracy in twenty-first-century society needs to be clearly recognised. It is also important to determine which public sector tasks can be given to the private sector, whether they are commercial enterprises or non-commercial entities dealing with relevant social issues.

Correia (2002) argues that an active, effective and responsible citizenship requires that more people are empowered to exercise rights and responsibilities towards other people, the community and the state. Increasingly, elements of civic life are reflected on the Internet, and there are signs that in years to come democratic politics will increasingly be conducted on-line (Arterton 2003). As Alexander (2003) points out, the legitimacy of participation is dependent on developing key aspects of citizenship rather than only providing access to a computer.

Barber (1992) suggests citizens need appropriate literacy levels to live in modern civic society. Democratic participation is educational and empowering. Learning, confidence and development of knowledge may be achieved during the process of participation. For Barbour, what is needed is competence to participate in democratic communities, ability to think critically and act deliberately in a pluralist world, and empathy that permits us to hear and accommodate others (p. 128). To help develop more inclusive and widespread public participation, we may benefit from tailored civic literacy programmes, which are aimed at politicians, officials in positions of power and ordinary citizens, to increase knowledge of what is possible in a more participatory democratic system supported by modern technology, and to outline areas of responsibility.

In similar vein to Barbour, Milner (2002) argues that only informed citizens will make participatory democracy work. He draws from previous research to suggest that more informed people tend to vote more. From comparative data, Milner points to indications that there is a higher turn-out in those countries where the average levels of knowledge of public affairs are higher. Further, he claims that 'a society's level of civic literacy reflects the proportion of adults possessing the knowledge required for effective political choice, a proportion that changes over time and varies among countries' (p. 6). It follows that if politically informed people participate more in democracy, then there is a responsibility on governments and their institutions locally to produce adequate and balanced information. There is also a responsibility, according to Stoker (1996), to provide adequate public forums for open political activity. In turn, the public's responsibility is to become informed by the information provided by governments and to participate actively in relation to public issues that concern them.

Several projects have been designed to help increase levels of civic literacy in the community. For example, the Public Broadcasting Service in Virginia, supported by 349 public television stations in the USA, produced an on-line democracy project aimed at raising awareness in young people,[23] and also to help adults build their knowledge of democracy.[24] In Miami-Dade County, in the USA, the Department for e-government developed a civic literacy project aimed at young people. Government has traditionally been an unattractive topic for children, and information about the nature and structure of local government and civic life has either been unavailable to children, or presented in terms that are confusing and difficult to grasp. The project, 'Under the Sea City',[25] is a technology-based initiative using the metaphor of an underwater world to foster a sense of community and civic knowledge, and also to promote understanding of political responsibility from an early age.

The project develops content for and in collaboration with children, to provide information and encourage them to participate in all aspects of civic life. The project website – using interactive games and quizzes – covers local culture, history, the environment, education, jobs, community diversity and county government processes. There are also links to approved kids' websites and events. In addition a bulletin board is available and kids can post requests for help with homework related to county government and history. The project benefits from volunteer input and the knowledge of in-house county council staff.

Key objectives are:

- to make topics about local government – its purpose, structure and relationship to the community – interesting, informative and relevant to children

- to engage youth in government interaction at an early age to create informed, civic-minded future citizens
- to share resources developed through this programme with educational institutions to enrich the classroom experience as it relates to public service
- to use a digital platform to address the broad goal that all children in Miami-Dade County, particularly the underserved, have access to the community's resources
- to facilitate cross-cultural interaction among children living in communities with culturally diverse and ethnically-rich backgrounds
- to consolidate information about County programmes and events for kids into a single place for easy access and use, available 24/7.

NGfL Scotland's[26] 'Connecting Communities' training programme[27] targets community and voluntary sector organisations to help them support the adoption of new technology. Community tutors from a wide range of backgrounds within the field of community education are identified initially by community strategy officers to receive three days of training. Learning is focused on basic ICT skills and a range of related topics that are part of a comprehensive 'Connecting Communities' training pack. One module introduces community sector professionals to the concept of e-democracy.[28]

A series of guides is also available from this website, providing information and advice on a variety of topics, related websites, organisations and products. Of particular note in the context of this chapter is the civic participation guide,[29] which outlines principles and policy developments regarding e-democracy and e-citizenship, and encourages community and voluntary sector organisations to visualise how and in what ways they might support development of e-democracy at community level.

Reservations about ICT and E-participation

While claims about contemporary ICTs often highlight positive aspects of their use, citizens may not in fact use technology designed specifically for them to participate in the ways expected of them. There is no culture of strong public involvement in traditional politics in the UK; and, after many years of not expecting to be involved in decision-making, it is doubtful that the general public will be automatically inclined to participate in traditional politics using any medium. Some will be wholly unaware of the new and more inclusive political will expressed by governments. Some of those who are aware of this new resolve may be cynical about government motives, and others may lack knowledge about the features of ICTs and new technological possibilities related to democratic practice.

Some commentators have advised caution in thinking that technology will change democratic politics for the better. For democratic renewal to work effectively, Winner believes political and economic institutions also have to be transformed. Institutions must respond to public views. However, there are fears that too much unrestrained public interaction will overload organisations and their officials. Without some form of on-line mediation, direct citizen participation could result in never-ending discussion and perhaps even massive delays to important decision-making processes. In addition, questions in regard to accountability and responsibility have been raised. Politicians and government officials are held accountable for what they do and say. However, it may be more difficult to ensure citizens act responsibly and are held accountable for their participatory actions. A key issue is to ensure that people act in the public interest rather than only in self-interest.

In addition, there are fears that open virtual spaces created for debate and democratic discussion might be co-opted by other interests. What is designed as democratic participation may in practice be found to have profound anti-democratic tendencies and unforeseen side effects. Permitting non-profit public sphere projects in local communities to be replaced by commercial profit-making enterprises elevates fiscal profit above the public interest, and may also make it possible for businesses outside the area to profile individuals and communities and develop niche market opportunities, potentially increasing their own profit but without necessarily bringing any real benefit to the local community. More unprincipled governments and state institutions might be tempted to survey the actions of citizens in local communities, and use information unscrupulously to engineer and manage local activities and behaviour socially from the bottom up. Too little knowledge of what is actually happening will mean some adverse developments may go undiscovered. Critical research in the field, along with wide dissemination of findings, will help identify and address problems.

In-depth knowledge and development of the theories of e-democracy and e-participation are needed to support the design of ICTs at different geographic levels. In addition, institutions and political authorities must prepare themselves to listen and act upon citizen input. Otherwise people will come to view poorly managed e-democracy exercises and on-line participatory democracy projects as trite, insincere, and little more than weak public relations exercises.

Suggestions for Further Research

As new ICTs evolve, the public will continue to be affected by fundamental changes to the State's strategic role and the reordering of social, cultural political, and economic organisations. Conceptualisations of community development practice and different models of democracy combined with fiscal support will be needed to support more participatory practices at community level, and to ensure a positive relationship between democracy and ICTs. There is need for systematic observation and theory development to support policy decisions underpinning the on-going design and use of ICTs in a variety of different community settings. An additional suggestion is that customised literacy programmes would help to spread information about the government's new political will, and would also broaden understanding about new democratic practices made possible by different kinds of contemporary technology. Civic literacy programmes would be made relevant by assessing local needs and contexts and tailoring information about new democratic practices to diverse groups and individuals living in very different neighbourhoods.

Raising literacy levels and broadening and deepening understanding may be supported by action research conducted with a range of different demographic and interest groups in diverse geographic areas. While many different small-scale projects to broaden participation have already been developed, there is very little empirical data that analyses actual use and significance for people, and evaluates changes in their routine practices. Besides noting advantages, problems and reservations need to be identified and openly discussed. Critical research is needed to illustrate the ways in which people routinely interact with ICTs. A blend of qualitative and quantitative research approaches would be useful in noting the perceptions and attitudes of citizens, their actual use of technology over time, and tangible changes in their routine life as a result of using ICTs. This chapter finally suggests going beyond anecdotal or thin self-supporting monitoring and evaluation exercises, to conduct in-depth, evidence-based research, which critically examines the ethical dimensions of citizenship/e-citizenship, practices associated with participation/e-participation, and off and on-line civic involvement in small-scale settings.

Notes

1. For example, world e-gov links may be found at http://www. egovlinks.com/world_egov_links.html (consulted 17 September 2002). Helpful resources on e-democracy developments and issues world-wide may be found at http://www.e-democracy. org/do/ (consulted 17 September 2002). See also RMIT resources at http://www.bf.rmit.edu.au/kgeiselhart/e-_democracy_ resources_.htm (consulted 23 September 2002).

2. http://www.statskontoret.se/gol-democracy/ (consulted 17 September 2002). See also John Gøtze's update on the portals project at http://www.governments-online.org/articles/12.shtml which discusses access, electronic public consultation and policy processes.

3. The Working Group on E-government in the Developing World came from countries in every region of the world – Brazil, Chile, China, Denmark, Egypt, India, Israel, Mexico, South Africa, Tanzania, Thailand, the United Arab Emirates and the United States.

4. *Roadmap for e-Government in the Developing World*, http: //www1.worldbank.org/publicsector/egov/e-gov.final.pdf (consulted 16 September 2002).

5. See http://www.oecd.org/EN/countrylist/0,,EN-countrylist-0-nodirectorate-no-no-159-0,00.html (consulted 25 September 2002).

6. http://www1.oecd.org/publications/e-book/4201131e.pdf (consulted 24 September 2002).

7. http://www.uni-mannheim.de/ed3/pdf/1994/ bangemann.pdf(NP).

8. There are three separate structural funds, two of which are relevant in the context of the CCIS study offered later in this thesis: the European Regional Development Fund (ERDF), which supports business development schemes and tourism projects, investment in infrastructure and environmental improvement; and the European Social Fund (ESF), which supports training, retraining and vocational guidance with particular emphasis on young people and the long-term unemployed.

9. http://www.archive.official-documents.co.uk/document/cm43/ 4310/4310-sm.htm(NP).

10. http://www.scotland.gov.uk/library5/government/iag_ framework.pdf (consulted November 2003).

11. www.ukonline.gov.uk (consulted November 2003).
12. http://www.openscotland.gov.uk/ (consulted November 2003).
13. http://www.scotland-legislation.hmso.gov.uk/legislation/scotland/acts2003.30001--d.htm#20 (consulted November 2003).
14. Available at http://www.communitiesscotland.gov.uk/communities/upload/SIPsCPPs.pdf (consulted November 2003).
15. http://www.communitiesscotland.gov.uk/ (consulted January 2004).
16. http://www.ltscotland.org.uk/communities/ (consulted January 2004).
17. Internet site: http://www.ltscotland.org.uk/communities/digital_inclusion_initiative_background.asp for more in-depth information.
18. Information about portal developments in various countries throughout the world is posted at the Government Online International Network (GOL-IN) website http://governments-online.org/articles/13.shtml (consulted January 2004).
19. http://europa.eu.int/yourvoice (consulted January 2004).
20. http://www.cabinet-office.gov.uk/servicefirst/2000/consult/code/ConsultationCode.htm (consulted January 2004).
21. A new global website acts as a single portal to promote ICT literacy http://ictliteracy.info (consulted January 2004). The site contains links to resources intended to raise awareness and promote debate about ICT literacy.
22. *21st century literacy in a convergent media world*. White Paper, Berlin. http://www.21stcenturyliteracy.org/White/WhitePaperEnglish.pdf (consulted April 2003).
23. http://www.pbs.org/democracy/kids/index.html (consulted January 2003).
24. http://www.pbs.org/democracy/ (consulted January 2003).
25. http://kids.miamidade.gov (consulted January 2004).
26. http://www.ltscotland.org.uk/communities/ (consulted February 2004).
27. See: www.ngflscotland.gov.uk/connectingcommunities (consulted January 2004).
28. See http://www.ltscotland.org.uk/connectingcommunities/files/context_e-demo.pdf (consulted January 2004).
29. http://www.ltscotland.org.uk/communities/civic_participation.asp (consulted January 2004).

References

Alexander, D. (2003), 'Foreword', in D. Rushkoff (2003), *Open source democracy: How online communication is changing offline politics* (London: DEMOS).

Arterton, C. (2003), 'Foreword', in D. Anderson and M. Cornfield, *The Civic Web* (New York: Rowman & Littlefield).

Backus, M. (2001), *E-Governance and Developing Countries: Introduction and Examples*. Research Report, No 3, April 2001, available at www.ftp11ed.org/files/research/reports/report3.pdf

Barber, B. (1992), *An Aristocracy for Everyone: The Politics of Education and the Future of America* (New York: Oxford University Press).

Cassell, P. (1993). (ed). *The Giddens Reader* (London: Macmillan).

Citizens as Partners: Information Consultation and Public Participation in Policy-Making (2001), OECD: http://www 1.oecd.org/publications/e-book/420113 1e.pdf (consulted 24 September 2002).

Communities Scotland: Integrating Social Inclusion partnerships and Community Planning Partnership (August 2003), available at http://www.communitiesscotland.gov.uk/communities/upload/SIPsCPPs.pdf.

Connecting Scotland: Our Broadband Future (2001) (Scottish Executive).

Correia, A. (2002), *Information Literacy for an Active and Effective Citizenship*, July 2002, White Paper prepared for UNESCO, the US National Commission on Libraries and Information Science, and the National Forum on Information Literacy, for use at the Information Literacy meeting of Experts, Prague, The Czech Republic.

Denhardt, R. B. (1993), *Theories of Public Organization*, 2nd edn (Belmont, CA: Wadsworth Publishing Co.).

Digital inclusion strategy: Connecting Scotland's People, (September 2001), available at www.scotland.gov.uk/digitalscotland.

Digital Transformation: A framework for ICT Literacy. Princeton NJ: Educational Testing Services (ETS) Retrieved

April 11, 2003 from http://www.ets.org/research/ictliteracy/ictreport.pdf

Duffy, K. (1995), 'Social Exclusion and Human Dignity in Europe: Background Report for the Proposed Initiative by the Council of Europe, Steering Committee on Social Policy, Council of Europe', in C. Oppenheim (ed.), *An Inclusive Society: Strategies for Tackling Poverty* (London: Institute for Public Policy Research (IPPR), 1998), pp. 227–52.

eEurope2002 (2000), http://www.europa.eu.int/information_society/eeurope/action_plan/pdf/actionplan_en.pdf.

eEurope2005: An information society for all, COM (2002) 263 final, Brussels, 28 June, http://europa.eu.int/information_society/eeurope/news_library/eeurope2005/index_en.htm.

Europe and the global information society: Recommendations to the European Council (1994), European Community (EC).

Evaluation of the Working for Communities Programme (2003), DTZ Pieda, 2003 – Research Findings No. 163/2003.

Fotopoulos, T. (1997), *Towards an Inclusive Democracy* (London: Cassell).

Giddens, A. (1993), *New Rules of Sociological Method* (London: Polity Press).

Gram, L. (1997), *Policy-making in the EU: Conceptual Lenses and the Integration Process* (London: Routledge).

Growth, Competitiveness and Employment (1993), EU White Paper.

Information Age Government in Scotland: A Common Approach, accessed at http://www.scotland.gov.uk/library5/government/iag_framework.pdf 20/10/2003.

Integrating Social Inclusion Partnerships and Community Planning Partnerships (August 2003), Communities Scotland, accessed 28/10/2003 at Internet site http://www.communitiesscotland.gov.uk/communities/upload/SIPsCPPs.pdf.

Living and Working in the Information Society: People First (1996), EU Green Paper.

MacKenzie, D. and J. Wajcman (1996), *The Social Shaping of Technology* (Philadelphia: Open University Press).

Malina, A. and A. Macintosh (2004), 'Bridging the Digital Divide: Development in Scotland', in A. Anttiroiko, M. Mälkiä and R. Savolainen (eds), *eTransformation in Governance: New*

Directions in Government and Politics (Hershey, PA: Idea Group), pp. 255–71.

Mansell, R. and R. Silverstone (1997), *Communication by Design* (New York: Oxford University Press).

Milner, H. (2002), *Civic Literacy: How Informed Citizens Make Democracy Work* (Hanover, New England University Press; and London: Tufts University Press).

Modernising Government (1999), UK White Paper.

Mosco, V. and J. Wasko (1988), *The Political Economy of Information* (Wisconsin: Wisconsin University Press).

The Net Result: Social Inclusion in the Information Society: Report of the National Working Party on Social Inclusion (INSINC), Internet site: www.uk.ibm.com/comm/community/uk117.html (consulted 1997).

Oppenheim, C. (ed.) (1998), *An Inclusive Society: Strategies for Tackling Poverty* (London: Institute for Public Policy Research (IPPR)).

Osborne, S. (ed.) (1996), *Managing in the Voluntary Sector: A Handbook for Managers in Charitable and Non-profit Organisations* (London: Thompson Business Press).

Pinkett, R. (2000), 'Bridging the Digital Divide: Sociocultural Constructionism and an Asset-based Approach to Com-munity Technology and Community-building', paper presented at the 81st Annual Meeting of the American Educational Research Association (AERA) (New Orleans, LA), 24–8 April, http://www.media.mit.edu/~rpinkett/papers/aera2oooo.pdf.

Pratchett, L. (ed.) (2000), *Renewing Local Democracy?* (London: Frank Cass).

Przeworski, A. (1999), 'Minimalist Conception of Democracy: A Defense', in I. Shapiro and C. Hacker-Gordon (eds), *Democracy's Value* (New York: Cambridge University Press), pp. 23–55.

Richards, D. and M. Smith (eds) (2002), *Governance and Public Policy in the United Kingdom* (Oxford: Oxford University Press).

Roadmap for e-Government in the Developing World: 10 Questions e-Government Leaders Should Ask Themselves (2002), Pacific Council on Internet Policy, consulted 1 October 2002, http://www.pacificcouncil.org/pdfs/e-gov.paper.f.pdf.

Rose, R. (2003), Oxford Internet Survey, available at http://users. ox.ac.uk/~oxis/index.html

Schon, D., B. Sanyal and W. Mitchell (1999), *High Technology and Low-Income Communities* (Cambridge, MA: Massachusetts Institute of Technology (MIT)).

Schiller, H. (1996), *Information Inequality: The Deepening Social Crisis in America* (London: Routledge).

Schuler, D. (1996), *New Community Networks: Wired for Change* (New York: Addison-Wesley).

Sclove, R. (1995), *Democracy and Technology* (New York and London: Guilford Press).

Stoker, G. (1996), 'Introduction: Normative Theories of Local Government and Democracy', in D. King and G. Stoker, *Rethinking Local Democracy* (Hong Kong: Macmillan), pp. 1–27.

Taylor, P., J. Richardson, A. Yeo, A. Marsh, K. Trobe and A. Pilkington (eds) (1997), *Sociology in Focus* (Bath: Causeway Press).

Thompson, J. (1995), *Media and Modernity* (Oxford: Polity Press).

Turner, N. and R. Pinkett, R. (2000), 'An Asset-Based Approach to Community Building and Community Technology', in the Proceedings of Shaping the Network Society, *The Future of the Public Sphere in Cyberspace, Directions and Implications of Advanced Computing Symposium 2000* (DIAC-2000) (Seattle, WA), 20–3 May, available at Internet site: http:// web.media.mit.edu/~rpinkett/papers/diac2000.doc (consulted 15 July 2003).

The 21st Century Literacy Summit White Paper (2002), Bertlesmann Foundation and AOL Time Warner Foundation, accessed 28/10/2003, at Internet site http://www.21stcentur yliteracy.org/.

Winner, L. (1996), 'Do Artefacts Have Politics?', in D. MacKenzie and J. Wajcman (eds) (1996), *The Social Shaping of Technology* (Milton Keynes: Open University Press), pp. 26–38.

Wiring It Up (2000), Performance and Innovation Unit, UK Cabinet Office (Consulted 1 October 2002): http://www.cabinet-office.gov.uk/innovation/2000/wiring/coiwire.pdf.

Innovation, Reform and E-democracy

Keith Culver

The new Information Communication Technologies (ICTs) are demonstrably innovative in their revolutionary effect on the way we can and do communicate with one another. Governments in industrialised democratic states now hope to use some of these technologies to revitalise atrophied relations between government and citizens.[1] The initial wave of improvement to the public face of government in its front-line service departments is in many ways complete, as jurisdictions such as the Australian state of Victoria report conversion of nearly 90 per cent of eligible government services to electronic delivery.[2] Many leading e-government jurisdictions are now turning to e-democracy (ICT-enhanced democratic practices) as the next step in improving government–citizen relations. The main idea seems to be this: just as technological innovation has driven innovation in communication, so technological innovation can drive social innovation in the communication and relation between government and citizens. In this chapter, I shall reflect on this analogical argument, and advance two theses about the purported causal link between technological and social innovation. In the first, general thesis I shall argue that leading e-democracy work to date is reformative rather than innovative. This thesis reminds us to avoid premature declaration of victory in democracy-enhancing use of ICTs. The second thesis addresses the gap between reform and innovation. I shall argue that where efforts in ICT-enhanced democracy are justified by its capacity to produce social innovation, that justification is adequate only to the extent that it reaches beyond generic democratic practices such as e-voting to find innovative solutions to problems of democratic practice in particular political cultures. This justification condition is not a simple matter. Social innovation is an elusive goal, whose achievement involves a kind of reversal of the current mutual alienation of government and citizens. Part of my argument will explore briefly in the context of Canada one way to understand what it might mean for the new ICTs to deliver social innovation. I shall close with an illustration of the distance between democratic reform and innovation using the new ICTs via an overview of recent experiences of the Delta Project in e-democracy in the Province of New Brunswick, Canada.

Innovation Is Not Reform: The State of E-democracy Today

Edmund Burke famously warns that 'To innovate is not to reform'.[3] Burke's supporting analysis argues that:

> Change is novelty, and whether it is to operate any one of the effects of reformation at all, or whether it may not contradict the very principle upon which reformation is designed, cannot be certainly known beforehand. Reform is not a change in the substance or in the primary modification of the object, but a direct application of a remedy to the grievance complained of.[4]

Innovation, then, accepts the risks inherent in a course of modification which may do away entirely with the objection of modification. Reform, by contrast, always maintains the essence of the object of modification. This distinction is a useful tool for the dissection of the claims made on behalf of ICT-enhanced democracy, especially when we evaluate the quantity and quality of our progress toward the social innovation. There is little point in cataloguing the claims made by advocates of e-government and e-democracy. Here I shall cite just one source to illustrate the general sense that e-democracy and e-government is thought to promise not merely reform but revolution. In the consulting firm Accenture's most recent sustained argument about the nature of e-government, Jupp and Astall write that:

> In the past, most democratic governments inched forward on the long path toward far-reaching reform. 'Today, a series of global demographic, socio-economic and political shifts are stressing the benefits of rapid and far-reaching response. Emerging waves of technology change have changed the art of the possible, allowing government to consider dramatic, not incremental change.[5]

On any reading, I think, this is a reflection of Burke's well-known distinction. What is sought, and what is thought valuable in e-government and e-democracy, is 'dramatic' innovation with the potential to replace the existing object of reform with an entirely new object. Yet what has occurred so far is reform and not innovation.

Let me illustrate the distance between innovation and reform through a quick review of leading examples of e-democracy, limited to those practices intended to have an immediate and substantial effect on government and governance.[6] The greatest initial blast of attention to the potential for the new ICTs to change practices of democratic citizenship came in 1999 in the Minnesota gubernatorial campaign of former wrestler and now Governor Jesse Ventura. Ventura's supporters blended politics with internet sales of Ventura merchandise, using a single website (www.jessenventura.org) to raise money and consciousness of the former wrestler's political aspirations.[7] Similarly intense attention was focused on the Arizona Democratic Primary in 2000. Democrats were able to vote electronically to select a Democratic Party candidate for President, using software provided by the private sector firm Elections.com.[8] As Joe Mohen, CEO of Elections.com, viewed the proceedings, it was 'a new milestone in democracy'.[9] A rather more intriguing use of ICTs in voting arrived in the practice of 'vote-swapping' which first emerged in the United States in the 2000 elections among supporters of Ralph Nader. Voters in jurisdictions where Nader had little chance of success agreed to vote for some other candidate leading in that jurisdiction, in trade for a vote for Nader by a voter in a jurisdiction where Nader stood a much better chance of success. In this way the Nader and non-Nader voter each aim to increase the likelihood of the preferred candidate securing victory in some jurisdiction even if not the voter's home jurisdiction. Perhaps the best example of the movement is www.votetrader.org, which promoted trading of votes between Gore and Nader sympathisers in order to protect Gore in swing states where Nader voters more favourably inclined to Gore than Bush might by voting for Nader cost Gore a crucial victory. The practice is also widespread in the UK (see, e.g., http://www.tacticalvoter.net), with rather more hope of enduring success to the extent that UK organisers have not yet suffered legal setbacks of the sort which brought a quick end to vote-swapping in the State of California.[10] More recently, quite exciting Scottish work in e-petitioning and e-consultation of formally disenfranchised youth shows signs of breaching assumptions about the nature of the electorate, and the way and frequency with which the electorate engages its representatives.[11]

These leading examples of e-democracy may be valuable reforms but it is unclear that they are innovations. They are instead modest milestones. Raising funds for a leadership race is a familiar task, as is the American process of voting in party-centred primaries. Vote-swapping shows dissatisfaction with the status quo, but is still firmly entrenched in the practice of voting for representatives. Gathering of support for petitions has an equally lengthy history. There can be little doubt that there have been improvements in speed and perhaps in security with the use of ICTs in these practices. Yet all of this falls far short of innovation as a course of reform which accepts as a possible outcome a doing away with the original object of reform, in this case those democratic institutions implicated in the decline in government–citizen relations.

I shall suggest here (with just the beginning of the supporting argument needed) that the relatively hesitant progress we have seen is due in part to the vagueness of the guiding ideal. Tony Blair's articulation of the ideal of democracy and its new needs is an instructive example, cited approvingly in the new HM Government consultation paper *In the Service of Democracy: A Consultation Paper on a Policy for Electronic Democracy*.[12] Blair writes:

> The democratic impulse needs to be strengthened by finding new ways to enable citizens to share in decision-making that affects them … The truth is that in a mature society, representatives will make better decisions if they take full account of popular opinion and encourage public debate on the big decisions affecting people's lives.[13]

It is difficult to know what to make of this as a statement of a guiding ideal to be realised through innovative use of ICTs. Why does Blair suppose that democracy is best strengthened by finding new ways for representatives to make better decisions, rather than devolved local governance, or perhaps distributed governance with norm-setting power vested in citizens themselves? Is a 'mature society' all we really want? Is that mature society uniquely British? And how is change toward that state of strengthened democracy to be assessed? These questions about Blair's statement of ideals are not in themselves especially alarming, I hope; but I do think the standard answer to them is. Socially innovative e-democracy is widely characterised as an ICT-driven change in the communicative relation between government and citizens from one-way to two-way, leading to a kind of renewed accountability of government to citizens, given expression in increased government responsiveness to citizens' deliberations on policy matters and transparency in government process and information, all without loss of security and privacy. Cruel as it may sound, I think this formulation captures the full sophistication of government-sponsored e-democracy today.

We are left with a complex slogan and ideas whose application conditions in daily life are not any clearer for addition of definition or deft conceptual analysis. 'Accountability', for example, is not an idea whose requirements in practice can be deduced from a better definition of the term. No amount of discussion of what it means to be accountable, or understanding of the history and diverse instances of what is said to be accountability, will help us to understand when we justifiably assess a government in Canada, Britain, France, or Peru as being accountable to its citizens to a lesser or greater degree than other governments. What is required to make sense of the loose ideal articulated by Blair and others is a coherent, fully expressed and well-justified political theory of democracy with appropriate adjustment for local variations. That theory must give content to the supporting ideal of accountability, which can develop a distinctive institutional character suited to the problems and aspirations of particular governments and citizens, and particular e-democracy tools can be devised to enhance pursuit of the ideal. To settle for anything less in support of the ideal of democracy is to accept a set of generic e-democracy practices which may do little more than reform existing practices at great effort and financial cost. Real social innovation requires careful thought about where we are going with the marvellous tools found in the new ICTs. And here, as the next section will suggest, the going gets difficult, as we must decide just who 'we' are for the purposes of social innovation driven by e-democracy.

Innovation and Ideals in E-democracy

I shall turn now to my second thesis, that we should only accept the general proposition that ICTs can drive social innovation in government–citizen relations (and so deserve public respect and public funding) once e-democracy has provided genuinely novel and better ways to realise the ideals of democracy in particular societies. I shall suggest that the test for achievement of social innovation through e-democracy is its capacity to add to our understanding of how we might face up to our largest problems as societies. This of course adds the further complication of deciding just which problems are the largest in a given society, but that we will not let that detain us unduly here.

One useful way to begin is to ask a question borrowed from Sir Isaiah Berlin. All social life involves loss, Berlin famously argued.[14] What can e-democracy do that orthodox democracy cannot to reduce that loss when independent-minded persons and groups live together? In Canada, social innovation is often thought to consist in new ways of instantiating key Canadian values in our social and political practices. Identification of those key values is of course contentious, and I shall do no more than assert the reasonableness of beginning by recourse to the Supreme Court's 1998 discussion of Canada's conceptual foundations in *Reference Re Secession of Quebec*.[15] In that decision the Court reflected on the right of the province of Quebec to secede unilaterally as a matter of right, and in its reflection one account of the underpinnings of the idea of Canada is expressed. The Court observes that:

> Those who support the existence of such a right [of unilateral declaration of independence] found their case primarily on the principle of democracy. Democracy, however, means more than simple majority rule. As reflected in our constitutional jurisprudence, democracy exists in the larger context of other constitutional values such as those already mentioned. In the 131 years since Confederation, the people of the provinces and territories have created close ties of interdependence (economically, socially, politically and culturally) based on shared values that include federalism, democracy, constitutionalism and the rule of law, and respect for minorities. A democratic decision of Quebecers in favour of secession would put those relationships at risk.[16]

What interests me most in this passage is the Court's refusal to separate the idea of democracy from the surrounding values which give democracy concrete meaning in the context of Canadian experience. Federalism is itself an optional characteristic of political order committed to democracy. Equally there is nothing inherently democratic about tolerance for minorities. Democracies typically though not necessarily exhibit this virtue – indeed, the problem of a tyrannical majority is explicitly identified by de Toqueville as a risk of unconstrained democracy. This particular combination of characteristics goes a very long way to giving the Canadian practice of democracy a distinctive content. Canadian commitment to tolerance of minorities, for example, is given special expression in constitutional acknowledgement of aboriginal peoples, and two founding nations. Yet later, largely non-European immigrants and other minorities emerging within established cultural groups are not ignored simply because they did not manage to have their identities specifically marked in the Charter. In the evolving conception of Canada, the ideal of

multiculturalism has emerged as a Canadian response to
the choice to assimilate or to tolerate. Canadian toleration
allows national and other internal minorities to maintain
their distinct cultural identities within Canada to the extent
they choose.[17] This particular brand of tolerance makes
possible a Canadian way of life which may ultimately be
far more respectful of individual, autonomous aspirations
than the great American experiment in the democracy of
overlapping consensus.[18]

Canadian respect for autonomy drives us to face up to
pluralism distinctively, even to the point where we must
accept with the evolving face of multiculturalism a kind of
enduring, managed conflict as the price of our respect for
the search for recognition,[19] played out in the individual
and collective preservation of cultural identities. We pay a
very high price for our autonomy-respecting explorations
of the boundaries of democratic pluralism.[20] Our respect
for the autonomy of individuals and groups rests uneasily
on hotly disputed arguments for the viability of collective
or group rights as mechanisms for securing cultural
recognition.[21] The practical output of this dispute in the
form of sovereignist movements has taken Canada to
the brink of collapse as a unitary state, on the back of
a democratic majoritarian referendum practice whose
bluntness played a significant role in the outcome of the
1995 Quebec referendum.[22] I suspect many Canadians have
an indelible memory of Preston Manning, then Leader of
the Opposition, standing in the House of Commons days
prior to the referendum, asking just what a majority is
in the context of secession. 'Fifty per cent plus one?' he
famously asked,[23] as others queried the viability of settling
the fate of a country by use of a badly phrased referendum
question up for simple assent or dissent, without special
space for the interests of internal minorities.[24]

What is important about all of this in the context of
e-democracy is not the details of my account of Canada's

foundational ideals. What is important is the way the intertwined elements of Canada's conceptual foundation, history and citizens have framed the practice of democracy in Canada. Our practices and the issues they face are Canadian, not generic, and the value of e-democracy as a part of social innovation lies in the potential of e-democracy to enable Canadians to face up to Canadian issues in ways which allow us to set aside our outworn institutions and practices. As Joseph Raz characterises the demands of tolerance expressed as multiculturalism, 'It calls on us radically to reconceive society, changing its self-image. We should learn to think of our society as consisting not of a majority and minorities, but as constituted by a plurality of cultural groups.'[25] Genuinely innovative e-democracy must offer us fresh tools for response to this challenge, to re-engage the question of how to devise democratic institutions with room for First Nations citizens, descendents of English and French colonisers, and more recent immigrants. But this is not all. Innovative e-democracy must provide us with fresh tools to discuss new problems of pluralism, new internal minorities and their claims to recognition, or failing that, a right of exit. The age of ICTs is equally the age of global travel and multiple citizenships. How might ICTs be used to drawn on the insight of the Canadian diaspora in democratic activity beyond mere voting? And how might ICTs help us to examine the boundaries of democratic pluralism? We need careful assessment of the assertion that those with multiple-citizenships and formal title to democratic participation in Canada ought, ethically, to withhold from doing so in certain circumstances. On this argument, multiple national allegiances, prolonged absence from Canada, or other factors may leave some citizens insufficiently acquainted with the facts, needs, issues and aspirations of a Canadian community faced with an issue requiring response from a moral community of which some citizens are not genuinely a part. We are equally in need of e-democracy tools to help us to make good on our commitment to tolerance by giving us new ways for internal minorities to advance their views. Can gender-equality organisations, or those united in their choosing to live in rural areas, be given better access to a participatory and deliberative brand of democracy? Can e-democracy permit limited self-governance as, for example, knowledge-intensive aquaculture industries might use ICTs to regulate themselves in a manner continuously open to public scrutiny – perhaps all the way to public availability of pollution data transmitted to the web from wireless instruments? Can e-democracy help us to refashion the role of representatives in Canadian democracy, permitting, perhaps, forms of proportional representation previously rejected as too technically unwieldy to be feasible in so large a country as Canada? These issues and possibilities matter, both for Canadians concerned to foster Canadian democracy, and as a basis from which to demonstrate to the world the benefits of Canadian e-democracy.

The Delta Project in E-democracy

In the preceding argument I have claimed that the difference between reform and innovation is mirrored in the current gap between the practice and the promise of e-democracy, and I have suggested that our sluggish progress toward closing the gap is due in part to the difficulty of imagining what innovative e-democracy might look like. I have tried to illustrate in the Canadian context an approach to this gap which argues that ICT-driven social innovation will have been achieved when some of the largest social questions facing Canada have been answered in wholly new ways. I do not know what that waypoint or end state might look like, of course, because an innovative, revolutionary approach is logically not the kind of thing whose content can be known clearly and precisely in advance. Here we arrive at a further difficulty in understanding what to make of the promise of e-democracy: how to assess, understand and begin to bridge the distance between reform and innovation driven by ICT-enhanced democracy. A full answer to that question is beyond the scope of this short chapter, but something of a beginning can be mustered through the lessons of the Delta Project in e-democracy. I shall try to focus in what follows on lessons about the process of seeking social innovation, so I will include some factual elements but will not dwell on them as I might in a case study.

The Delta Project gains its name from the association of the Greek Δ with the idea of change, and the rich fertility of a river delta. The Delta Project is less a particular project with a beginning and end than a group of researchers and practitioners who have come together to ask one question: how do and how can the new ICTs affect the nature and structure of government, methods of governance, and the practice of citizenship? Members of the Delta Project come from several departments of the Government of the Province of New Brunswick, the University of New Brunswick, and private sector ICT firms CGI Group and Xwave. An international dimension was added to early stages of the project through our contact with the City of Sunderland in the UK, and research partners at the Centre for Law and Society at the University of Edinburgh. In our initial formation, members of the Delta Project attempted to use our diverse capacities to deliver and evaluate an ICT-enhanced public policy consultation,[26] on an issue provided by the Department of Environment and Local Government, but delivered to the public by Service New Brunswick. Private sector partners were to use this experiment to examine technical issues, and university researchers were to examine the progress of government as a learning organisation. University researchers additionally proposed to focus on the place of senior citizens in this consultation, as a particularly interesting group of citizens ordinarily least exposed to ICTs yet typically most at leisure to participate in civic activities. All of this, we hoped, might be replicated in parallel in the UK, to establish a cross-cultural comparison. This quite rigid initial formation of the Delta project foundered when the academic partners were unable to secure research funding, as funding bodies shied away from a project identified as excessively ambitious. This conclusion had a predictably negative effect on the morale of project members, for whom the project was largely a labour of love, sitting as it did outside the sole mandate and jurisdiction of any one of the participants.

Our morale was revived recently by the decision of the City of Saint John, in the Province of New Brunswick, to conduct a public consultation on its budget priorities. The context of the consultation is of interest for a number of reasons beyond the City's eventual choice to use ICTs to enhance the consultative process. The City of Saint John is Canada's oldest city, incorporated in 1785, and governed by an elected mayor and ten Councillors elected at large to form the City's Common Council. Saint John is known for its blue-collar character, expressed in an average annual income of $20,772 in contrast to the national average of $25,196.[27] The City is also affected by a slow decline in population. Between 1991 and 1996 the population of the City contracted by 3.3 per cent, from 74,969 to 72,494. This population change only exacerbated a range of other difficulties facing the city, all culminating in the need to cut $5 million from the City's budget for 2003. Councillors and city administrators agreed that reductions of this size required public consultation. This much of the story is a reasonably familiar picture for a city in an economically depressed region of any country. The picture is somewhat less familiar when we look to the kind of public consultation advocated by city administrators.

Finance Commissioner Andrew Beckett and IT Director Bill Todd suggested to Common Council that the City undertake an e-consultation to inform and survey citizens, and use a discussion forum to gather citizens' considered opinions regarding policy options for a city forced to live more frugally.[28] Consultation alone is a significant shift in practice in a city government traditionally run by a mayor and at-large councillors whose representative function is limited by their lack of responsibility to geographically fixed jurisdictions. The decision to add a discussion forum to the admittedly non-binding format of the consultation moved beyond an attitudinal survey to a search for solutions, visibly opening dialogue between citizens and city government as city administrators went on-line to answer posted questions. Citizens using the discussion forum took up the opportunity to offer fresh policy options, including suggestions that the city issue bonds as part of securing more favourable conditions for debt repayment, or save money on snow-removal by requiring property owners to care for public walkways traversing their properties. The more unusual move on the part of city administrators came in their choice of partners to deliver this consultation on-line, bilingually and at low cost. The administrators of the City of Saint John took a fundamentally collaborative, interdisciplinary approach. They enlisted the help of Service New Brunswick, the service delivery arm of the New Brunswick Government,[29] private sector ICT consulting firm CGI in its capacity as on-site advisor to Service New Brunswick and University of New Brunswick researchers skilled in survey design and program evaluation. This formation of a purpose-specific, interdisciplinary cluster of expertise all occurred prior to the design of the consultation and its questions and methods. The e-consultation integrated the efforts of the private sector, university sector and two levels of the public sector, reaching from planning through execution, and on to data synthesis and program evaluation.

Over the four weeks of the e-consultation, brochures containing information and survey questions were mailed to all Saint John households, and made generally available at City offices and in public libraries. A total of 317 persons participated in a survey instrument beyond the on-line forum, and 218 of those persons participated on-line. Participants answered eleven questions with subsections containing quantitatively analysable requests for statement of degrees of satisfaction with various city services, together with qualitatively analysable free-form text boxes permitting citizens to offer their views in their own words. The results of the consultation were posted for citizens' information, and brought before Common Council for consideration. Common Council directed 'that this report be referred to the City Manager for consideration as part of the 2003–2004 budget process'.[30] A typical danger of any consultation is evident in the result of this e-consultation: consultations are typically only politically binding on authorities, so improvements in the quantity or quality of participation in deliberation on policy matters may matter very little if there is no political incentive for authorities to put consultation results into practice. In this case it is too early to say whether e-consultation marks a fundamental social innovation in the City of Saint John. The City budget planning process is ongoing, and the City appears keen to carry out further e-consultations.

The role of several, but not all Delta Project members here is significant, and significantly changed from the early intentions of the Delta Project group. Our original formation was a monolith, intended to proceed as a kind of unified point of view maturing over a series of consultations in an effort to generate a reasonably comprehensive picture of the merit and demerits of e-consultations. Our initial inclination toward controlling all aspects of e-consultations to be devised and evaluated was overcome by the need for sheer speed to capitalise on the willingness of Saint John officials to engage in an e-consultation. Only a few members of the Delta Project were able to move as quickly as the opportunity demanded and as we proceeded, we found this to be less a dissolution of our original intention than a change in the way we brought expertise to bear on the e-consultation. Delta members engaged directly in the e-consultation were able to rely on the advice and reflections of others members outside the e-consultation, all the while making forward progress in understanding the potential of e-consultation.

We are aware of the relatively small size of the step we have taken. This is certainly not a 'small step for man, and a giant step for mankind' in the wake of Neil Armstrong. Rather, this is a small step forward in an atmosphere where the rhetoric of innovation often runs hard against a wall of political realities. Those political realities include a perceived need to spend public funds on projects where success is guaranteed, and the related perception that successful projects must not simply be successful in the end, but successful in all stages of execution. Perhaps unsurprisingly, then, what I want to emphasise here are the twin benefits visible in the City of Saint John budget e-consultation. The consultation itself has independent value as an innovation in municipal governance in Saint John; but the larger lessons arrive in what we learned about conduct and evaluation of an e-consultation. In at least the early days of use of new technology to enhance time-worn democratic practices, would-be innovators must be intellectually and practically flexible. Innovators must be flexible in the form in which they collaborate in pilot program design, flexible in execution of the program, and flexible in finding ways to the general goal of understanding whether ICTs can provide genuine innovation in the atrophied relations between citizen and state. None of this flexibility restrains the enthusiasm of the Delta Project members for larger leaps where they are possible. Flexibility has simply led us to be open to the

possibility that incremental changes may, with proper guiding foresight, amount to the great leap forward properly
characterised in hindsight as innovation.

Formation of this kind of diverse team prior to a project
is rare. Government silos and institutional cultures generate
the so-called political realities mentioned above. These
factors are often blamed for a kind of inflexibility which is
the death knell for collaborative projects. As significant as
these problems are, I think emphasis on them draws away
from the larger problem in e-democracy development: e-
democracy as it stands is an ambiguous goal and process, and,
as our experience shows, there are plenty of opportunities
for missteps, embarrassments and worse. It is unsurprising
that ready recruits for a risky event are not always easy to
find. Yet in an era of diminished internal policy-making
and research capacity in government, collaborative, multi-
sector effort is a precondition of successful effort to find
innovative solutions to the mutual alienation of citizens
and government. By the same token, careful collaborative
work in program evaluation is the key to understanding
whether small steps forward in e-democracy pilot projects
can plausibly be said to connect to a wider set of democratic
ideals in Canadian democracy. These observations may
sound trivial, but their lesson has yet to penetrate the daily
practices of government. The Organisation for Economic
Cooperation and Development (OECD) reports that 'No
OECD country currently conducts a systematic evaluation
of government performance in providing information,
conducting consultation and engaging citizens in policy-
making.'[31] However limited our first step forward, the Delta
Project has in place the key elements necessary to learn from
reform to drive toward innovation in e-democracy.

Conclusion

Let me close with a few final words on innovation, reform and e-democracy. I have argued that there is a gap between the rhetoric of e-democracy's promise of technologically driven social innovation, and the reality of hesitant reform of a few democratic practices. This itself should not be too great a worry at this early stage in e-democracy work. We should be worried, however, about just what it is that we propose to drive with ICT to create a better public, political life for Canadians and other citizens of democratic societies. Canadian democracy is not a generic thing; it is a many-splendoured thing. Generic tools will likely fail to inspire and aid those who attempt to build socially innovative forms of Canadian democracy to give fresh life to the union of government and citizens of a multicultural society striving to reduce the loss any of its members suffer for the sake of membership in the society. Canadian e-democracy will lead the world in reviving the relation of government and citizens only through imaginative reconception of democratic practices in light of the distinctly Canadian ideals incorporated into the conceptual foundation of the country. That reconception of democratic practices risks innovation in which old ways are thrown aside, but that risk must be taken if democracy is to survive the new ICTs. Without viable guiding ideals, the new ICTs may gradually revolutionise democracy in a wholly unsatisfactory way. E-democracy may become a strange pastiche, where instant polling and unfettered direct democracy give life to the worst fears of Plato and de Toqueville, as we mistake pursuit of popular whims for support of defensible ideals, and tyrannise those minorities who protest.

Notes

1. There is an extensive and varied literature on the collapse of participation in community-level voluntary associations, and an apparently concomitant collapse in participation in the institutions of democracy. Leading academic work often departs from Robert Putnam's *Bowling Alone: The Collapse and Revival of American Community* (New York: Simon & Schuster, 2000). A general overview of the role of ICTs in democracy may be found in Pippa Norris, *Digital Divide? Civic Engagement, Information Poverty & the Internet in Democratic Societies* (Cambridge: Cambridge University Press, 2001). Comprehensive statistical data on declining voter turnout is available at the International Institute for Democracy and Electoral Assistance (www.idea.int). The OECD has recently set out an institutional manifesto for response to the loss of social capital claimed by Putnam. Considerable attention is being given the OECD's *Citizens as Partners: Information, Consultation and Public Participation in Policy Making* (OECD 2001) (available at http://www1.oecd.org/publications/e-book/4201131e.pdf). A very useful summary of citizen-disengagement data driving various approaches to ICT-enhanced democracy is Stephen Coleman and John Gøtze, *Bowling Together: Online Public Engagement in Policy Deliberation* (London: Hansard Society, 2001).

2. See *Government Online – A Report Card 1996–2001* at http://www.egov.vic.gov.au/Victoria/StrategiesPoliciesandReports/Reports/ReportCard/GOLtargets.htm.

3. Edmund Burke, 'Letter to a Noble Lord on the Attacks Made Upon Mr. Burke and His Pension, in the House of Lords, by the Duke of Bedford and the Earl of Lauderdale, Early in the Present Session of Parliament 1795', in Peter J. Stanlis (ed.), *Edmund Burke: Selected Writings and Speeches* (Garden City, NY: Anchor Books, 1963), p. 561.

4. Burke, 'Letter', p. 560.

5. Vivienne Jupp and Lis Astall, *Technology in Government: Riding the Waves of Change* (Accenture, September 2002), p. 3.

6. By this qualification I mean to rule out experimental on-line communities and other activities whose exploratory character and lack of connection to a specific institutionalised political

process disqualifies them from claiming to make a substantial impact on the way the authority of the state is constituted, expressed and obeyed.

7. G. R. Anderson, 'Jesse Ventura, Inc.', *Salon*, 23 March 1999 (http://www.salon.com/news/1999/03/23news2.html (accessed 9 October 2002)).

8. Elections.com has recently agreed with consulting giant Accenture to take its e-voting products to the international market.

9. James Ledbetter, 'Net Out the Vote', *The Industry Standard*, 27 March 2000 (http://www.thestandard.com/article/display/0,1151,13004,00.html (accessed 9 October 2002)).

10. James Ledbetter, 'Vote-Swapping Hits the UK', *The Industry Standard*, 4 May 2001, reposted at CNN.com. (http://www.cnn.com/2001/TECH/internet/05/04/uk.vote.swapping.idg/).

11. This work was led by Napier University's International Teledemocracy Centre (http://itc.napier.ac.uk/).

12. Office of the e-Envoy, *In the Service of Democracy: A Consultation Paper on a Policy for Electronic Democracy* (London: Office of the e-Envoy, The Cabinet Office, 2002).

13. Tony Blair, *The Third Way: New Politics for the New Century* (London: The Fabian Society, 1998), cited in Office of the e-Envoy, *In the Service of Democracy*, s. 3.1.

14. Berlin makes this claim in 'Two Concepts of Liberty', *Four Essays on Liberty* (Oxford: Oxford University Press, 1969), pp. 167ff.

15. *Reference re Secession of Quebec* [1998] 2 S.C.R. 217.

16. *Reference re Secession of Quebec*, para. 131.

17. As Joseph Raz records this Canadian advance in political theory: 'The term [multiculturalism] was used first in, and applied to, Canada. "Multiculturalism" means – among other things – the coexistence within the same political society of a number of sizeable cultural groups wishing and in principle able to maintain their distinct identity.' Joseph Raz, 'Multiculturalism', *Ratio Juris*, 3 (1998), p. 197.

18. I borrow here from John Rawls, 'The Idea of an Overlapping Consensus', *Oxford Journal of Legal Studies*, 7 (1987), pp. 1–25. The ideas introduced in this article are given fuller expression in John Rawls, *Political Liberalism* (New York: Columbia University Press, 1993). It is of course controversial whether the United States' institutions are representative of an

overlapping consensus; but I take it as relatively uncontroversial that the United States is closer than Canada to the practice of overlapping consensus. By parity of reasoning, I take it that Canada is closer than the United Sates to expression of a perfectionist style of liberalism.

19. On the historical and conceptual roots of this idea see Sir Isaiah Berlin, 'The Search for Status', in Henry Hardy (ed.), *The Power of Ideas* (London: Chatto & Windus, 2000), pp. 195–9. See also Charles Taylor, *Sources of the Self* (Cambridge, MA: Harvard University Press, 1989) and 'The Politics of Recognition', in Amy Gutmann (ed.), *Multiculturalism and the Politics of Recognition* (Princeton: Princeton University Press, 1992), pp. 25–73.

20. On the conceptual foundations of this search see, e.g., Alon Harel, 'The Boundaries of Democratic Pluralism', in Arend Soetemann (ed.), *Pluralism and Law* (Dordrecht: Kluwer Academic Publishers, 2001), pp. 133–53. See also Leslie Green, 'Pluralism, Social Conflicts, and Tolerance' in Soetemann (ed.), *Pluralism and Law*, pp. 85–105.

21. On the conceptual confusions involved in some of these conceptions of rights-ascription, see Michael Hartney, 'Some Confusions concerning Collective Rights', *Canadian Journal of Law and Jurisprudence*, 2 (1991), pp. 293–314, reprinted in W. Kymlicka (ed.), *The Rights of Minority Cultures* (New York: Oxford University Press, 1995), pp. 202–27.

22. Sometimes we accept tactics for response to conflict even when those tactics fly in the face of global good graces, as in the case of the United Nations-condemned practice of public funding of separate Roman Catholic schools in Ontario. See, e.g., Michael Valpy, 'Not our problem, is Ottawa response on UN Bias ruling. Panel says Canada allows discrimination through Ontario's funding of RC schools', *The Globe and Mail*, 4 February 2000, A6.

23. From Question Period, Monday, 18 September 1995: 'Mr. Speaker, Canadians want this Quebec referendum to be decisive and conclusive. They do not want any confusion or ambiguity concerning the meaning of the vote, before or after. Yet the Leader of the Opposition clouds the issue when he says that he is prepared to accept a yes vote as binding and conclusive but not a no vote, and the Prime Minister does not help things when he implies that he is prepared to accept a no vote as binding

and conclusive but waffles on the meaning of a yes vote. 'For the benefit of all Canadians including Quebecers who want clarity and certainty in interpreting the Quebec referendum, will the Prime Minister make clear that a yes vote means Quebec is on its way out, that a no vote means Quebec is in the federation for the long haul, and that 50 per cent plus one is the dividing line between those two positions?' Available electronically in Hansard at: http://collection.nlc-bnc.ca/100/201/301/hansard-e/35-1/225_95-09-18/225OQ1E.html#14530.

24. Consider, for example, the limited consideration of the autonomy of aboriginal nations within the boundaries proposed by Quebec as the edges of its newly sovereign territory.

25. Joseph Raz, 'Multiculturalism', p. 197.

26. I give a stylised account of some of the difficulties encountered by the group in Keith Culver, 'The Road to E-Democracy', in Carolyn Johns (ed.), 2002 *Institute of Public Administration of Canada Case Studies in Public Administration* (Toronto: IPAC, 2002), pp. 1–5.

27. Statistics Canada, Census 1996 data.

28. See the City of Saint John Common Council Minutes for 16 September 2002 for a record of the original presentation of the idea by city administrators to Common Council: http://www.cityofsaintjohn.com/downloads_static/CC_Minutes_Sept_16_2002.pdf.

29. The Province of New Brunswick has designated the Crown Corporation Service New Brunswick as the central provider of government services to citizens. In that capacity Service New Brunswick has a highly developed single-window service system with over-the-counter, telephone and web delivery of more than 100 services from municipal, provincial and federal governments. For Service New Brunswick's mandate and function see their website at www.snb.ca.

30. See City of Saint John Common Council minutes of 12 November 2002, 89–365, item 5. http://www.city.saint-john.nb.ca/downloads_static/CC_Minutes_Nov_12_2002.pdf.

31. 'Engaging Citizens in Policy-making: Information, Consultation and Public Participation', *OECD Public Management Policy Brief, PUMA Policy Brief No. 10*, July 2001, p. 4.

'Big Brother or New Jerusalem?' Anti-Utopia and Utopia in an Age of New Technologies

Elaine Graham

The movie *eXistenZ* (1999), directed by David Cronenberg, is one of a number of cinematic explorations of humanity's encounter with information and communication technologies during the past decade. *eXistenZ* explores the implications of digitally-generated multi-sensory 'virtual reality' (VR), its title referring to the name of a software program that runs a complex interactive role-play game. It is intriguing to see how the two main characters, one male and one female, are made to represent two very different reactions to technology. The 'heroine', Allegra Geller, a games designer, loves the exhilarating rush of entering the virtual domain, and sees it as a stimulus to the imagination and the intellect. In a neat reversal of gender stereotyping, it is the male character, Ted Pikel, who expresses the greater anxiety – close to hysteria – when asked to undergo his first journey into cyberspace, fearing a loss of personal integrity and control when 'under the influence' of the digital program.

I like eXistenZ because throughout the film these two approaches are held in tension. *eXistenZ* deliberately plays with that ambivalence, switching between euphoria and dislocation as it shifts from one virtual world to another.

We are presented here, in fictional form, with two contrasting representations of the effects of information and communication technologies on the way we live, work and communicate. Reactions to the impact of technologies on human society frequently polarise on the question of 'liberation' or 'enslavement' (Cooper 1995), ushering in either a utopian 'new Jerusalem' of unlimited prosperity and wealth or the dystopia of a panoptic, 'Big Brother'-type society.

In truth, this polarisation is more realistically a continuum of responses, embracing a variety of philosophies of technology, of social change and even doctrines of human nature (E. L. Graham 2002); but such a stark coincidence of fear and fascination is a vivid indication of our uncertainty as to the future trajectory of human engagement with technologies. We find ourselves asking, therefore, what choices and opportunities are implicit in the hopes and anxieties engendered by new information and communication technologies: not only choices to do with access and distribution; but also what kind of human beings we will be in such a technological future. These present themselves as questions about interpersonal encounter, about community, about the body politic; yet, as we shall see, implicit within the debate about ICT is a level of discourse about human nature often ignored by secular humanism. For there is a strong religious subtext at work, especially in some writers' expansive pronouncements on the mystical and metaphysical dimensions of cyberspace, their equation of new technologies with a kind of demi-urgical power, and their expectations of technologies effecting the liberation of the human race from the limits of embodiment, finitude and mortality.

'New Jerusalem': Digital Utopia

The Net makes a type of equation: Data = information = knowledge = wisdom = truth = freedom. (*Interrogate the Internet* 1996: 126)

One of the most frequently occurring models of ICT, and especially the Internet, is that they are inherently powerful democratic media, serving to create a global virtual forum, free of restraint, in which freedom of expression will reign. It is argued that ICTs are democratic by virtue of their accessibility for ordinary people: they circumvent mediating processes that may distort or divert the authentic wishes of the people, and they draw more people in to participate by virtue of their immediacy of impact. ICTs thus provide the technological means to deliver mass participation in the political process, free of the bureaucracy and conservatism of party machinery, circumventing the manipulation of conventional news media or institutional parliamentary protocol. Email and the world wide web thus put into the hands of ordinary citizens powerful and effective means of communication (and influence) which were formerly the property of a wealthy elite. For example, new information and communication technologies have been suggested as one means of attracting groups of voters currently alienated by politics. After the election in the UK in 2001, it was suggested by the Electoral Commission itself that voting might take place in future by mobile telephone (MORI 2001).

Such an optimistic view finds echoes in scholarly literature and research, especially in the United States, where the 'new frontier' of ICT is often likened to the early days of the American nation (Kapor 1993) in which new democratic forms are enabled to flourish unconstrained by forces of tradition or entrenched political interests. New media offer ideal opportunities to create genuinely democratic communities, albeit based in virtual, rather than geographical constituencies. It is not that new technologies are eroding people's ability or willingness to participate, but merely providing new patterns of democratic access (Rheingold 1991).

Such a vision of the on-line utopia of the New Jerusalem reflects broadly 'technocratic' views. These are single-mindedly positive about the ability of technological advance to facilitate problem-solving and advance human interests. ICTs do not threaten or render human activities obsolete, but simply free our human creativity to achieve new limits. In that respect, too, there is what we may term an 'instrumental' attitude to technologies, in that they are regarded as quintessentially neutral, neither good nor bad, merely instruments for achieving purposes and values enshrined elsewhere. Underlying this is a version of Enlightenment humanism in which the rational subject, uninhibited by the external constraints of superstition, fear or conservatism, is enabled to scale new heights of intellectual and technological achievement. And this link with secular humanism is, I believe, quite significant when we come to consider the theological dimensions to this.

> The Net has ... become a simulacrum of a possible libertarian world: an unregulated plenitude where technological wizardry and a clean hack can overcome the inertia of embodied history, where ossified political and economic structures will melt down into the liquid flow of bits ...' (Davis 1998: 115)

There are, however, at least two objections to the utopian vision of the digital new Jerusalem. First, when it comes to mustering resources to influence public opinion or make a political intervention by establishing a presence on the Internet, then it is the corporate interests rather than private individuals or pressure groups who will have the requisite financial resources. Research suggests that the economic inequalities already present in other media – TV, radio, newspapers, billboards and so on – will simply be reproduced on-line (Norris 2001: 95–111).

> The language of cyberspace is English and cyberspacetime itself is a Western, post-industrial and specifically American creation. For most people on the planet, this reconstruction

of reality is far from being of paramount importance or relevance. It remains to be seen what effects this reality gap will have on relations between the West and the Rest, and on humanity's ability to deal with the very real problem of earlthly scarcity and limitations: resources, population, pollution. (Nguyen and Alexander 1996: 104)

Second, although the number of outlets for expression has increased exponentially, our ability to access them does not necessarily increase at the same rate, if at all. If most people are selective in what they can absorb, then research suggests that we tend to gravitate towards sources that already confirm our views. Indeed, there is evidence that those participating on-line are activists already involved in politics, rather than a significantly broader constituency (Norris 2001: 18–19). Similarly, the law of diminishing returns may also apply; that is, as more information is generated, the chances of any of it making any significant impact are reduced.

This suggests that rather than helping to create an accessible, coherent *polis*, electronic media will actually serve to fragment public debate and political intervention. The populist nature of media such as the Internet comes about because there is very little gate-keeping; but we know that it is also very indiscriminate and varied in quality: 'the ability simply to surf a vast unstructured web of material which both expresses and provokes an enormous variety of tastes and interests gives scope to mere congruence rather than co-ordination' (G. Graham 1999: 99).

'Big Brother': Virtual Dystopia

Gordon Graham has characterised resistance to new technologies, and the Internet in particular, as 'a neo-Luddite reaction' on the part of those who forecast that the ubiquity of computers and electronic media will herald the death of the book, contribute fatally to the dumbing-down of culture as our attention spans shorten and individuals retreat into the atomistic solepcism of virtual reality (G. Graham 1999: 7).

Within this framework, digital technologies are both the cause of social fragmentation and also a sanctuary from the resulting *anomie* and alienation. Indeed, many commentators derive their critiques from a kind of digital Marxism, in which the ideological superstructure (cyberspace) is parasitic upon the material – 'real' – infrastructure of organic life, physical bodies and face-to-face interaction. Thus, Jean Baudrillard argues that digital technologies such as virtual reality represent a kind of technological substitute or prosthesis for reality (Baudrillard 1983). The shift from the real to what Baudrillard terms 'the hyper-real' takes place when *representation* (of a presumed pre-existent reality) is displaced by *simulation*:

> popular culture preempts the exchange of symbols between individuals, introducing another layer of experience that undermines the subject's ability to define and to grasp the truth. Electronic mediation cripples the modern system of representation, folding it into a new mode of signification in which signs are divorced from their referents in the object world, becoming reorganized into a 'hyperreal' of screen surfaces. (Poster 2001: 133)

This blurring of the real and the unreal marks Baudrillard's analysis of postmodern space and place wrought by the development of cyberspace and electronic communications. The Internet is a virtual community in the way Disneyland is virtual, capable of existing only insofar as it is a simulacrum, a simulation; but in faking reality, it distracts us from realising that the community it simulates actually no longer exists anywhere. It feeds us the vision of inclusive community, personal liberty, freedom of speech, unlimited information as a strategy of 'deterrence' – in Marxian terms, an ideology – against the fact that these things have in fact dissolved. In *Le Crime Parfait* (1995), Baudrillard speaks of the 'theft' of truth by the simulacrum, in which the idea of the real has been stolen by the virtual, which then takes its place as the semblance of reality.[1]

Many critics argue that the disembodied nature of cyberspace and ICT is responsible for the erosion of conventional patterns of association, for which networked, on-line communication is a poor substitute. On-line, there is autonomy and freedom; yet ICTs serve to erode traditional networks of association, so that we have more communication with friends via email than our next-door neighbours. Having lost their moorings in physical association, our politics begin to dissolve, to become as 'fragile, airy, and ephemeral' (Heim 1993: 68) as cyberspace itself. And for some, the fragility of cyberspace and the virtual communities it engenders has something to do with its essentially disembodied nature:

> Our virtual life in cyberspace paralyses our bodies. Cyberspacetime promises us liberation from the constraints of space, time and materiality. However, without the experiences of our bodies, our thoughts, our ideas, our ethics and politics must all suffer. We know ourselves and our world mainly because we live and move in the world through our bodies ... In cyberspace we no longer need to face and live with the presence of others. What then becomes of our ethical and political consciousness? (Nguyen and Alexander 1996: 117–18)

While some commentators warn against the panoptic nature of ICTs, arguing that our every movement will soon be tracked electronically, that we cannot help but leave digital traces of ourselves wherever we go in a networked world, others argue, more prosaically, that any need for coercive, external surveillance is obviated by the fact that we are all too prepared to collude in our own oppression and passivity.[2] Who needs 'Big Brother' the surveillance technology, when we have *Big Brother* reality TV?

> Before the television monitor, the individual participates in a new cultural space in which the definition of truth is altered. No longer a correspondence to reality, no longer posing the critical question ('What relation does what I see bear to what I know?'), televisual epistemology asks rather, 'Does what I see hold my attention or urge me to switch channels?' (Poster 2001: 24)

Technological Re-enchantment/Disenchantment

Fundamentally, these are questions of whether an essential human nature will be compromised or consummated through new technologies. But underlying the discussion too are questions of the re-enchantment or disenchantment of the world; for it is intriguing to see how much of the utopianism towards new technologies and especially the Internet evokes themes of spirituality and transcendence. For many, new technologies are demiurgical devices, enabling humanity to transcend physical limits, such as bodily finitude, illness and mortality, or to transport their users to a higher plane of existence. For others, the very existential and spiritual integrity of human beings is threatened by the encroachment of rationalisation. Despite the assumptions about the incompatibility between science and religion, therefore, these new explorations into what it means to be human in a digital, cybernetic and information age call forth theological deliberations. But these, too, reflect the utopian and dystopian pairings of the more politically driven debates.

Cyberspace as Sacred Space

> [T]echnologies of communication are always, at least potentially, technologies of the sacred. (Davis 1998: 8)

One strand of futuristic speculation captures the trend towards the 're-enchantment' of public discourse often associated with a move into postmodernity at the end of the twentieth century. This sensibility is strongly optimistic about the prospects for technologically enhanced and assisted development; but it dwells on the *spiritual* opportunities offered by the digital age – cyberspace as 'sacred space'.

Erik Davis has argued for a strong continuity between users of ICT with ancient traditions of spirituality, especially Hermetism and Gnosticism (Davis 1998). Despite the secular, technical-rational nature of modernity, the potential of information and communications technologies for reawakening dormant instincts for the spiritual is widely celebrated. He maintains that advanced technologies are a means of realising utopian dreams, apocalyptic fantasies and drives towards infinite knowledge and immortal existence. Davis calls this new movement 'techno-paganism': like neo-paganism, a characteristically modern movement, but one inclined to equate the sacred with technology rather than nature. In regarding the tangible, material world as an elaborate cipher for divine power, in which the codes and bytes of digital information serve as the vehicles of transport into a higher reality, many adepts continue the arts and practices of earlier magi and demiurges. In this respect, Davis suggests that techno-paganism may be regarded as a continuation of early modern Hermetism; although we may also trace elements of more ancient Platonic, even Gnostic, tendencies, in which the fallen, prosaic, material – and illusory – world is but a pale shadow of a higher, secret, spiritual realm of perfect order and information (Davis 1998).

Michael Heim renders this Platonic connection most explicit, when he argues that our fascination with cyberspace is a function of a perennial erotic drive to transcend the material world in search of 'a sensationless world of pure ideas' (Nguyen and Alexander 1996: 115). What we are pursuing are the Platonic forms themselves, drawing the mind away from the meat of the body into its realm of perfection. 'With an electronic infrastructure, the dream of perfect FORMS becomes the dream of inFORMation' (Heim 1993: 82). This sacralising of the technological extends to other activities: the Internet as teeming with religious activities, from the staging of virtual rituals to the posting of cyber-shrines and digitalisation of sacred texts in cyberspace (Brasher 2001), and the celebration of the noösphere, a vast, global intelligent system encompassing the earth like a benevolent Spirit (Davis 1998: 280).

Once more, this contradicts interpretations which regard science and religion as antipathetic, for here are new technologies as – in David Noble's words – *instruments of deliverance* (Noble 1999): the tangible, material means by which humanity can manipulate elemental and hidden powers, thereby ascending into a sacred realm of 'transcendence', no longer inhibited by the inconveniences of embodiment. Cyberspace invites us, therefore, to consummate the timeless human quest to transcend the physical world in search of perfection and immortality; but note how this vision is heavily infected with a startling dualism of mind and body: 'The animating archetype of the information economy, its psychological spunk, lies in a gnostic [sic] flight from the heaviness and torpor of the material earth, a transition from the laboring body into the symbol-processing mind' (Davis 1998: 115).

Disenchantment

> We are the moths attracted to flames, and frightened by them too, for there may be no home behind the lights, no secure abode behind the vast glowing structures. There are only the fiery objects of dream and longing. (Heim 1993: 86)

Just as there are those who speak of technologies as facilitating spiritual as well as political enlightenment, there are those who regard them as anathema to human spiritual flourishing. Such technological pessimists believe that the intensification of new technologies can only degrade human uniqueness. While his reflections on the trajectory of modern culture's fascination with technology predated computers, the Internet and cyberspace, Martin Heidegger (1889–1976) articulated some very prescient themes which have provided some very powerful material for later commentators (Heim 1993; Myerson 2001).

In *The Question concerning Technology*, written towards the end of his life, Heidegger links what he regards as nihilistic tendencies of technology with earlier themes about the nature of authentic human existence. Heidegger claimed that 'technology's essence is nothing technological' (1993: 4): in other words, not to be understood or approached through its design or function, or even in terms of productive processes, but rather in its potential to yield or 'enframe' the inner essence of Being. Technology thus assumes for him an ontological status; more than a mere instrument, or manufactured tool, it is the means by which potential being is brought forth (*aletheia*) into tangible form. So technology is not something created or forged by human activity, but the manifestation or unconcealing of a ubiquitous, elemental force.

Thus technology becomes an overarching system, a way of understanding and relating to the world as a whole; but a system that ultimately masters and determines all human activities. Everything, including human labour, is reduced to 'standing reserves', or mere raw materials awaiting disposal according to the inexorable trajectory of technological manufacture. Technology is insidious in its effects, which will be to distort and impoverish humanity's openness to the richness of their existence (in his terms, an openness to *Dasein*, or Being). The imperatives of technology now serve to determine the ways in which the world is revealed to us, and the nature of our engagement with it. Eventually the logic of technological framing is so dominant that it obscures other more authentic revelations of the nature of being. Humanity may believe that it is in control of technology in an instrumental sense, but Heidegger's warning was that technology as an ontological force is potentially all-encompassing, at the expense of authentic and spontaneous human apprehension of the world.

> The danger of technology lies in the transformation of the human being, by which human actions and aspirations are fundamentally distorted. Not that machines can run amok, or even that we might misunderstand ourselves through a faulty comparison with machines. Instead, technology enters the inmost recesses of human existence, transforming the way we think and know and will. (Heim, 1993: 61)

The chief danger of the effects of technology, for Heidegger, lay in its engulfing of the human spirit and its capacity to distort human intentions and actions. It was the ability of technology to transform humanity from within, and not so much a fantasy of assimilation as ontological transformation (as in the amalgam of human and machine in the figure of the cyborg), that constituted technology's fundamental alteration of the essence of human experience. In a technological age, human labour has become so contaminated by the demonic forces of reification that the inner truth of artefacts is obliterated by (to use a rather more Weberian term) technical-rational instrumentality. The solution is a reinvigoration of spiritual values (a *poesis*) and a return to a more organic medium in which humanity is not alienated from its own existence. As Heidegger puts it, 'Only a god can save us' (1976).

Heidegger's concerns echo those of other philosophers and sociologists of modernity (such as Max Weber and Karl Marx) in his presupposition that the essence of modernity is to be found in its underlying characteristics of rationalisation, bureaucratisation, disenchantment and reification of human labour and commodities alike. However, one of the problems with Heidegger's model of technology is that, like modernisation, it is a monolithic and ahistorical phenomenon independent of human agency or cultural and historical variations. Inevitably, perhaps, this means that Heidegger's concept of technology is one of an impersonal force against which human beings are merely passive, helpless victims: 'Technology is often treated as unitary both from the favourable perspective of toolmaking and progress and from the negative standpoint of degredation and loss' (Poster 2001: 34).

In thinking about the nature of technology and its impact on our lives, however, it is important to consider how, empirically, it has developed and how in different circumstances economy, culture and technology will interrelate. Indeed, the history of one of the most pervasive and fundamental technologies of contemporary times, the Internet, is a good example of this. Developed originally as a means of communication for use in the event of nuclear war or other total catastrophe, electronic and web-based communication have now evolved in far more populist and diverse directions (Ross 1991: 75–100). Technological development can have unexpected consequences, a reminder that histories of technology do not simply conform to patterns of unbroken and progressive innovation (Pinch and Bijker [1987] 2003). It is valuable to preserve Heidegger's insight that technologies are more than neutral tools and instruments, but rather possessing the power to reconstitute human relations in which they are embedded; but other aspects of his evocation amount to a somewhat deterministic and abstract model of the impact of technology on human experience. Under Heidegger, technology reifies into destiny, and his retreat into eco-spirituality as the only option descends into mystification and abstraction.

Posthuman Thinking

Viewed all together, therefore, we can perceive a crucial fault-line running throughout. Do new ICTs represent promise or endangerment, mastery or extinction? This is a question regarding the future trajectory of human engagement with technologies: whether new communications technologies foster greater interaction, nurturing new forms of democratic participation and freedom of information, creating vibrant, networked, global communities, or whether they represent an attentuation of healthy political and civic association, a narrowing of cognitive horizons encouraging introverted individualism which substitutes 'virtual' relationships for their 'real' counterparts; whether they expand our lexicon of space, time and place or remove us from embodied, face-to-face authentic living. But what does it mean to be human, if our very humanity has itself been so transformed, so circumscribed, by new ways of technological living?

The impact of new technologies blurs many of the taken-for-granted categories of space, place and time; the boundaries of the body; the interface of machine and human. In the case of the Internet, it collapses physical distance, transcends national boundaries, reinvents conventions of text and reading, transforms human interactions into the flow of information, creates new artificial environments and machinic intelligences. This necessarily calls forth some radical rethinking of what it means to be human in an age some call the 'posthuman': 'We need to re-question the uniqueness of that which is human, and to redefine differences between human and animal, human and machine. This is, in a sense, the age-old investigation into the nature of mind and body, reason and intelligence' (Nguyen and Alexander 1996: 113).

Notions of the posthuman argue powerfully not simply for the power of new technologies on our economic, cultural and political existence, but as an ontological force, too.

For certain, we cannot disinvent the technologies, but at a more fundamental level, nor can we conceive of 'human nature' untouched by our engagement and interdependence with our tools, artefacts and environment. This is perhaps most lucidly expressed in Donna Haraway's seminal essay, 'A Cyborg Manifesto', first published in 1985 (Haraway 1991). In a high-tech world, she argues, the only political and ethical vantage-point to make any sense is one in which we regard ourselves as 'cyborgs', fusions of flesh and machine, human and cybernetic. This means we cannot ground our ethics on the high ground of essential humanity, uncorrupted spirit or pristine body. 'Bodies can no longer serve as the last outpost of a vanishing world of finite spacetime and bounded order' (Nguyen and Alexander 1996: 121). Instead, we need to learn to think ethically, politically, even theologically, from a position of complicity with the technologies. That means refusing the polarities of instrumentalism or determinism, because both deny human agency, the heterogeneity of technologies and the reflexive nature of human engagement with our tools, artefacts and technologies.

Both instrumentalism and determinism maintain a rigid dualism of agents and tools, action and fabrication (Kaufman-Osborn 1997). On the one hand, instrumentalism conceives human agency in relation to technologies to be supreme, unlimited; the material world of tools and artifacts, not to mention non-human nature, is relegated to mere matter to be manipulated according to the will of human self-aggrandizement. On the other, human agency seemingly plays no constructive part in the building of worlds; the 'essence' of human distinctiveness is somehow conceived as independent of the processes of invention and fabrication.

> It is therefore not enough to ensure that a technological activity or product is examined in its context, exposing the

human and environmental implications and even, asking questions about its purpose: it has to be acknowledged that technologies *are* the context. Technology is itself shaping the value judgements we are making about it. (Conway 1999: 109)

While we may wish to argue that technology transforms what it means to be human, that there is no extra-cultural human essence independent of material culture, therefore, it is necessary to articulate an alternative approach which would attribute a radically different place to the role of human agency in the making and remaking of humanity, nature and culture, and one which attends to the vagaries of specific technological activities and forms.

Andrew Feenberg has argued that theories of technology fall into one of two major categories: the instrumental theory and the substantive theory. The instrumental theory, exemplified by the technocratic model surveyed above, 'offers the most widely accepted view of technology. It is based on the common sense idea that technologies are 'tools' standing ready to serve the purposes of their users. Technology is deemed 'neutral', without valuative content of its own' (Feenberg 1991: 5).

The substantive model of technology, by contrast, understands technologies as embedded in, and emerging to shape, social, cultural and economic conditions. Technology needs to be regarded as a form of social practice (Pinch and Bijker [1987] 2003); so to assume, as the technocratic perspective does, that technologies can be conceived independently of context or implementation, is to deny the extent to which economic interests, scientific world-views and cultural values are embedded in the design and utilisation of tools, artefacts and other technologies, not to mention their portrayal back to us as instruments of mastery or extinction. It is also to evade questions of access, power and distribution.

The issue is not that machines have 'taken over,' but that in choosing to use them we make many unwitting cultural choices. Technology is not simply a means but has become an environment and a way of life: this is its 'substantive' impact. (Feenberg 1991: 8)

No Place for No-Place

In their different ways, Baudrillard and Heidegger are, in their protest against the illusory or ideological nature of technologies, pointing towards the danger of their being elevated above their origins in material contexts, social conventions and human labour. The 'reflexive' model of technological design and deployment, similarly, reminds us of technologies' very embeddedness and complicity in such processes, and defies notions of instrumentalism or determinism that invite us to 'bracket out' questions of human agency in relation to technologies.

It is fine to want to defend the claims of the suffering body and human warmth against the cold universality of scientific laws. But if universality stems from a series of places in which warm flesh-and-blood bodies are suffering everywhere, is not this defence grotesque? Protecting human bodies from the domination of machines and technocrats is a laudable enterprise, but if the machines are full of human beings who find their salvation there, such a protection is merely absurd. (Latour 1993: 124)

Reflexivity calls attention to the origins, interests and applications inherent in the design and use of new technologies; that, in the words of Bruno Latour, our machines are already full of human labour. In other words, human beings cannot be considered to be the sole actors or agents in a world of interdependent humans, machines and nature where all are mutually constitutive.

In virtual reality participants merge with a computer-generated world; object and subject combine and interact;

the boundaries of the body become indeterminate. Similarly, whereas when machines became predominant for the means of production, as for example in the manufactories of the industrial age they were part of a fixed, quite inflexible system of production, supply and demand dedicated to the manufacture of particular commodities, in the information age they are interactive, inserted into a network of non-hierarchical communications with no overarching plan of production, amounting to 'combinations of machines and humans in surprising and unanticipated configurations' (Poster 2001: 27).

Within such a reflexive, hybrid (posthuman) model of our engagement with technologies, the boundaries between object and subject, determinism and agency, enframing and Being, are irrevocably blurred. Our response can no longer be the protest against the distortion of an essential humanity by invasive, instrumental machines, but a question of acquiring appropriate knowledge concerning the most equitable means of configuring humans, nature and machines, of living alongside and intermingled with our tools, technologies and artefacts: a truly 'cyborg ethic'. And there seems nowhere better to begin this critical process than with the very notions of utopia and dystopia themselves, and whether these alternative visions are themselves working according to the assumptions of instrumentalism and determinism or by a more reflexive, substantive model.

The tradition of utopian thinking goes back to Plato's *Republic* (350 BCE) in which he speculated on how a perfect society might be ordered. But ever since, writers have been conjuring up imaginary good societies (utopias) and bad ones (dystopias, anti-utopias, negative utopias) as a recognisable exercise in imagining new worlds. But it is Thomas More's *Utopia* (1516) which first uses the word, taken from two other Greek terms: 'eutopia', the good place, and 'outopia', no-place (Pringle 1997: 11–14). The conflation of these two terms intrigues me. As a good place, utopia performs a didactic purpose, suspending reality through the exercise of imagination, the better to serve as critical lens to its own day. But this 'fantastic' function of the fictional, non-existent 'no-place' is a far cry from the creation of an imaginary place that bears no relationship to anywhere else. To visit the 'no-place' of the imagination (or virtual domain) without any intention of building the 'good place' to which it points is, arguably, to sell utopia short on its ethical or political substance.

Yet in relation to cyberspace as good/bad space or no-space, therefore, it seems to me that much of the utopian appeal of cyber communities and communications rests in their very *inability* to reproduce the complexities of gender, race, dis/ability, thus freeing participants to play with personal identity, to suspend reality: but this is not so much a transcendence of these issues of power and difference, as a bracketing out. The fatal choice, however, is to behave as if the virtual world were not connected to other worlds in any way at all – in other words, to absolutise that world, to seal it off from any political interventions or moral debate: to refuse to see that world as, in fact, 'full of human labour'.

It may be more appropriate, therefore, to acknowledge that humans are capable of building and inhabiting all kinds of worlds – some material, others virtual – but that they are all bound by the relations of their production, albeit working according to different conventions. So when Kevin Robins says that 'I think it is time that this real world broke in on the virtual one' (Robins 1995: 137), I hear this not so much as a return to Baudrillard's rather rigid distinction between the virtual and the real nor necessarily a denial of cyberspace as a legitimate sphere of operation so much as a plea to regard the creation of new synthesised domains, however seductive, as always requiring accommodation within a 'political economy of cyberculture' (Escobar 2001: 58).

Theological Reflection

Neither a deterministic model of technological development, which affords little scope to human agency or choice, therefore, nor an instrumental understanding, which assumes human freedom to transcend material limitations to be absolute, are consistent with a theological anthropology which understands humanity in the image of God as bounded, finite and relational.

First, I think we can affirm the creative activity represented by human engagement with its tools and technologies, an understanding of science and technology as entirely consistent with traditional notions of the *imago Dei* (Herzfeld 2002). As Ted Peters puts it, humanity cannot *not* be inventive and innovative (Peters 1997: 15); yet he maintains that an understanding of creativity and personhood as relational and responsible would preclude the treatment of nature as a mere commodity to be manipulated at will. To place human creativity – including new technologies – within the context of its divine giftedness (Peters's notion of 'created co-creators') fosters a different sensibility in which such activity is afforded an alternative horizon other than expediency. It argues that human will is, ultimately, bounded by the integrity of Others; that natural resources, non-human animals and subordinated human groups are not to be reduced to 'standing reserves' for our disposal. Rather, everything retains its own purpose, to be routed back into the life of God; and human self-sufficiency – secular or merely self-regarding – is fatally fragile.

> Should we play God? No, we should not play God in the promethean sense. But we should play human in the *imago Dei* sense – that is, we should understand ourselves as created co-creators and press our scientific and technological creativity into the service of neighbour love, of beneficence. (Peters 1997: 161)

This links back to my discussion of utopia. To pretend that our building of worlds – material, literary or virtual – bears no relationship to questions of how we live in these worlds is unacceptable because it is a denial of their necessary interdependence. We can regard technological endeavour as that which results in the 'concealment' of the political and economic interests, human labour and social conventions that go into their construction; or as that which serves to reveal the artefactual nature of technologies, their role in bringing human creativity into material and tangible form.

Amid the discussion of technological innovation as a legitimate sphere of human creative activity, therefore, it is also necessary to recognise the limits of such discourse. The notion that humanity can seek redemption via technocratic means alone – whether this be the inhabitation of a perfect, pure virtual environment or the achievement of bodily perfection via genetic modification, cybernetic or prosthetic enhancement, even social engineering – represents the ultimate in the pursuit of human perfection as the apotheosis of our technological, moral or political endeavours. I have already argued that to talk of humanity as in some degree self-constituting via its own technologies, of being capable of influencing the course of its own development is to fall prey to what we might term 'hyper-humanism': a distortion of modernity's faith in the benevolence of human reason, producing the hubristic belief that humanity alone is in control of history. Hyper-humanism may even be regarded, in theological perspective, as a kind of *idolatry*: the elevation of human, finite creation as ultimate reality; a confusion of the fabricated with the ineffable. To affirm humanity as simultaneously creative *and* creaturely is one corrective to this, as a counterweight to the self-interest of technocratic humanism as, for example, in the tendency of the global elite to manufacture technological visions in its own image and self-interest, to the neglect of wider questions of equity and distribution.

Similarly, we have seen how celebrations of the 'technological sublime' as facilitating human ascent from material embodiment into the ideal realm of disembodied, detached omniscience are regarded by some as the outworking of humanity's eternal, enduring and universal 'religious' instincts. Yet these ideals betray only a predilection for qualities of detachment, omniscience, immutability and incorporeality, motivated by 'fear of death, loathing of the body, desire to be moral and free of error' (Mazlish 1993: 218). A theological anthropology, by contrast, sees things differently, not least in its eschewal of a symbolic of transcendence premised on omnipotence, individualism and immortality. Rather than regarding the immanent, embodied, material world as an impediment to genuine spirituality, or – reminiscent of Gnostic world-views – as the profane, flawed, pale reflection of the authentic divine world, this vision sees it as the very realm of divine-human encounter. This is perhaps best encapsulated theologically in a distinction between 'magical' and 'sacramental' action.

I have already alluded to the similarities between ideas of cyberspace as sacred space and Gnostic world-views. This teaches that underlying external, material reality is an inner, spiritual world perceptible only through access to a higher knowledge or superior consciousness. The material world is but a shroud for the spiritual realm, which is the true home of higher beings and cosmic energies. As with the Hermetic world-view, however, signs and symbols are tangible manifestations of the higher powers: thus numerology, the movements of the stars, mysterious configurations of the alphabet, can all give access to the deeper, hidden world of the sacred. Hence, I think, the flight from the body, but the enduring fascination with what is surely the *magical* nature of information and communication technologies – insofar as they use digital data, bytes and codes, these can be seen as the potent keys to unlock the vital energy of creation.

By contrast, a sacramental understanding of matter and spirit regards the physical world as the outward form that communicates inner grace; but it does not seek 'transcendence' so much as 'transformation' of matter in order to experience the sacred. Once again, the attitude towards embodiment is revealing:

> Both ... the spiritualized divine and human body, and the noncorporeal existence of humans allied to cyberspace, picture the body not in terms of fallen corporeal 'nature' requiring transformation, but in terms of a necessary transcending of the gory messiness of the flesh in a technologically or spiritually rarefied version ... (Oliver 1999: 343)

In sacramental activity, the mundane, even the profane is taken and transformed, via human labour, into something that can be considered a divine epiphany. Yet this does not discard, but essentially sacralises, the material in order to point to the spiritual; and it does this by being reordered, rather than destroyed: 'We do not encounter God in the displacement of the world we live in, the suspension of our bodily and historical nature' (Williams 2000: 207). Yet the significance of sacraments, as Rowan Williams argues, is not to mimic the power of the divine but to *make humans holy* through their interaction with the material world. This is not achieved, however, by discarding, but by embracing material, contingent and embodied experience for these ends. Yet in embracing it, we discover too, that it evades our grasp: that the world of representation and world-building (physical or symbolic) is always inadequate fully to express the divine. So again, far from being infused in themselves with divine or supernatural powers, signs and symbols, material objects and practices rather point away from themselves to a reality they can never capture. This is reflected in theological traditions that speak of the non-representability of the divine, the impossibility of speaking the name of the Holy One; and the injunctions against believing that human creative powers can ever rival those of God. In an age when all energy, reality and information is becoming digitalised – the flesh becoming word – it is perhaps important to remember that language, that quintessential mark of divine (and human) creativity, will always fall short of that it attempts to signify. Hence the intriguing detail in the Jewish legend of the Golem, in which a clay man is animated via the magical powers of incantation, but where the artificial being, once given life, heralds its essential imperfection – its artefactual rather than creaturely status – by being unable to speak (E. L. Graham 2002: 92–4). Made through words and signs, it remains outwith the economy of language by virtue of its human and not divine origins. This is an understanding that, whilst human creativity can reflect that of the Creator (and in particular by calling existence into being through the Word), human invention is always contingent, bounded and flawed.

Conclusion

> At the highest level, public life involves choices about what it means to be human. Today these choices are increasingly mediated by technical decisions. What human beings are and will become is decided in the shape of our tools no less than in the action of statesmen and political movements. The design of technology is thus an ontological decision fraught with political consequences. The exclusion of the vast majority from participation in this decision is the underlying cause of many of our problems. (Feenberg 1991: 3)

In surveying the range of responses to the impact of ICT on personal identity, patterns of community and the public domain, we have seen how the information age is regarded as simultaneously 'threat' and 'promise' to human integrity. Yet crucially, this only serves to illuminate implicit philosophies of the relationship between human agency and creativity, and its products: our tools, artifacts and technologies. An insistence on the determinative – but not deterministic – nature of technologies, and the importance of the political and economic choices imbuing human design and interaction with technologies, provides an alternative to models of technology as monolithic, impersonal and instrumental. To conceive, instead, of technologies as *reflexive* phenomena is to see them as simultaneously products of our own creative energies and possessing a capacity for shaping, in turn, the environments and cultures we inhabit. It also reminds us that important value-judgements lie at the very heart of our engagement with technologies: what kinds of humans we may become, how humanity will use the resources, commodities and artefacts granted to it, questions of access, equity and distribution. These are, ultimately, questions of how we use our creative abilities – abilities to build and inhabit all kinds of worlds, material, virtual and imaginary; but worlds which, nevertheless, can either enhance or diminish the image of God within all of us.

Notes

1. See also Kroker 1996.
2. This view is perhaps best expressed by Neil Postman, in works such as *Amusing Ourselves to Death* (London: Methuen, 1987) and *Technopoly: The Surrender of Culture to Technology* (London: Vintage, 1993).

References

Brasher, Brenda (2001), *Give Me That Online Religion* (San Francisco: Jossey-Bass).

Baudrillard, J. (1983), *Simulations* (New York: Semiotext(e)).

Baudrillard, J. (1995), *Le Crime Parfait*, Collection L'espace critique (Paris: Galilee).

Conway, Ruth (1999), *Choices at the Heart of Technology: A Christian Perspective* (Harrisburg, PA: Trinity Press International).

Cooper, D. E. (1995), 'Technology: Liberation or Enslavement?', in R. Fellows (ed.), *Philosophy and Technology* (Cambridge: Cambridge University Press), pp. 7–18.

Davis, E. (1998), *Techgnosis; Myth, Magic and Mysticism in the Age of Information* (London: Serpent's Tail).

Escobar, A. (2001), 'Welcome to Cyberia', in D. Bell and B. M. Kennedy (eds), *The Cybercultures Reader* (London: Routledge), pp. 56–76.

Feenberg, A. (1991), *Critical Theory of Technology* (Oxford: Oxford University Press).

Graham, E. L. (2002), *Representations of the Post/Human: Monsters, Aliens and Others in Popular Culture* (New Jersey: Rutgers University Press).

Graham, G. (1999), *The Internet: A Philosophical Inquiry*, London: Routledge.

Haraway, Donna (1991), 'A Cyborg Manifesto: Science, Technology, and Socialist-Feminism in the Late Twentieth Century', *Simians, Cyborgs and Women: The Reinvention of Nature* (London: Free Association Books), pp. 149–82.

Heidegger, M. (1976) [1966], '"Only a God Can Save Us Now": An Interview with Martin Heidegger', *Philosophy Today*, 20(4), pp. 267–84.

Heidegger, M. (1993) [1954], 'The Question of Technology', in D. F. Krell (ed.), *Basic Writings* (London: Routledge), pp. 307–42.

Heim, M. (1993), *The Metaphysics of Virtual Reality* (Oxford: Oxford University Press).

Herzfeld, N. (2002), *In Our Image: Artificial Intelligence and the Human Spirit* (Minneapolis, MN: Fortress Press).

Interrogate the Internet (1996), 'Contradictions in Cyberspace: Collective Response', in R. Shields (ed.), *Cultures of Internet: Virtual Spaces, Real Histories, Living Bodies* (London: Sage, pp. 126–32.

Kapor, M. (1993), 'Where is the Digital Highway Really Heading?', in *Wired Magazine* 1.03, http://www.wired.com/wired/archive/1.03/kapor.on.nii_pr.html, accessed 28.06.02.

Kaufman-Osborn, Timothy V. (1997), *Creatures of Prometheus: Gender and the Politics of Technology* (Lanham, MD: Rowman & Littlefield).

Kroker, Arthur (1996), 'Virtual Capitalism', in S. Aronowitz, B. Martinsons and M. Menser (eds), *Technoscience and Cyberculture* (London: Routledge), pp. 167–79.

Latour, B. (1993), *We have Never been Modern*, trans. Catherine Porter (Cambridge, MA: Harvard University Press).

Mazlish, Bruce (1993), *The Fourth Discontinuity: The Co-Evolution of Humans and Machines* (New Haven: Yale University Press).

MORI, 'How Britain Voted in 2001' (on-line), http://www.mori.com/polls/2001/election.shtml (2001), accessed 31/7/01.

Myerson, George (2001), *Heidegger, Habermas and the Mobile Phone*, London: Icon Books.

Nguyen, Dan Thu and Jon Alexander (1996), 'The Coming of Cyberspacetime and the End of the Polity', in R. Shields (ed.), *Cultures of Internet: Virtual Spaces, Real Histories, Living Bodies* (London: Sage), pp. 99–124.

Noble, David F. (1999), *The Religion of Technology: The Divinity of Man and the Spirit of Invention*, 2nd edn (New York: Penguin).

Norris, Pippa (2001), *Digital Divide: Civic Engagement, Information Poverty, and the Internet Worldwide* (Cambridge: Cambridge University Press).

Oliver, Simon (1999), 'The Eucharist before Nature and Culture', *Modern Theology*, 15(3), pp. 331–53.

Peters, Ted (1997), *Playing God? Genetic Determinism and Human Freedom* (London: Routledge).

Pinch, Trevor J. and Wiebe E. Bijker [1987] (2003), 'The Social Construction of Facts and Artifacts', in Robert C. Scharff and Val Dusek (eds), *Philosophy of Technology: The Technological Condition* (Oxford: Blackwell), pp. 221–32.

Poster, M. (2001), *What's the Matter with the Internet?* (Minneapolis, MN: University of Minnesota Press).

Pringle, David (ed.) (1997), *The Ultimate Encyclopedia of Science Fiction* (London: Carlton).

Rheingold, Howard (1991), *Virtual Reality* (London: Secker & Warburg).

Robins, K. (1995), 'Cyberspace and the World We Live In', *Body & Society*, 1(3–4), pp. 135–55.

Ross, A. (1991), *Strange Weather* (Cambridge: Verso).

Williams, R. (2000), 'The Nature of a Sacrament', in *On Christian Theology* (Oxford: Blackwell), pp. 197–208.

Some Social, Political and Theological Perspectives on the New Media

Andrew R. Morton

The electronic media or Information and Communication Technologies (ICTs), which are associated with computers, the internet and the web, are leading to significant transformation of the economy, both in production and in consumption, and consequently of wider aspects of life.

A few years ago this transformation was exaggerated, with unrealistic and inflated expectations, some over-optimistic and others over-pessimistic (including the anticipated collapse of capitalism – is that over-optimistic or over-pessimistic?). This has been followed by a deflation of expectation, in part associated with the bursting of the e-investment bubble. Now there is a danger of *under*estimating the actual and potential transformation both of economy and of life.

The development of the technologies is rapid, and although access to them is far from universal, being uneven and largely confined to the 'north' or 'developed' world, it is also expanding rapidly. The technological advance is such that those in their teens are leaving behind those in their twenties and so on through the deciles.

The uses and effects of ICTs, as of all tools, are a matter of human choice and can be either benign or malign, though it may be that good outcomes take more human effort than bad. For example, the individual citizen may use them in order to be open to a wide range of information and so to be much engaged in the affairs of the world; equally she may use them to select a narrow range of information and filter out all else, reading only 'The Daily Me', and thus be *dis*engaged from the affairs of the world. Similarly they may be instruments in the hands of citizens who wish to change the power relations in their society or instruments in the hands of their rulers who wish to maintain the existing relations. In other words, they will tend to reflect the environing pattern of power, whether it be in flux or stable.

One illustration of this concerns the civil service. For a long time in representative democracy there have been two classes, the political class, that is, the parliamentarians, whose members have been visible and removable, and an administrative class, that is, the civil service, whose members have been invisible and immovable. The wider the franchise has become, the more entrenched the latter have become. But ICTs are now making them and their work transparent and accountable, bringing them out into the public domain. This may reduce their relative power; alternatively they may respond to it by engaging with the public in a way which leaves the politicians behind, thus forming a new configuration of power.

The over-optimism and over-pessimism attached to ICTs have been associated with large philosophies or world-views. Along with other modern technologies, they have played a role in both utopian and 'dystopian' thinking. The utopian visions of their potential have at times had a mystical or millennial quality, with their apparent transcendence of physicality and their 'virtual' character even being interpreted as promising infinite knowledge and immortal existence, and there have almost been echoes of Plato's forms or Teilhard de Chardin's noösphere. In this way the disenchantment associated with modernity has been reversed in a re-enchantment. At the same time and by contrast, these modern technologies have been regarded as highly dangerous, sources of darkness rather than light, enslaving rather than liberating, as in Heidegger's writings in the 1950s on the nihilistic 'darkening of the world' through the demonic reification of technology so that it becomes master not servant. Such dystopian thinking is a deepening of disenchantment.

The truth is probably in neither of these views. The hopes of the one and the fears of the other are alike excessive. There is a position on the nature of the relationship of human beings to their technology which is somewhere in the middle, between instrumentalism, according to which technology is merely human beings' instrument and therefore subordinate to them, and determinism, according to which technology determines their life, rendering them subordinate to it. According to this middle position, human beings have a 'reflexive' or 'substantive' relation with both their environment and their technology, so that the three – humans, nature and machines – are all interconnected. Human personhood is not separate or detached from materiality (in a 'defended self' or 'essential humanity'); personhood is defined by space, time and bodily boundaries. So there is a mutual embeddedness or complicity between humans, nature and machines. Humans invest and embed themselves in their technologies, so that machines can be said to be full of human beings because full of human labour; then in the reciprocity of interaction the technologies embed themselves in the humans, shaping their environment, their culture and their life; the relation of technology to humanity is thus not determinist but determinate. If there is this kind of blending interaction between humans and machines and between humans and nature, there is a not dissimilar blending between machines and nature.

This discussion of the relation between human beings and their tools could be further illuminated by a very early yet highly sophisticated human tool, namely, language, an instrument which is clearly also a culture and an environment and therefore an important item of human embedding in both the active and the passive senses.

This 'middle' position is congruent with a theology of humanity or theological anthropology based on the *imago dei*. On this view, humans are both originative and derivative, being both creative and creaturely (or *co*creative), both free and dependent, both capable and fragile.

A major social change, which has been taking place in North America, Europe, Japan and Australia, has been described as 'dispersal of community'; this is a change from *groups* to *networks*. The inner structure of these societies is becoming less a set of discrete groups relating to one another as groups and more a set of diffused and overlapping networks in which individuals relate to one another as individuals. In this new pattern, people's identities are multiple rather than singular, as they tend to belong to many networks rather than to one group and do so more loosely. This is accompanied by a movement 'indoors', with a shift of the location of the significant social component from workplace to household to individual. ICTs appear to be consonant with this development; they do not cause it, for it is a wider phenomenon and it started earlier; but they assist it.

This 'dispersal of community' and its replacement by networks awaits assessment for gains and losses. One apparent loss is suggested by the Pauline image of the physical body for a community such as the Church; according to this image, multiple functions are integrally combined in a working unity of diversity. The possibility of such interfunctionality or acting as a body is fairly clear in, say, a church congregation, but not in a network. This is one question over networks, whether in general or more specifically associated with ICTs.

Analysis of the ownership and usage of ICTs around the world shows a number of 'digital divides'; in other words some categories of people have access while other do not. Three main factors are socio-economic status, political liberty and knowledge of English; for lack of access is associated with being poor or living in an illiberal society or not knowing English (which has become overwhelmingly the main medium).

Two other factors which were initially significant but are becoming less so are age and gender; what tended earlier to be the preserve of young males now involves old as well as young and women as well as men (though in Scotland there is still a male preponderance and a noticeable absence of over-60s). Level of education is becoming less important. Doubtless there are other factors, which may or may not have been measured. It seems, for example, that in Scotland single people are greater users than the married and cohabitant. Owners are not to be equated with users; one estimate in North America is that out of half a billion people 'on-line' a quarter billion do not use the facility. Given the great variations between countries in culture and custom, there is likely to be considerable variation in ICT usage; for example, in Catalonia, though 35 per cent are on-line, usage is low, which may reflect the popular custom of eating out in the evening!

Research into the social effects of ICTs is largely confined to North America (with the notable exception of the University of Essex) and is inevitably tentative given the relative newness of this development. However, it has had some fairly clear results. A main feature of the effects on social interaction is that ICT links have not replaced either telephone or face-to-face links but have been added to them, with the latter continuing substantially at the same level. So social linkages have grown in volume and velocity. (It has been noted that a high proportion of email communication, as well as by mobile telephone, is personal i.e. between kin and friends.) It appears that this growth in the quantity of interaction has not adversely affected its quality, except that it seems that communication by email, with its absence of visual contact, is rather harsher. By contrast, there is evidence of some reduction in the quality of intra-household relations, with less face-to-face communication and some strain on relations.

The use of ICTs for citizen participation in the political process could be called e-democracy. There is a view that e-democracy and parliamentary democracy do not readily mix, because parliamentary democracy, at least as at present, is a process for centralising politics, managing its demands and simplifying its complexity, by reducing choices and aggregating opinions and generally gatekeeping, and is therefore resistant to the unmanageable, decentralising and complexifying potential of e-democracy, which would tend to break the circle of the electoral chain of command, which involves tight links of representation from-elector-to-parliament-to-government and thence of accountability from-government-to-parliament-to-elector.

If there is such a conflict, ICTs may be used by the present political system to control political communication, to influence public opinion and to keep electors under surveillance. Contrariwise they may be used by those dissatisfied with the present system to produce a new politics that reflects the richness and complexity of life and the negotiated, multiple and transnational nature of identities and communities.

The existing system of parliamentary democracy is in fact being criticised, because of its centralising, controlling, narrowing and oversimplifying tendencies, coupled with more particular features such as powerful party discipline, the subordination of parliament to executive, the displacement of much decision-making to policy networks, as well as the excessive influence of the unelected media.

The system of parliamentary democracy is also being questioned in a more radical way by those who wish the state to be slimmed down. To some it should be no more than an arbiter of what is just. To others justice itself is no more than an agreed set of procedures and the state therefore no more than an aggregation of those procedures. To yet others – the out-and-out postmodernists – both justice and the state dissolve even further into mutual respect for incommensurable interests and views.

Associated with this is a radical redefinition of citizenship. It is claimed that whereas nineteenth-century models of citizenship presupposed a single omnicompetent state jurisdiction, each individual is now a citizen of a multiplicity of constituencies, geographical and non-geographical, some of which come and go. It might be retorted that membership of multiple and fluid constituencies does not mean multiple and fluid citizenship, since citizenship implies some overall polity and constituency, without which power cannot be authorised and accountable, indeed without which the common world and the common good dissolve.

However, two less extreme and probably more widely held views are that e-democracy and parliamentary democracy, though to some extent in conflict, can coexist, uncomfortably perhaps but nonetheless creatively, or that there is no conflict at all between them, so that ICTs can quite smoothly bring benefits to parliamentary democracy.

On the assumption that there can be such a creative and beneficial relationship between ICTs and existing political processes and that in this sense ICTs can enhance representative democracy, making it also participatory democracy or citizen democracy, what are the beneficial uses? Again, opinion is broadly divided in two, between more modest and more ambitious hopes, that is, between 'revivalists' who see ICTs putting new life and vigour into the *existing* practices and procedures and 'reformers' or perhaps 'transformers' who see them creating quite *new* practices and procedures. (One should add that a third and even more radical view, associated with the already mentioned view that the state is obsolete, is that ICTs should neither revitalise nor reform existing political processes but replace them entirely.)

Four kinds of ICT enhancement of parliamentary democracy can be envisaged. They form a progression or ladder, moving from intra-parliamentary mode to increasingly intense extra-parliamentary modes in the sense of interaction between parliament and citizens.

The first mode of ICT use improves internal parliamentary procedures by giving parliamentarians electronic access to (1) library and information services (2) expert sources (3) agendas, minutes, draft bills, etc., and, through electronic voting for both (4) parliamentary votes and (5) (externally) parliamentary elections.

The second mode improves communication from parliament to citizens by giving the latter electronic information about (1) parliamentarians' availability, voting, positions (2) parties' manifestos and their candidates' positions (3) parliamentary proceedings, votes, documents, drafts and reports, and by webcasting parliamentary proceedings.

The third mode improves interaction between parliament and citizens, that is, two-way communication between them, by (1) exchange of e-mail correspondence between parliamentarians and citizens and (2) on-line mutual advice bureaux.

The fourth mode involves more intense interaction or two-way communication whereby citizens become participative and in that sense more internal to the process and less on the outside looking in. Its forms can include on-line participation in (1) election hustings (2) petitions and campaigns (3) focus groups (4) discussion forums (5) citizen juries and deliberative panels (6) proceedings of parliamentary committees.

ICTs are called the *new* media to contrast them with the not-so-new media of press and broadcasting. The latter have certainly become central to the political process and not necessarily to its benefit. It has been said that this form of mass media, at least as it has developed, has become like a rushing torrent or self-consuming wave, that it is monopolistic and narcissistic, that it commodifies information and, worst of all, that it blots out thought and memory. It is claimed that by contrast ICTs, which can keep a complete archive, can be instruments of thought and memory (working indeed with a different kind of time), can be genuinely interactive, can overcome the national myopia of most of the mass media, and above all can break the latter's monopoly. The strongest critics of the mass media claim that they are eroding public culture, whereas ICTs have the capacity to enhance it.

This case for ICTs to make up for the deficiencies or even counteract the damaging effects of the more conventional media has been made particularly sharply in Scotland, on grounds of the unrepresentative political stance of many of the newspapers and the absence of appropriately localised television news coverage.

Scotland has been praised for its traditions of 'moral community' and 'democratic intellect'. These express the truth that politics and citizenship are an engagement that is both social and intellectual; they are about a people thinking together. This brings out that a major part of politics is deliberation. Of course it is also about decision-making and decision-implementing; but a prerequisite of both is deliberation, which provides them, as it were, with their oxygen. If this distinction is recognised, the fear of some parliamentarians, that participative or citizen democracy is a threat to representative democracy and therefore to them, can be dispelled. The fact that the many, the citizens, engage in deliberation is no infringement of the prerogative of the few, the parliamentarians, to decide and to implement those decisions.

Scotland, as well as having a new parliament and executive, also has an instrument which is particularly designed to help develop citizen democracy or 'negotiated governance' and so specialises in deliberation. It is the Scottish Civic Forum, which is officially recognised by the Scottish Executive, though not as yet by the Scottish Parliament. Though constitutionally it is a partnership of non-governmental organisations, its function is not to represent those organisations far less to make representation ('lobby') on their behalf to the Parliament or the Executive. Its function is to be an open space, hence 'forum', for the widest possible public deliberation on public affairs, including but not solely those which are or may be the subject of legislation or other governmental or parliamentary action. This deliberation is open to all citizens, hence 'civic'; it follows from this that it is open to parliamentarians, who do not cease to be citizens on election. It could be said that the Forum's aim is to help surround politics with an atmosphere of public discourse, thus giving political decision-making the oxygen of civic deliberation. It has not so far given special attention to the use of ICTs in the service of citizen deliberation, but it is now being encouraged to do so and, as it were, to 'elongate' its forum sessions into a more continuous 'e-forum'.

The Scottish Parliament itself has a high level of ICT output, probably as high as any parliament anywhere, as Neal Ascherson's contribution to this volume indicates. This includes website, webcast, forums and public access points (in libraries). However, this high output is met with low uptake, through lack of publicity and of user-friendliness, with an absence of thematising and indexing and the like. It is arguable that information is confused with interaction and that there is a 'vomiting' of too much too undigested.

An interesting sidelight on the Scottish Parliament and ICT use is that ICT users in Scotland have greater confidence in the Scottish Parliament and Executive than non-users, and the more intense the usage, the greater the confidence. By contrast, the intensive users and the non-users have less confidence in the UK Parliament and Executive than the moderate users. One can only speculate on the reasons for this correlation between increasing ICT use and increasing confidence in the Scottish institutions; is it a consequence of the Scottish Parliament's own highly developed use of ICTs? or is it that the Scottish Parliament is living up to the widespread hope that it would be better than the UK Parliament at encouraging democratic participation? or what?

The Scottish Executive is also active in relation to ICTs. It has a 'Digital Inclusion' policy. Its unit for this purpose has six aims: educating the public, focusing on what ICTs can do (not how they work); increasing access, from Scotland's current level of 36 per cent (compared with England's 42 per cent and the USA's 50 per cent) to 100 per cent by 2005; developing skills; creating 'digital communities', at the time of writing as a pilot project freely giving the facilities to every household in one urban and one rural area; encouraging business use; creating public access points, in shops, banks, pubs, bus stations, etc., 200 at the time of writing, with a target of 1,000.

A recurring theme in the discussion of the the use of ICTs is that they can be either an aid or an alibi for change and that they must be seen within the wider context of the many forms of human communication and interaction and relationship and above all in the context of human will. Change in institutions does not come easily, given their inherent inertia and the vested interests in the status quo. The Scottish Parliament and Executive, like other institutions, are liable to the temptation to treat ICTs as an alibi for citizen participation rather than as an aid to it. This happens if in the other forms of communication, face-to-face, telephonic and other, the institutions are not open and transparent and engaging. One aspect of this is that ICTs can be, as it were, too cheap a form of communication for the sender in that a large proportion of responsibility and cost is with the recipient. None of this is to imply that ICT communication does not have its special contribution or to suggest that the different forms of communication can be easily put on a scale of value. For example, abused women may find ICT communication with the abuser preferable to face-to-face communication, and the Samaritans find that some desperate people prefer ICT to the telephone.

At least one Scottish parliamentarian (MSP) considers the main issue to be the need for change in the whole under-standing and practice of interaction between politicians and the people. This MSP longs for politicians to have 'engagement *with*' and 'dialogue *with*' citizens rather than 'consultation *of*' or even 'participation *of*' them. The present consultations are unsatisfactory, as they are too many, too perfunctory and too paper based, and consequently overloading, mechanical and a 'comfort blanket' for the politicians with their semblance of openness. Real openness between politicians and citizens involves engagement and dialogue in a continuous or iterative process rather than in a disjointed series of isolated episodes (e.g. there should be use of the more sustained methods of market research rather than one-off requests for opinion). This criticism of the present practice of consultation is related to two other concerns. One is the danger of regarding the politicians' role as being simply to follow the public and not also to lead it; the politicians' response to the dialogue and engagement with citizens should be to *appropriate* what they hear, not necessarily to accept it (and presumably for the citizens to appropriate what *they* hear). The other is the tendency to focus too much attention on the process of *forming* and legislating policy to the neglect of the process of *implementing* and making it operational.

Paradoxically, politicians' greater openness and information-*giving*, by exposing weaknesses of government, has undermined confidence in it; does a public that receives more information need more education in the use of it? At the same time, politicians' greater information-*receiving* through the advent of ICTs (those endless emails) has added to their time overload.

The MSP also considers that politicians are increasingly constrained by media that are cynical about politics and tend to misdescribe healthy debate and disagreement as unhealthy division and disloyalty. Excessive party discipline, which may reflect loss of party ideological identity, colludes with this debasement, trivialisation and oversimplification of political discourse.

Scottish standards for governance have been set by the Consultative Steering Group, a body which, at the time of the creation of the Scottish Parliament and Executive, laid out four criteria for them, namely, accessibility, accountability, equal opportunity and power sharing. This has tended to become, in the absence of a proper constitution, a surrogate one; it was never intended to be so, having a more specific and properly limited purpose. There is need for a genuine constitution or supreme law, if there is to be full citizen democracy (with 'citizens' not 'subjects'). In this regard, one proposal is that there be a Scottish Constitutional eConvention.

Questions of jurisdiction, authorisation and accountability may arise in relation to the governance of ICT communication. The International Committee for Assigned Names and Numbers is a potential instrument of governance of the internet in the interests of its users; but the method of election to it is uncertain and there is as yet no 'internet public' in any constituted sense. Some fear that in the absence of such a public or publics, large corporations or large states may take over the effective governance.

If ICTs are to be a real help to citizen participation or e-democracy, in the sense of enabling citizens effectively to influence political decision-making, a great deal of work needs to be put into design. This is a clear message from www.openDemocracy.net, a London-based ICT global channel 'for knowledge, participation and understanding that gives a depth of coverage to the ideas and issues that shape society but are given only scant attention in conventional media'. In this context at least, content cannot be separated from form, which could be said to be the relationship that content has to people. Self-articulation by the many, as they 'find their voice', is essential, but it is not good enough if it does not advance the argument, if it is only 'noise'. To produce the quality that is required to make a difference, that is, to affect decision-making, it is necessary, for example, to edit or moderate the input without misrepresenting it, in order both to enable further development of the argument by the many and to assist the ultimate decision-making by the few. Designing ICT programmes for e-democracy is a high-level skill. Any new Scottish initiatives will require to give it great attention.

Internet Reflections

Alison Elliot

The encounter between human beings and their technology is one that is regularly fraught with threat as well as opportunity. Human identity is seen to be a fragile plant when confronted with the potential of its creations for domination, be it benign or anarchic. In the past, a constructive accommodation has been achieved between humankind and its technological developments in communication and it is likely that the same will happen with current developments in electronic communication. However, in the process, they throw up opportunities for modest insights into aspects of interpersonal relations and their organisation, whether in virtual or in pre-electronic form.

The Internet can be regarded as a mirror in which human relationships are reflected, distorted and reconstructed. These reflections can expose weaknesses in aspects of social organisation that are customarily seen as beneficial or can expose limitations to the values a group is thought to espouse. In selecting the following reflections, it is convenient to characterise the Internet as falling into two different functional categories: as disembodied space and as shop window.

The Internet as a Disembodied Space

The disembodied nature of the Internet has two aspects to it.

In the first place, the communication that it sets up between individuals has a flat structure; it is a web, rather than a corporate body. By contrast, the kinds of civic organisations that traditionally enable and promote citizenship in the population are often highly structured, with the functions of the organisation strictly distributed through its members. The metaphor of the functioning of, and interrelationships between, different parts of a body can readily be applied to such an organisation. Roles carry with them responsibilities and tasks are compartmentalised, so that, for example, the treasurer and the secretary observe strict boundaries between their remits, much as eyes and legs do in a physical body. The advantage of this demarcation of roles is that the organisation can capitalise on the specialist skills of its members. The downside is a territoriality that can impede communication and can lead to members feeling excluded from important decision-making.

Associated with such organisations are civic skills (Putnam 2000) such as minute-taking or chairing meetings. These skills are readily transferable, and people possessing them are well placed to be influential in civil society. Churches have frequently nurtured these skills in their members, and Putnam comments on this characteristic. In former Communist countries, it was noted that the churches were places not just where an alternative vision was kept alive but where an alternative resource of civic skills could be found when new leadership was needed.

As civic organisations weaken, and their associated skills become less valued, and less common in the population, the attraction of direct Internet communication, unmediated by a hierarchy of office-bearers, becomes evident. Whether organisations can function effectively with such a flat structure or whether familiar roles and responsibilities will emerge among the participants of virtual associations is a fascinating question. However, for the purposes of this argument, the important observation is that the flat structure of Internet association exposes some of the shortcomings of traditional community organisations, as excluding those without the skills or the confidence to participate effectively within them. It also offers the possibility of widening participation beyond the previous range of activists.

One area in which inclusion can be increased relates to a second aspect of the Internet as a disembodied space, namely, that communication is possible without people coming face to face with each other. The dangers inherent in this situation are well known, with liaisons being established between adults and children which can lead to sexual exploitation. Less dramatically, people's fantasy lives can interact with each other in ways which can be educational but also have the potential to do psychological damage.

It is frequently observed that communication over the Internet is impoverished because it lacks the quintessentially human element of non-verbal communication, the body language and gestures that convey an extra dimension to the message of the words. However, that fails to account for the negative aspects of being visible to your interlocutor, which can sometimes be a barrier to civic participation.

For example, Coleman and Normann (2000) report on an on-line consultation into domestic violence carried out by the Westminster All-Party Parliamentary Group on Domestic Violence. This enabled women who had lived with domestic violence to give direct evidence to the MPs in circumstances which protected their anonymity, but which allowed discussion and development of their evidence. Participants were recruited through women's groups, disability groups and Women's Aid refuges, and their identity was kept confidential through the use of false names. Support was on hand from the staff of the refuges, and also from one of the Moderators, if women found the experience distressing at any time. The consultation was greatly valued by over 90 per cent of those who took part. They felt that their story was listened to by far more people than would otherwise have been the case. Although there was disappointment that the MPs did not appear to be as engaged as the participants had expected, the MPs themselves appreciated the value of the exercise. Many of the participants welcomed the support they found among their own group and found the experience creative and healing.

For this vulnerable group, therefore, the face-to-face nature of natural communication can be a barrier to civic participation, and the Internet can be used creatively in this way to include such people in decision-making. This example shows how the new technology can reveal not only gaps in the reach of the democratic process but also weaknesses in models of participation otherwise given high positive value.

The Internet as Shop Window

It is often hard to realise just how extensive the reach of the Internet is. Websites may be designed with a particular, local audience in mind, but that does not stop people with other interests, or living on the other side of the world, reading the information on them and drawing their own conclusions, which may be false, about the nature and purpose of the organisation. The Internet can be an excellent tool of publicity, but it can also be mercilessly revealing. How an organisation presents itself through its website therefore has to be thought through very carefully to ensure that it offers a valid impression of the organisation's values and purpose.

It has been noted that churches and congregations are organisations that have done well in preparing people for civic life. Moreover, the Scottish church tradition is one which has had no hesitation in contributing to civic and political debate and development (Storrar and Donald 2003). If traditional forms of civic engagement are changing, and the Internet is one of the ways forward, the question arises of how congregations are adapting to the challenges and opportunities of the new situation.

As Neal Ascherson's chapter records, it was decided to conduct a survey of the websites of a small sample of Church of Scotland congregations to see how they presented themselves. To what extent could they be said to be using the Internet creatively as a tool of engagement with the concerns of their local community? Did they simply give information about church activities for their own members? Did they give evidence of being concerned about activities in the wider community? What kinds of links did the congregations have to other websites?

Every eighth congregation on the list of Church of Scotland congregational websites (thirty-seven congregations) was sampled in June 2002 by Dr Heidi Campbell. Note was made of the structure and servicing arrangements for each website. Any information about the local community was noted and links were listed and categorised as to whether they were to other church-based sites, to community sites, to the Scottish Churches Parliamentary Office, or to international organisations.

The websites varied tremendously and showed considerable individuality and imagination. Most of them concentrated on highlighting what was happening inside the congregation. Many of the websites did not appear to encourage involvement beyond their own congregational activities. Only 11 per cent listed information about their local community, and 19 per cent had no links to another site.

Analysis of the links that were offered indicated that most were to other church-based sites. Sixty-two per cent were linked to the Church of Scotland website and 46 per cent to other Church of Scotland weblinks, such as the local Presbytery. Thirty-eight per cent were linked to websites of other denominations or other religious organisations (such as Action of Churches Together in Scotland).

Links to community groups were offered in the case of 38 per cent of the congregations. These included the websites of the local council or community council, occasionally including a tourist guide or weather report. Some were to charities with a Christian origin, such as Cyrenians or the Children's Hospice Association Scotland.

Cultural links were noted separately, in the expectation that, since many church buildings are of historic interest, tourism might provide a connection with other community activities. Nineteen per cent of the congregations had links which were categorised as cultural, and covered links to Christian artistic sites as well as ones with a genealogical or historical focus.

Wider political engagement was identified by noting reference to the link to the Scottish Churches Parliamentary Office (only 3 per cent of congregations) or to international sites. Thirty-two per cent of congregations offered links to international sites, with Christian Aid being the commonest link.

An email questionnaire was sent to the webmasters of these congregations, where they could be identified, to explore further how the congregation understood the purpose of the website and what effect it had had, or was hoped to have, on the congregation itself. Eleven replies were received, many of them capturing the evident commitment and enthusiasm of the webmasters themselves.

Most of the replies indicated that the purpose of the website was to provide information about the congregation, although one saw the purpose as that of providing access to good-quality Bible-based teaching on-line. Some identified the value of the site in keeping former members of the congregation in touch with its activities, or keeping a link with students who had left to go to university. One had been set up to celebrate the church's centenary.

Asked whether the website had had a noticeable influence on the congregation, most indicated that it was too early to say. One congregation did notice an increase in the hits at Summer Club time, suggesting that this might be reaching younger people. They also noted an increase in non-members attending church, which might indicate an effect of the website, although they had not set out to measure this.

It was suggested in the questionnaire that having a website might alter the degree of face-to-face communication within the congregation, or encourage the congregation to have a more outward-looking focus. One reply indicated that the website was a talking point among the enthusiasts in the congregation and so had increased the face-to-face communication for this particular group, and another said that an aim of the site was to increase awareness of the missionary linked to the congregation. However, the suggestions did not resonate with the experience of other webmasters.

On the basis of the content and presentation of the congregational websites sampled, the impression is of churches more concerned with their own internal activities than with outreach to, or engagement with, the wider community. This is rather at odds with the results of the recent study on the social capital of Church of Scotland congregations commissioned from the Department of Urban Studies of Glasgow University (Flint, Kearns and Atkinson 2002). They found that the congregations they sampled (one-third of all congregations) were engaged, on average, in almost half of the social capital-generating activities identified in the questionnaire to which they responded. There were differences between congregations, with those in poorer, urban areas showing more of these activities than those in other areas. Their study gives a picture of congregations reaching out to their local community, though not utilising as many ways of doing this as they might.

It is possible, therefore, that the potential of a website for increasing communication between a congregation and its local community has yet to be fully realised in many cases. At the time of sampling, only 245 websites were listed on the Church of Scotland site, and the correspondence with the webmasters indicated that they considered it still to be early days in exploring the value of this tool. It may also be the case that the congregations that were first to develop a site were ones with less interest in community issues.

If the Internet is becoming an important tool in civic activity, and if the churches wish to maintain a prominent role in this process, this study indicates that they have some way to go in developing that potential. In time, if they wish it, websites can connect them much more closely into the wider social and political concerns of their community. The opportunities are there for creative engagement both locally and on the national and world stage with people's pressing needs and hopes. How churches develop this tool in the future will be a telling measure of how they regard their civic responsibilities.

References

Coleman, S. and E. Normann (2000), *New Media and Social Inclusion* (Hansard Society E-Democracy Programme).

Flint, J., A. Kearns and R. Atkinson (2002), *The Role of Church of Scotland Congregations in Contributing to Social Capital and Community Development in Scotland* (Edinburgh: Church of Scotland).

Putnam, R. (2000), *Bowling Alone: The Collapse and Revival of American Community* (New York: Simon & Schuster).

Storrar, W. and P. Donald (eds) (2003), *God in Society: Doing Social Theology in Scotland Today* (Edinburgh: Saint Andrew Press/Centre for Theology and Public Issues).

The Message of the Text in an Age of Text Messaging

Johnston R. McKay

It was a throwaway remark on a programme about the alphabet, in Melvyn Bragg's Radio 4 series *In our Time*, which was the starting point for this chapter. One of the contributors was Allan Millard, the Emeritus Professor of Hebrew and Semitic Languages at the University of Liverpool, and he was describing how, in his view, language was first analysed when a Canaanite scribe, round about 1800 BC, working in the city of Biblos, discovered that neither the hieroglyphic signs of the Egyptians nor the cuneiform strokes of the Babylonians could represent his Canaanite language. He took from the Egyptian hieroglyphic the picture which represented a door, for example, and, in his language, used it to stand not for the door itself but for the sound 'd' of the beginning of the word 'door'. Since the word which represented what the picture was never began with a vowel, he constructed an alphabet which did not require vowels. His words consisted purely of consonants and the reader was left to supply the appropriate vowels according to the context. An alphabet with vowels began to emerge when Canaanite traders visited Greece and introduced their Greek customers to their alphabet. Some Greek words did begin with vowels, so, in the construction of their alphabet, Greeks adopted the Canaanite letters which represented sounds Greek did not use for the vowels they needed. For example the sound of the Canaanite aleph was unnecessary so it was adapted to give the Greek alpha. As Professor Millard was describing his scribe in Biblos constructing an alphabet without vowels, he said, 'Exactly what has happened with text-messaging today'.

I will return to what might link the Semitic languages' lack of vowels and the conventions of today's text messaging later on. However, it is worth noting that I learned what I did about the Canaanite alphabet from a programme of serious, well-informed, educative discussion, which is an exception to much of today's radio. Even the 'flagship' programme *Today* on Radio 4 involves the presenters soliciting and then reading out emails or text-messages.

Thirty-five years ago, when I was first invited to take part in a television programme, I sat in the BBC canteen with the legendary Dr Ronald Falconer, then Head of Religious Broadcasting for BBC Scotland, who explained to those of us who were sitting round the table that the BBC had just discovered the cheapest form of broadcasting. It was later to be called the 'phone-in'. These first, hesitant, crackly broadcast phone calls have now become the staple diet of most radio programming. For example, the morning schedule on BBC Radio Scotland today involves programmes which invite and encourage either e-mails or text messages from listeners for six hours out of the first seven and a half hours.

The phone-in programmes which Ronald Falconer described were introduced because they provided cheap broadcasting. Now audience involvement through emails and texts has become essential to radio broadcasting, and to a lesser extent television broadcasting, because news is offered in an interactive format: essential in the sense that programme makers have discovered from research that what appeals to listeners is not just the news, but what the person with a mobile phone and able to call or text *thinks about the news.*

Is this the democratisation of the air-waves, or is it popularising them? Access broadcasting or dumbing down?

Some years ago the first piece of real research into what the audience expected of religious broadcasting was undertaken for BBC Scotland. The research was conducted among people aged 35–45, all of whom said they were interested in spiritual issues, but who had no formal connection with any of the churches: the audience for whom most religious broadcasters try to make their programmes. The research showed a distinct aversion to anything which smacked of institutional religion, which in itself is not necessarily bad, but it also showed that this audience wanted from religious broadcasting whatever would enhance people's personal happiness, provide the 'feel-good factor' and increase their experience of personal well-being.

There was no interest in programmes which explored issues of social justice, or in deep questions of life and death. When asked to comment on words which they rejected, they chose 'suffering', 'God', 'mystery', 'belief', 'values', 'silence'.

The challenge for religious broadcasting, but much more the challenge for the church today, is to find a way of talking about these themes without mentioning the words which make the audience switch off.

I am not only a believer in public service broadcasting, I am a believer in public service religious broadcasting. My reaction to this research was not to ask how we could provide this audience with what it wanted (which is the question I would certainly have been expected to ask in the days when John (now Lord) Birt was the BBC's Director General) but rather to ask what the style and content of programmes should be which would convince this audience that there was more to life than *personal* experience, and more to religion than feelings of personal satisfaction, that concern for the other and the neighbour as a matter of social justice was something which should engage us all, and that questions of faith and life and death were worth exploring.

I spoke about that research to two in-service training courses run by the Church of Scotland. The first was for ministers who had been ordained for seven to ten years. Their very strong, immediate reaction was to insist that the research was flawed, based I suspect on the 'shoot the messenger' school of responses. A couple of months later I spoke to a group of newly ordained ministers who accepted the research without question. I reflected afterwards that the difference in response between those who had been ordained longer and dismissed the research and those newly ordained who accepted it might have had to do with the closeness of those just ordained to the world outside the church.

Much has been made recently of a vision of a 'church without walls', but if that slogan is to have any meaning whatsoever then those who are leaders in the church must begin to discover what people outside the walls think about, believe and aspire to in the sphere of religion. That is why, when I was involved as a producer of religious broadcasts in programmes which I hope were regarded as preaching (in the broadest sense) I was trying to make programmes which spoke to that audience.

That involved abandoning church services as the *primary* form of religious broadcasting both on radio and in television. Whatever sort of religious communication is appropriate on radio and television it cannot be the conventional form of preaching from a pulpit. I believe that even more strongly than I did when I started working in religious broadcasting: then my conviction was based on the obvious fact that the number of people who could make the imaginative leap from their kitchen to a church was diminishing, and no broadcaster wants to hitch their programme wagon to a plummeting audience. Now I believe it because I recognise the nature of the audience has changed in that it does not make the equation that the audience of the mid-twentieth century would have made between spiritual development and membership of the church. It is also true that the nature of religious broadcasting has changed too. In the 1950s and 1960s, Ronnie Falconer could say without any embarrassment that 'we' (the BBC's Religious Broadcasting Department) are the broadcasting arm of 'the Church', and commit BBC resources to an evangelistic 'Tell Scotland' campaign.

Let me offer several theological reflections on all of this.

The first is that every revolution in communications has had a profound effect on both the form and the content of Christian faith. I began with what I learned about the alphabet and the formation of what we now recognise as 'words'. The concept of a word, something which symbolised, encapsulated, demonstrated and described the nature of a reality by which human beings communicated with each other had a fundamental effect on religious ideas through the Hebrew *dbr* and the Greek *logos*, and was the outcome of this revolution in communication.

Later on the *copying* of books so influenced the content of the Gospels that even today we are having to wrestle with issues caused by changes, errors, glosses and interpretative additions introduced to the transmission of the Gospels and which has not only bred a whole science of textual criticism but has influenced theological reflection.

The first sermon class I ever attended was run by John O'Neill, who later became New Testament Professor in Edinburgh but then was teaching in Cambridge. I was asked to draft a sermon on Mark 3.28, 29: 'Truly I tell you, people

will be forgiven for their sins, and whatever blasphemies
they utter, but whoever blasphemes against the Holy Spirit
can never have forgiveness.'

Many years later, John O'Neill sent me an article he
had written,[1] arguing that the word 'Holy' (*hagios*) is
an intrusion, inserted by a scribe who, when he read the
original 'anyone who blasphemes against *this spirit*', for
example, the spirit of forgiveness which Jesus has been
speaking about, asked himself, 'what spirit would that be?'
and answered his question 'It must be the Holy Spirit' and
so wrote the word 'Holy' in the margin. In a later copy in
the phrase 'whoever blasphemes against "this" spirit', the
word 'holy' was included in the text instead of 'this'.

Many centuries later, communication was further transformed by Gutenberg's invention of the printing press which
made the Bible available to people in their own language and
so contributed immensely to the transformation of theology
and the fracturing of Christendom at the Reformation.

In the last century there has been the broadcasting
revolution: first radio and then television. Ronald Falconer
actually recognised thirty years ago that they would have
a profound effect on the Christian faith when he observed
that 'there is something about the nature of television which
makes events larger than life, thus distorting the truth about
them'.[2]

In a symposium produced by the Centre for Theology
and Public Issues at Edinburgh University, Derek Weber
writes, 'It is the technology of camera and screen, of
microphone and receiver that separate speaker and hearer,
that redirects attention from the real to the fantasy, from
the important to the trivial'.[3]

What radio and television did to the Christian gospel
was to help transform it from indirect communication to
direct communication. In the Mair Lectures[4] in Glasgow
University, I argued that Kierkegaard was right to say that
'whenever we turn Christianity into direct communication,

it is altogether destroyed. It becomes a superficial thing, capable neither of inflicting deep wounds nor of healing them.' But television (and to some extent radio too) is always happier with direct communication and so, I believe, has contributed to the falsification of the Christianity which is offered to a mass audience.

There have been, and still are, producers who recognise that if the language of religion has much more in common with the language of poetry than that of the journalist then the images they use to convey religious ideas have to be oblique, more evocative than literal, more often counterpoint than harmony, learning from the poet Emily Dickinson:

> Tell all the truth but tell it slant –
> Success in Circuit lies
> Too bright for our Infirm Delight
> The Truth's superb surprise
> As lightning to the children eased
> With explanation kind
> The Truth must dazzle gradually
> Or every man be blind.[5]

Too often, however, the nature of the media demands that instant truth be met with instant opinion, and so the gradual is dismissed and the complex reduced to direct communication in simple statements.

One of the reasons why it is vital to see Christianity as 'indirect communication' is that, despite the tendency of the broadcast media to gravitate towards the aggressively direct, it is possible (and as I have hinted, religious broadcasting is one of the few areas of broadcasting where it is still possible) to use an ambiguous, tangential approach to an area of interest or concern to explore the very themes which lie behind the words rejected by those in BBC Scotland's research and so introduce them seductively, surreptitiously and subversively to the audience.

My next theological reflection follows on from that because it is possible to argue that it was not radio and television which turned Christianity into 'direct communication' but the Church's preaching itself. At opposite ends of the theological spectrum, Rudolf Bultmann states in Kerygma and Myth that 'The preacher in his sermons must not leave his hearer in any uncertainty as to what he requires them to believe to be true',[6] while Karl Barth famously declared that 'Preaching is the Word of God which he himself speaks'.[7]

From what I have said about Christianity as indirect communication it will be clear that I take issue on this subject with both Bultmann and Barth. However, I suspect that a good number of ministers, who might not agree with the basic theological stance of either Barth or Bultmann, would nevertheless agree with them about preaching.

In that case, I believe they have a problem. The world of text messaging does not like the message of the text to be communicated in certainties and propositions and convictions and beliefs which people have to accept. The world of text messaging wants to be able to argue with those who, as a famous prayer for broadcasters puts it, 'speak where many listen'. The audience which wants not just the news, but what the person with the mobile phone thinks about the news, does not want to hear the message of the text as binding. He or she wants to express an opinion about it or to hear what others have to say about it. The person on the mobile phone does not want to be left in any doubt as to the truth of what Bultmann's preacher wants them to believe, or what Barth's preacher says is the unquestionable Word of God, any more than he or she wants news to be presented in a form which denies both the right and the opportunity to comment on it. The presumed (or assumed) power of the broadcast journalist or the religious authority have been challenged.

Let me return, briefly, to the Canaanite scribe who discovered that neither the hieroglyphics of Egypt nor the cuneiform strokes of Babylon were able to represent his Canaanite language. The written languages of Egypt and Babylon were the preserve of the elite, of the power-systems represented by the gods and the kings. This Canaanite scribe in the alphabet he developed without vowels was implicitly rejecting that world of power and undermining the world of authority. I simply ask whether the vowelless alphabet of text messaging, which began not in the world of power and authority which eventually embraced it but in a culture of youthful revolt might not be a similar rejection of the sort of authority systems of which religion has traditionally been one?

A further theological reflection is to ask whether both in the life of the Church and in the life of Biblical scholarship there have been trends which are (depending on your point of view) either a response to all of this and an attempt to reach an accommodation with it, or else a trend which has accelerated the whole process.

It is quite common today for ministers to form worship committees and to engage in group construction of sermons. My suspicion is that this trend has contributed to the undermining of any sense of a specific role for the ordained ministry of word and sacrament which, in turn, is reflected in a good deal of the confused soul-searching there is about what ministers of religion are actually for. However, in the context of the subject of this chapter, I suspect that this trend is based on the premises that (a) everyone's view of what a Bible passage means or is about is equally valid (which is the philosophy behind the use of emails and text messages in broadcasting) and that (b) Bible passages are fundamentally about whatever they mean to the individual reader.

That is exactly the conviction behind what is now called 'reader-response criticism' in literary studies in general and Biblical studies in particular. The Biblical scholar Margaret Davies writes,

According to this view, meaning is created by the reader construing the text. The potential of the writing is realised by the reader in making sense of words, phrases, sentences, paragraphs, and eventually the whole complex of the work, forging a comprehensive meaning from the parts.[8]

There are some, like myself, who are still sufficiently conservative to regard the uncovering of a Gospel writer's intention as not only possible but as integral to the way in which we hear Scripture speaking, who will be acutely suspicious of this trend; while others, like Margaret Davies, will see reader-response criticism as offering 'refreshing vistas' to interpreters of the Bible.

My final theological reflection occurred to me when listening to Professor Elaine Graham at the 'Netting Citizens' conference. She said (see p. 157 above),

> The impact of new technologies blurs many of the taken-for-granted categories of space, place and time; the boundaries of the body; the interface of machine and human. In the case of the Internet, it collapses physical difference, transcends national boundaries, reinvents conventions of text and reading, transforms human interactions into the flow of information, creates new artificial environments and machinic intelligences. This necessarily calls forth some radical rethinking of what it means to be human in an age some call the 'posthuman'.

Professor Graham argued that the posthuman age involves not just a quantitative change in humanity's development, involving, for example, Jesus' ignorance of the shape of the world or its place in the universe, which does not inherently undermine his essential humanity. This posthuman age involves a qualitative change to humanity's essence. If that is so, then it raises a serious theological issue put starkly by Gregory of Nazianzus in the fourth century, when debate was raging over whether Christ was truly human, or whether, perhaps, he had a divine soul: 'That which he has not assumed, he has not healed'.[9] In other words, only the true and full humanity of Christ is sufficient to provide a true and full salvation. But, if there is a qualitative change in the nature or essence of humanity as a result of the impact of new technologies, can traditional theological categories deal with a posthuman reality which is qualitatively different from the humanity assumed by the Son of God?

Professor Graham makes the point that the new technology 'transforms interactions into the flow of information': which brings me back to the central point of all my reflections, both as a broadcaster and a preacher, on the present situation. The world of text messaging, the world of information technology, is a world of information, and often of dogmatic assertion, whereas the language of religion is the world of engagement, of debate, *of story*.

The staccato code of the text message is far removed from the discursive style of the storyteller. The typical assertiveness in the responses to the radio presenter's invitation to send emails or text messages commenting on the news or a discussion about the news on a radio programme is very different from the narrator's art. When religious discourse has been conducted in the language of slogans, it has been no different from the assertiveness of the text-message 'discussion', but when it has taken the form of engaged debate allowing for shifts of opinion and subtle changes of position it has become part of the story of ecclesiastical or doctrinal development.

The form of news broadcasting which encourages listener-response assumes that what matters about truth is factual, verifiable information, the stuff of journalists who seek to discover the facts. Have we too readily assumed that public truth requires to be expressed in the form of the news broadcast and the coinage of the journalist? Is there a place for indirect communication and narrative in the arena of public truth? Presumably Jesus of Nazareth thought so or he would not have adopted the parable as his principle means of communicating truth both privately and publicly.

In an earlier conference organised by the Centre for Theology and Public Issues, Bishop Stephen Sykes pointed out that the National Health Service owed at least as much to Mrs Gaskell and Charles Dickens as it did to Aneurin Bevan and Lord Beveridge in that the novelists showed with such clarity the extent of poverty in the country and the inability of charity and philanthropy to combat it.

It is, however, surprising to say the least to find how patronising those who have some responsibility to follow the methods of Jesus of Nazareth can be about the telling of stories. Recently I was invited to speak to a presbytery conference about communicating the gospel. I referred to the story and how powerful a story can be. One of the ministers said to me, 'Of course stories are important in communicating Christian faith, but don't we have to show that the faith is intellectually respectable as well'!

Notes

1. 'The Unforgivable Sin', *Journal for the Study of the New Testament*, 19 (1983), pp. 37–42.

2. Ronald Falconer, *Message, Media and Mission* (Edinburgh: Saint Andrew Press, 1977), pp. 41ff.

3. Derek Weber, 'Making Graven Images', in Peter Elvy (ed.), *Opportunities and Limitations in Religious Broadcasting* (Edinburgh: Published for Jerusalem Trust by Centre for Theology and Public Issues, New College, University of Edinburgh, 1991), pp. 149–55.

4. Johnston McKay, *This Small Pool* (Glasgow: Trinity St Mungo Press, 1997).

5. Emily Dickinson, *Complete Poems* (London: Faber & Faber, 1970), No. 1129.

6. Rudolf Bultman, *Kerygma and Myth* (New York: Harper & Row, 1961), p. 23.

7. Karl Barth, *Homiletics*, trans. Geoffrey W. Bromiley and Donald E. Daniels (Louisville, KY: Westminster John Knox Press, 1991), p. 56.
8. Margaret Davies, 'Literary Criticism', in R. J. Coggins and J. L. Houlden (eds), *A Dictionary of Biblical Interpretation* (London: SCM Press, 1990), pp. 402–5 (404).
9. Quoted in J. Stevenson, *Creeds, Councils and Controversies* (London: SPCK, 1966), p. 98.

The Internet as Social-Spiritual Space

Heidi Campbell

The Internet means different things to different people. According to Annette Markham (1998), individuals can conceive of the Internet as a tool, a place or a state of mind. This spectrum of conceptions provides a helpful starting point to describe ways the Internet is seen and used by individuals. It also encapsulates the diversity of approaches in Computer-mediated Communications (CMC) research in the past two decades. CMC, according to John December (1997), is 'a process of human communication via computers, involving people, situated in particular contexts, engaging in processes to shape media for a variety of purposes'. It is an interdisciplinary area of study considering questions related to psychology, communications, sociology and even philosophy. In the 1990s, studies of the social side of computers began to emerge such as investigating how the Internet influences personal identity and social structures. This raised awareness that the Internet is not simply used for utilitarian or information-based pursuits. By the mid-1990s, research began to show the Internet was being integrated into numerous social and even religious pursuits. The Internet increasingly functions as a social and spiritual place for many people, as information technology intersects with awakened postmodern spiritual desires and a search for meaning in an information age.

The purpose of this chapter is to highlight and explore social and spiritual facets of the Internet. This is done by investigating how this conception and perspective of study has emerged in CMC research in the past decade. First, the Internet is contextualised by considering specific aspects of its roots and history. Then several conceptions of the Internet are outlined, presenting the different facets of how the Internet has been conceived and utilised. Next, how the Internet can function as a social-spiritual space is outlined through describing 'The Internet as sacramental space'. This conception unpacks how and why the Internet is being employed in a variety of spiritual pursuits.

Contextualising the Internet

In order to understand how the Internet is conceived of as a new social-spiritual space, it is important to highlight the roots of this information technology. The beliefs that underlie the Internet's history have affected how and why this technology has been used for distinct purposes.

Through a historical analysis of the emergence of the Internet[1] two key themes emerge which characterised this technology: fear and promise. Beginning in the 1960s cold war's culture of suspicion, Internet technology and ARPANET were created in response to the fear of looming devastation produced by the advent of nuclear technology (Sardar 1996). Created to sustain communication in the midst of catastrophe, the Internet from its inception came out of an underlying current of alarm and mistrust. Yet, the Internet's development and expansion in the 1980s and 1990s also illustrate the belief in a positive view of progress, universal rights to access and promotion of freedom of information. The Internet was presented as a new land of opportunity and a 'wonderful pluralistic world' opening society up to new potential ways of governing, relating and being (Dyson et al. 1996: 28).

This tension between fear and promise within computer and Internet technology is also seen when exploring the idea of cyberspace and its roots in science fiction. Cyberspace is a metaphoric image of an imaginary world existing beyond the computer screen.[2] In science fiction, cyberspace illustrates a desire for humans and technology to merge. It is a virtual space offering the opportunity to create a new reality, where the virtual world presents escape from the real world. Yet, cyberspace also presents a dichotomy. Technology is portrayed as offering both hope for the future and a dark dystopia, as the technological world oppresses and exerts control over humanity. Many advocates and critics of the technology have used this dichotomy to support claims that the Internet is either utopia or dystopia (Wellman 1997b). The roots and rhetoric of the Internet highlight the possible extreme responses towards this technology. The Internet is either criticised as potentially destructive or lauded as potential saviour. It is presented as a tool or place that creates a distinctly helpful or harmful technological environment.

Yet the Internet is not a medium that can be branded as simply good or evil. When studying the Internet as a social phenomenon, increasing numbers of people engaging in social interaction on-line, we find both strengths and weakness manifest in the technology. Here the Internet blurs the boundaries of what is real and virtual, as technology which both unifies and alienates. Therefore, a different and more balanced approach is necessary to understanding the complexity of the Internet. Nardi and O'Day use the label of 'critical friend' as an alternative response for evaluating technology and investigating its outcomes (Nardi and O'Day 1999: 27). Emerging somewhere between technophobe and technophile perspectives, critical friends consider both positive and negative effects of the Internet. They focus on identifying how a given technology operates and suggest individuals embrace technology with caution. This is characterised by the Technorealist Manifesto <www.technorealism.org> which seeks 'neither to champion nor dismiss technology, but rather to understand it, and apply it in a manner more consistent with basic human values'.

The critical friend is similar to the position of 'prophetic resistance' promoted by Clifford Christians in *Responsible Technology* as a Christian-based response to the 'technicistic worldview'. Prophetic resistance advocates revealing weaknesses of other positions and resisting oversimplified prejudices, while not rejecting outright the technology itself. Therefore the prophet does not rail against the existence of the technology. Technology only becomes a problem when it becomes sacralised or when it seduces our language and being. To bring 'prophetic witness into the existing technological order' Christians claims it must first be raised in the Christian community and then brought to the larger human community. As the prophetic witness addresses the human tendency to allow technology to serve the interest of power, 'our technological activity can be freed at last and inspired to follow the biblical path of loving God above all and our neighbour as ourselves' (Christians et al. 1986: 221). Identifying this perspective is important as a religious or spiritual response to technology extends this evaluation to consider how Internet technology affects and shapes the soul. The history of and reaction towards the Internet are laden with distinct beliefs about the technology of Internet choices. These underlying assumptions inform how people approach the Internet and to what ends they use it.

Conceptions of the Internet

There are many different approaches to the Internet. Along with Markham, one of the first attempts to describe how individuals operate on-line was presented by Phil Agre in his article 'The Internet and Public Discourse' (Agre 1998). In it he presents several conceptions of the Internet and ways they influence life on-line. He describes the Internet as a communications medium, a computer system, a discourse and a set of standards. While Agre's models are helpful, and will be noted in this section, essentially they do a better job of addressing legal and political concerns than looking at the Internet as a social phenomenon. Markham – who characterised the Internet as a tool, a place or a state of mind – sought to describe general user approaches to the Internet (Markham 1998). By combining the ideas of Markham and Agre with reflection based on a recently completed study of on-line communities, several other models or conceptions emerge that seek to highlight a particular use and study of the on-line context. Here the Internet will be identified as: information space, a common mental geography, an 'identity workshop', a social space and a sacramental space. These descriptions seek to capture people's perceived and actual use of the Internet. This spectrum shows the Internet can be seen as being utilitarian, conceptual, experimental, social or even spiritual by users. Discussing these particular conceptions also helps to introduce various trends in CMC research relevant to these discussions of the Internet.

The Internet as Information Space

The Internet as information space highlights information exchange occurring on-line. The Internet allows individuals to utilise a variety of software and technologies to interact with data. Here the Internet is often referred to as the realm of pure information and the World Wide Web is seen as its holding house. The Internet exists for the utilitarian purpose of transferring messages or data. Individuals use the Internet as a tool to locate their desired data.

One of the unique aspects of the Internet is that it allows each netizen simultaneously to be 'a publisher as well as a consumer of information' (Rheingold 1993: 97). With minimal resources, in comparison to public access television or pirate radio, individuals can publish their own website or start an email list on their preferred topic. Thus, people on-line often focus on generating and discovering information of personal interest. Internet technology is valued for its ability to retrieve and store data.

The CMC studies began by focusing on users' interactions on texts. These studies can be traced to the 1970s, when CMC focused primarily on the technological capabilities of computers by exploring how particular technical, economic and ergonomic characteristics of computers affected organisational efficiency and effectiveness (Kiesler, Siegel and McGuire 1984). In the early 1980s, while research grew into the context of computer interaction, it still had an informational focus on organisational communication on-line, and how individuals exchanged information and developed informational networks. Studying the net as an information space is still prevalent within discussion of copyright, navigation of information spaces and cyber-law.

According to Spears and Lea, 'CMC reflects a shift of the attentional focus to the content and context of the message' (1992: 40). The attention is on the message over the producer, the textual creation instead of the text creator. These texts focus individuals on representations of reality. Importance is placed on conceptions of what they are interacting with on-line, over what is behind the words. Numes argues in the virtual world of the Internet, 'our words are our bodies' (Numes 1995: 326), where people become known by their words or their taglines. The texts presented become the defining factor of who one is in cyberspace and what one does. Through text, readers construct mental images of the other. Information space dictates that individuals become known as data producers. Texts produced are seen as representing the totality of the particular producer, limiting interpersonal engagement with them at a deeper level. Information becomes abstracted from its author or creator; the focus becomes gathering data.

This conception highlights a negative tendency towards de-personalising those who generate the text. Roszak in *The Cult of Information* argues that this occurs as those in the information society mistake access to information for knowledge. He states that society is now based on an 'information economy'; those who control information are the new power brokers (Roszak 1986: 91). This is often central to debates on the 'Digital Divide' where discussion of the Internet is framed in terms of the 'information rich' versus the 'information poor'. The focus is utilitarian, promoting the most access to the most information for the most people.

The Internet as Common Mental Geography

The Internet as common mental geography[3] views the Internet as providing more than a tool for communication, but a structure for individuals to construct a common world-view. Computers are meant to supply standardised methods of processing data. These processes are meant to link computer operators to a common platform of language and interactions.

This platform provides a common mental geography, a way to describe how the real world functions using computer-ese and technological imagery; the machine is used to understand humanity. This can be associated with 'technobabble', where the 'human condition is frequently explained in terms of technological metaphors' (Barry 1993: xiii). Technobabble involves using mechanistic language to describe human processes. This has connotations outside the realms of computing as individuals use anthropomorphic ideas, attributing human characteristics to material objects, to describe computers and their processes.

By merging technobabble with cyber-philosophy the Internet becomes a distinct way of viewing reality, the physical world interpreted through the screen. Research such as the work of Sherry Turkle on hacker culture at MIT (Turkle 1985) and philosophical writings in the early 1990s, such as Michael Benedikt in *Cyberspace: First Steps* (1992), characterised investigations of this sort. This ran alongside studies of CMC in the areas of: group norms and social identity, social identity within communities of users (Lea 1992). Developments in digital art and cyber-literature also utilise the Internet as a new space for creativity. Cyberspace creates a digital canvas for new artistic and technological expressions, from interactive poetry to 3-D game imaging. Merging technology and human creativity has also spawned dialogue on cyborg philosophy and posthuman discourses, which encourage a new philosophical framework, and language has been used to describe and frame the innovations of cyberspace (Haraway 1991).

This conception brings together elements of science fiction fantasy with computer networking images. Cyberspace can be seen as an environment shaped as much by story and myth as it is by networked computers. Here cyberspace can be seen as a real place, the place where people see themselves while 'surfing the net'. Yet cyberspace is a simulated territory; it is a metaphor and media image that does not truly represent the actual computer network architecture of computer connections and telephone lines. However, some users chose to let fantasy inform their reality. This extreme can be seen in the lives of computer hackers. Turkle describes hackers as individuals obsessed with their computers whose chief aim is to engage the world through computers and technology. As one hacker, whom Turkle quotes, commented, 'I have assimilated the process to the point that the computer is like an extension of my mind ... Once I know in my mind exactly what I want to do, I can express it on a computer without much further effort' (Turkle 1985: 218).

A common mental geography can evoke a mystical image of the Internet facilitating a global consciousness. In writing about the projected potential of Virtual Reality (VR) to share its created reality with the physical world De Kerckhove states this as 'VR technology would allow many minds to collectively process a kind of "group consciousness"' (De Kerckhove 1995: 47). Seeing the Internet as common mental geography supplies those who create computer technology, as well as users, with a common system of communication and a new meta-narrative to be used to make sense of the world. If kept in balance, it can provide cohesion and a sense of social support for like-minded netizens. Internet users see the on-line environment as a place to build utopia or pursue a 'better' reality.

The Internet as
Identity Workshop

The Internet as 'identity workshop'[4] enables people to see the on-line context as a place to learn and test social skills. (Parks and Floyd 1996: 83). The Internet is characterised as a space of freedom and experimentation. Individuals are able to 're-present' themselves by either highlighting certain attributes or hiding others, or by creating new persona for themselves. The focus here is on personalised use, as the Internet 'has provided a forum in which users can re-create themselves' (Block 1996: 5). Changing one's identity on-line can be done easily as electronic communication is essentially blind. The Internet erases social cues so status, power and prestige are not communicated contextually or dynamically (Kiesler, Siegel and McGuire 1984: 125). What is seen are words on a screen with which individuals can construct both themselves and the 'bodies' or presence of others with whom they are communicating.

One discussion area in CMC research attempts to distinguish real from the virtual identity on-line by exploring the question of 'embodiment', what the body is in cyberspace. How Internet users identify their body on-line can influence how they see themselves and communicate with other net users. This perspective was the focus of much CMC research in the mid-1990s as focus turned to various facets of on-line communities, ranging from describing patterns of life found on MUDs or MOOs such as described by Bruckman and Resnick (1995) and Mnookin (1996), to the development of community on Usenet and IRC systems done by individuals such as Reid (1995). Many researchers were drawn to investigate these groups because they included a unique mixing of aspects of the 'real' social world with a computer-created 'virtual' world. This intersection creates what some have referred to as an 'identity workshop' (Parks and Floyd 1996: 83), an opportunity for individuals to create new personas and relationships utilising options often unavailable to them in their embodied social context.

In cyberspace, people are seen as 'disembodied', detached or freed from the constraints of the physical. On-line bodies are constructed through words. People present their bodies by the words they select. The Internet gives individuals the ability to recreate their personal identities. Some see the Internet as a mecca of 'multi-personality possibilities' where the Internet unties the mind from the body offering new ways of expression and opportunities for equality. This not only allows for experimentation, such as gender swapping, but also creates a space in which prejudices can be eliminated (Stone 1995). People are judged on the basis of their text response, not their status or appearance.

For example, on email lists individuals receive all postings made by other members of that group. They select a message and open it, coming face-to-screen with a piece of text, most likely generated by an individual they have never met. Typically they have no access to a visual image of the individual. Social and non-verbal cues for the most part are absent. In email, individuals are portrayed as standardised computer block letters, the type-written word; it is up to the reader to construct the body of the persona they are communicating with. Also, individuals who are primarily written rather than oral communicators often thrive in interactions on-line, finding it a medium conducive to their communication style (Myers 1987).

While options for anonymity and the absence of social cues on-line allow individuals a sense of freedom, they also create some unpleasant by-products. The dissolution of boundaries can result in de-individualisation where there is a 'loss of identity and weakening of social norms and constraints associated with submergence in a group or a crowd' (Spears and Lea 1992: 38). Thus, the on-line anonymity, which promotes equal participation within a group, can also lead to reduced self-regulation and promote uninhibited behaviour.

Disembodiment creating freedom on-line can also lead individuals to confusion, dishonesty and deception. This is expressed by Dibble's classic account of 'A Rape in Cyberspace' where a character in a Multi-User Dungeon (MUD) hacked into another character's person to 'virtually' assault her. The incident received significant media attention and showed how involvement in a fantasy-based on-line environment can have real world psychological and sociological effects on participants (Dibble 1996). Positively, it centres on freedom and potential, wherein people are not bound by social class or physical appearance. Negatively, it creates a very egocentric view of the Internet, where individual choice dominates and undesirable social behaviour can surface.

The Internet as Social Network

The Internet as social network portrays the on-line context as a social space where making connections with people is the primary goal. This inter-personal focus highlights relationships formed on-line; individuals see their central reason for being on-line as to connect with others. The Internet is a place of unlimited connections, where through a few clicks of a mouse or punches of a keyboard people find themselves in communication with others, and not just information.

The 1990s saw the pioneering and establishment of social CMC research. This was particularly noted in the emergence of virtual or on-line community studies pioneered by the likes of Rheingold (1993) and Wellman (1997a). Questions of communication of social information, group meanings and identities, forms of relationship and social negotiation were explored. As Paccagnella states, 'Cyberspace constitutes a wonderful example of how people can build relationships and social norms that are absolutely real and meaningful even in the absence of physical, touchable matter' (Paccagnella 1997).

Referring to the Internet as a social sphere has become a significant trend in CMC research. Jones focuses much of his work around this idea and in 'The Internet as a Social Landscape' describes the Internet as a 'human constructed' sphere: 'Cyberspace is promoted as social space because it is made by people and thus as the 'new public space' it cojoins traditional mythic narratives of progress with the strong modern impulses towards self-fulfilment and personal development' (Jones 1997: 22).

Much has been written on the social nature of the Internet. Studies have found that people use email and other forms of CMC to socialise, maintain relationships, play games and receive emotional support (Parks and Floyd 1996: 83). While some see on-line relationships as shallow and impersonal illusions, others argue that the Internet liberates inter-personal relations and creates communities. As Parks and Floyd wrote, 'one vision is of relationships lost, while the other is of relationships liberated and found' (1996: 81).

The Internet as social network has a communal orientation. It involves not just creating individual social connections, but a social web. Research into the social nature of the Net often focuses on on-line communities which 'embody a new kind of social interaction that no one had predicted' (National Research Council 1994: 30).

On-line communities allow individuals to select their neighbours and seek out new friends with common interests. Borders are erased as the person in the next room or on the next continent is only an email away. Rushkoff states that the Internet has become a metaphor for a new model of human social interaction: 'It allows for communication without limitations of time or space, personality or body, religion or nationality ... a fractal approach to human consciousness' (1994: 57).

Yet the Internet as social space does have its problems. on-line, the veil of the screen separates individuals from each other. With freedom come complications as 'communicators must imagine their audience, for at a terminal it almost seems as though the computer itself is the audience' (Kiesler et al. 1984: 125). If individuals wish to move past this veiled interaction, they must reach beyond the screen. This is often a disappointing move (Katz and Aspden 1997).

The Internet as Sacramental Space

The Internet as sacramental space acknowledges technology's ability to alter individual and communal religious practice as it is brought on-line. Using the Internet as a sacramental space involves the adaptation of symbols, rituals and practices as technology is used in spiritual pursuits. While contemporary society often feels isolated and disconnected, the Internet has come to represent an other-worldly space allowing people to re-engage with issues of spirituality. Margaret Wertheim, in *The Pearly Gates of Cyberspace*, argues that cyberspace allows people once again to engage spiritual yearnings, silenced in a world where science has dominated religion:

> The 'spiritual' appeal of cyberspace lies precisely in this paradox: It is a repackaging of the old idea of Heaven, but in a secular, technologically sanctioned format. The perfect realm awaits us, we are told, not behind the pearly gates but the electronic gateways labelled .com and .net. and .edu. (Wertheim 1999: 21)

Locating themselves in the seemingly timeless, boundless realm of computers, a new breed of spiritual pilgrim has emerged. Some choose to seek out traditional forms of religious expression from the 20 million religious websites said to exist on-line. On their own terms and in the privacy of their own homes, they can visit cyber-cathedrals or temples. Others experiment with newer forms of religious expression: combinations of ancient beliefs altered and adapted for this technologically mediated environment (Brasher 2001).

As in the off-line world, there is no unified spiritual belief on-line. The Internet functions as a marketplace of religions. Every major ideology and religious system existing in the real world is likely to be represented on some website or discussion group. From Islam (Bunt 2000) and Christianity (Veith and Stamper 2000) to Zoroastrianism (Chama 1996), most traditional religions have some form of representation in cyberspace (Zaleski 1997). Also new religions unique to the Internet such as Technopaganism, neo-paganism adapted and celebrated in a technological context, have also been birthed on-line (Davis 1998). While different schools of spiritual thought can be found in the digital world, all have one thing in common – digital technology is seen to provide tools allowing the user to engage in spiritual activities on-line in a variety of ways.

Cyber-religion also allows spiritual seekers the opportunity to explore diverse religions with variable ease. Brenda Brasher surveys a spectrum of new religious expressions on-line from cyber-pilgrimages through virtual shrines to cyber-seders helping people reconnect with their Jewish faith. By invigorating concepts of sacred time, presence and spiritual experience cyber-religion is 'a crucial contemporary cultural outlet for our meaning heritage from the past' and can 'make a unique contribution to global fellowship' and inter-religious understanding (Brasher 2001: 6).

Exploring the characterisation of the Internet as sacramental space is central to this study. It highlights this new uses of the Internet and the fact that it can creates space for spiritual reflection. The idea of taking religious practice on-line challenges many people's conceptions of religion and religious ritual, as well as what religious community should look like. The Internet as sacramental space involves both social interactions between people of faith and spiritual engagement through technology. Therefore understanding the Internet as a social sphere that can encourage religious networking and spiritual engagement needs to be further unpacked.

The Internet as a Social-Spiritual Network

For many signing on to the Internet is a transformative act. In their eyes the web is more than just a global tapestry of personal computers. It is a vast cathedral of the mind, a place where ideas about God and religion can resonate,

> where faith can be shaped and defined by a collective spirit.
> (Chama 1996: 57)

While contemporary society often feels isolated and disconnected, the Internet has come to represent a place of
connection enabling the forging of relationships, as well as
an other-worldly space allowing people to re-engage with
spiritual pursuits.

How the Internet can be perceived as a new model of
human social interaction has been addressed. Internet
technology allows humans to transcend boundaries
of time, space and the body to form communicative
relationships with others. In the past decade many CMC
researchers have focused on studying this new social sphere.
Cyberspace or the Internet studied as primarily a social
space allows people to see on-line relationships in new
and innovative ways. The rise of social network analysis
research acknowledges that in modern society people are
not wrapped in traditionally densely knit, tightly bound
communities, but are floating in sparse, loosely bound,
frequently changing networks. Community ties are seen as
narrow, specialised relationships. Relations and emerging
patterns become the focus of study. This understanding
of community as social network has been readily applied
to the study of on-line social relationships. As Wellman
states,

> When a computer network connects people it is a social
> network. Just as a computer network is a set of machines
> connected by a set of cables, a social network is a set of
> people (or organisation or other social networks) connected
> by a set of socially meaningful relationships. (Wellman
> 1997a: 179)

Studying computer-mediated communication as a social
technology means recognising that these social networks
are not simply 'virtual' but are also embedded in the real

world. On-line and off-line community cannot be neatly separated from each other. People's engagement in face-to-face communities is often linked to their participation in on-line communities. Katz and Rice's Synoptia Project found being an Internet user involved in on-line social interaction was positively associated with being a member of a community or religious organisation (Katz and Rice 2002: 155). Pew's study of religious use of the Internet too affirmed that most active religious surfers are also off-line participants in their faith (Larsen 2001). While the technology may force the communities, especially religious ones, to restructure their forms of interaction they often represent consciously imported off-line styles of interaction or interest on-line (Campbell 2001).

While religion is one area that has readily been imported on-line, trying to summarise and categorise cyber-spirituality can be challenging. Michael Bauwens identifies three conceptions of spiritual engagement on-line. He describes these as the 'Electric Gaia' where technology is seen 'as a necessary adjunct to make improvements in consciousness possible', 'The God Project' in which technology becomes a 'crude substitute for spiritual powers' or enables a search for a literal 'Machine-God, Deus Ex Machina' and 'Sacramental Cyberspace' in which the Internet is seen as a place to further the aims of various religions or even to serve as a tool for 'transmission of spiritual energy' (Bauwens 1996). Christopher Helland also provides two helpful classifications of how people use the Internet for spiritual purposes: religion on-line and on-line religion (Helland 2000: 214–20). Religion on-line occurs when religion transports traditional forms of communication of a one-to-many fashion into the on-line environment, such as through establishing a religious organisational website. On-line religion refers to how religion adapts itself to create new forms of communication through many-to-many networked interaction, such as on-line prayer or worship services. Both Bauwens and Helland agree that on-line religion gives religious practitioners the ability to re-present their beliefs and practices on-line leading either to religious innovation or repackaging.

In the mid-1990s, a focused exploration of religious aspects of CMC began to emerge. Research that investigated the Internet as a spiritual space has taken many different approaches. These include looking at the general phenomenon of cyber-religion (Brasher 2001), religious ethics and VR (Houston 1998), how technology reconnects people with spiritual beliefs (Cobb 1998; and Wertheim 1999), adaptations of traditional religious practices on-line (Bunt 2000; and Zaleski 1997) and new religious expression (Davis 1998). A range of Christian critiques of the Internet has been produced from strong critiques (Brooke 1997) and enthusiastic advocacy (Dixon 1997; and Wilson 2000) to a critically friendly approach of addressing both the benefits and weaknesses of Internet technology (Schultze 2002). At the beginning of the twenty-first century, religious CMC research has begun to be considered as a serious field of inquiry. J. K. Hadden and D. E. Cowan's *Religion on the Internet: Research Prospects and Promise* (2000) was the first noteworthy academic attempt to survey and address different theoretical approaches to studying religion on-line. Focused investigations of issues such as identity, community and social consequences of religious use of the Internet are increasing and raising the profile of the religious use of the Internet for both practitioners and academic researchers (Campbell 2003). Other recent research such as Dawson and Cowan's *Religion Online* (2004) continues to probe the myriad religious rituals and expressions appearing on-line as well as the general phenomenon.

While information-gathering is a prime motivator for many using the net, this does not devalue the Internet's potential for facilitating other forms of interaction. Exploring the Internet as sacramental space demonstrates how this technology offers both social and spiritual dimensions. In this respect, the Internet can be a place where social relations are cultivated, as well as spiritual encounters pursued or enhanced. Social network analysis offers a viable way of understanding relationships formed through on-line interaction. This approach presents an image of an underlying network of loosely bounded relationships which encourages fluid interactions. This dynamic structure translates well into a spiritual context, where encounters with meaning and transcendence are also seen as malleable and experiential. Social network analysis combined with a sacramental view of the Internet opens up new possibilities as the Internet is recognised as a social-spiritual network.

The Internet can be seen as both a humanly constructed, social space and a spiritual space capable of facilitating transcendent engagement. As a public sphere, the Internet is a gathering place for people and their stories. In the process of seeking connections with like minds, people can be drawn into communities of faith, spaces of religious interaction and even spiritual encounters on-line. Investigating the Internet as sacramental space argues that cyberspace can aid humanity's spiritual progression, described as an 'important way station' on humanity's journey towards a greater spiritual evolution (Cobb 1998: 97). While more study needs to be given to the implications and effects of on-line spirituality and socialisation within a networked society, this chapter has sought to outline current discussions concerning social and spiritual dimensions of the Internet. It also offers a framework for categorising and evaluating other forms of Internet use and engagement.

Notes

1. An ideological and historical analysis of the Internet is best summarised by Roy Rosenzweig, 'Wizards, Bureaucrats, Warriors and Hackers: Writing the History of the Internet', *American Historical Review*, 103(5) (December 1998), pp. 1530–52.
2. For an introduction to the concept of cyberspace, see William Gibson, *Neuromancer* (New York: Ace Book, 1984). For discussion of science fiction and virtual reality and their intersection with the Internet, see Rushkoff (1994).
3. Metaphoric image taken from Benedikt (1992), p. 2.
4. Terminology attributed to Amy Bruckman's study 'Identity Workshop: Emergent social and psychological phenomena in text-based virtual reality' found at: http://media.mit.edu/pub/MediaMOO/Chapters/identity-workshop/ (accessed June 1998).

References

Agre, P. (1998), 'The Internet and Public Discourse', at *First Monday* (2 March 1998), accessed 25 June 1998, http://www.firstmonday.dk/issues/issue3_3/agre.

Barry, J. (1993), *Technobabble* (Cambridge, MA: MIT Press).

Bauwens, M. (1996), 'Spirituality and Technology: Exploring the Relationship', at *First Monday* (4 November), accessed 6 September 1998, http://www.firstmonday.dk/issues/issue5/bauwens/index.html.

Benedikt, M. (1992), *Cyberspace: First Steps* (Cambridge, MA: MIT Press).

Block, J. (1996), 'The Internet Relationship', *Overland*, 143: 4–10.

Brasher, B. (2001), *Give Me That Online Religion* (San Francisco: Jossey-Bass).

Brooke, T. (1997), *Virtual Gods* (Eugene, OR: Harvest House).

Bruckman, A. and M. Resnick (1995), 'The MediaMOO Project: Constructionism and Professional Community', *Convergence*, 1 (1) (Spring), accessed 20 February 1999, http://www.cc.gatech.edu/fac/Amy.Bruckman/papers/index.html#convergence.

Bunt, G. (2000), *Virtually Islamic: Computer-Mediated Communication and Cyber Islamic Environments* (Lampeter, Wales: University of Wales Press).

Campbell, H. (2001), 'An Investigation of the Nature of Church through an Analysis of Christian Email-Based Online Communities', unpublished PhD thesis (University of Edinburgh).

Campbell, H. (2003), 'A Review of Religious Computer-Mediated Communication Research', in S. Marriage and J. Mitchell (eds), *Mediating Religion: Conversations in Media, Culture and Religion* (Edinburgh: T&T Clark/Continuum), pp. 213–28.

Chama, J. C. (1996), 'Finding God on the Web', *TIME* (16 December), pp. 57–61.

Christians, C. et al. (1986), *Responsible Technology: A Christian Perspective* (Grand Rapids, MI: Eerdmans).

Cobb, J. (1998), *Cybergrace: The Search for God in the Digital World* (New York: Crown Publishers).

Davis, E. (1998), *Techgnosis* (New York: Random House).

Dawson, L. and D. E. Cowan (eds) (2004), *Religion Online: Finding Faith on the Internet* (New York: Routledge).

December, J. (1997), 'Notes on Defining of Computer-Mediated Communication', *Computer-Mediated Communication Magazine*, 4 (January), accessed 4 November 1997.

De Kerckhove, D. (1995), *The Skin of Culture* (Toronto: Somerville House Publishing).

Dibble, J. (1996), 'A Rape in Cyberspace; or How an Evil Clown, a Haitian Trickster Spirit, Two Wizards and a Cast of Dozens Turned a Database into a Society', in Peter Ludlow (ed.), *High Noon on the Electronic Frontier: Conceptual Issues in Cyberspace* (Cambridge, MA: MIT Press), pp. 375–95.

Dixon, P. (1997), *Cyberchurch, Christianity and the Internet* (Eastbourne: Kingsway Publications).

Dyson, E. et al. (1996), 'Cyberspace and the American Dream: A Magna Carta for the Knowledge Age', in *The Information Society* 12.3, 295–308.

Hadden, J. K. and. D. E. Cowan (eds) (2000), *Religion on the Internet: Research Prospects and Promises* (London: JAI Press).

Haraway, D. J. (1991), *Simians, Cyborgs and Women: The Reinvention of Nature* (New York: Routledge).

Helland, C. (2000), 'Online-Religion/Religion-Online and Virtual Communities', in J. K. Hadden and D. E. Cowan (eds), *Religion on the Internet: Research Projects and Promises* (New York: JAI Press), pp. 205–23.

Houston, G. (1998), *Virtual Morality* (Leicester: Apollos).

Jones, S. (1997), 'The Internet and Its Social Landscape', in Steven Jones (ed.), *Virtual Culture* (Thousand Oaks, CA: Sage), pp. 7–32.

Katz, J. and P. Aspden (1997), 'A Nation of Strangers?', *Communications of the ACM*, 40(12) (December), pp. 81–6.

Katz, J. and R. Rice (2002), *Social Consequence of Internet Use: Access, Involvement and Interaction* (Cambridge, MI: MIT Press).

Kiesler, S., J. Siegel and T. McGuire (1984), 'Social Psychological Aspects of Computer-mediated Communication', *American Psychologist*, 39(10) (October), pp. 1123–34.

Larsen, E. (2001), 'CyberFaith: How Americans Pursue Religion Online', *Pew Internet and American Life Project* (23 December 2001), URL: http://www.pewinternet.org/reports/toc.asp?Report=53

Lea, M. (1992), *Contexts of Computer-Mediated Communication* (London: Wheatsheaf/Harvester).

Markham, A. (1998), *Life Online* (Walnut Creek, CA: AltaMira Press).

Mnookin, J. (1996), 'Virtual(ly) Law: The Emergence of Law in LamdaMOO', *Journal of Computer Mediated Communication*, 2(1, 2) (June), accessed 14 June 1998, http://www.ascusc.org/jcmc/vol2/issue1/lamda.html

Myers, D. (1987), 'Anonymity Is Part of the Magic: Individuals Manipulation of Computer Mediated Communication Contexts', *Qualitative Sociology*, 10, pp. 251–66.

Nardi, B. and V. O'Day (1999), *Information Ecologies: Using Technology with Heart* (Cambridge, MA: MIT Press).

National Research Council (NRC), Computer Science and Telecommunications Board (1994), *Realising the Information Future: The Internet and Beyond* (Washington DC: National Academy Press).

Numes, M. (1995), 'Jean Baudrillard in Cyberspace: Internet, Virtuality and Postmodernity', *Style*, 29(2), pp. 314–28.

Paccagnella, V. (1997), 'Getting the Seat of Your Pants Dirty: Strategies for Ethnographic Research on Virtual Communities', *Journal of Computer Mediated Communication*, 3(1) (June), accessed 10 February 1999, http://www.ascusc.org/jcmc/vol3/issue1/paccagnella.html.

Parks, M. and K. Floyd (1996), 'Making Friends in Cyberspace', *Journal of Communication*, 46(1) (Winter), pp. 80–97.

Reid, E. (1995), 'Virtual Worlds: Culture and Imagination', in Steve Jones (ed.), *CyberSociety* (Thousand Oaks, CA: Sage Publications), pp. 164–83.

Rheingold, H. (1993), *The Virtual Community* (New York: HarperPerennial, 1993).

Roszak, T. (1986), *The Cult of Information* (Los Angeles, CA: University of California Press).

Rushkoff, D. (1994), *Cyberia* (New York: HarperCollins-Flamingo).

Sardar, Z. (1996), 'alt.civilizations.faq--Cyberspace as the Darker Side of the West', in Ziauddin Sardar and Jerome Ravetz (eds), *Cyberfutures* (London: Pluto Press), pp. 24–36.

Schultze, Q. (2002), *Habits of the High Tech Heart* (Grand Rapids, MI: Baker Academic).

Spears, R. and M. Lea (1992), 'Social Influence and the Influence of the 'Social' in Computer-mediated Communication', in Martin Lea (ed.), *Contexts of Computer-Mediated Communication* (London: Wheatsheaf/Harvester), pp. 30–65.

Stone, A. (1995), 'Sex and Death among the Disembodied: VR, Cyberspace and the Nature of Academic Discourse', in Susan Leigh Star (ed.), *Culture of the Internet* (Oxford: Blackwell Publishers and the Sociological Review), pp. 242–55.

Turkle, S. (1985), *The Second Self: Computers and the Human Spirit* (London: Granada Publishing).

Veith, G. E. and C. L. Stamper (2000), *Christian in a .com World* (Wheaton, IL: Crossway Books).

Wellman, B. (1997a), 'An Electronic Group Is Virtually a Social Network', in Sara Kiesler (ed.), *Culture of the Internet* (Mahwah, NJ: Lawrence Erlbaum).

Wellman, B. (1997b), 'The Road to Utopia and Dystopia on the Information Highway', *Contemporary Sociology*, 26 (July), pp. 448–51.

Wertheim, M. (1999), *The Pearly Gates of Cyberspace* (London: Virago).

Wilson, W. (2000), *The Internet Church* (Nashville, TN: Word Publishing).

Zaleski, J. (1997), *The Soul of Cyberspace: How Technology Is Changing Our Spiritual Lives* (San Francisco: HarperSanFrancisco).

Changing Voices:
Email, the Internet and
Theological Engagement

Marjory A. MacLean

In the conference 'Netting Citizens', the Centre for Theology and Public Issues lived up to the Church of Scotland's noble tradition of reflecting on issues that belong beyond the peculiar scope of the Church's own life. In this chapter, however, the self-indulgent question is raised how the life of the Church has been affected by the advent of the new technologies, and whether issues are raised that are particularly theological or ecclesiological.

As an ancient institution with a slight tendency to conservatism, the Church has probably come late to these questions asked of itself, and late to the benefits that may be available for its work and mission. Heidi Campbell's recent doctoral thesis[1] explores the phenomenon of ecclesial communities created on the internet; and there are probably hundreds of thesis topics waiting to be identified even in the more conventional use of email and the internet by churches locally and centrally.

This short chapter takes some tiny first steps in identifying some of the theological issues that present themselves on the smallest reflection on current practice and usage of the technologies available.

Email: Quizzing the Specialists and Querying the Answers – a Question of Church Polity

Every day there arrive at the Church of Scotland's administrative offices dozens of emailed questions. Many of them come from ministers and office-bearers who direct their queries to the right department because of prior knowledge or an existing working relationship. Others come from new correspondents who write out of curiosity, personal need or discontent: these are directed to the writer's best guess of the appropriate department, or come with a request for IT/webmaster staff to forward the message to the relevant official. This often produces food for theological thought: it has become obvious in the internet age, for example, that the Church does not have a single department dedicated to issues relating to the topic 'God', and for this much ribbing is received. (Most departments are relieved that this is not the monopoly topic of any one of them.)

Through the facility of the office server, emails find their way to the appropriate person within minutes or hours; and sometimes two or more departments will cooperate through an email conversation to produce an answer. This has produced a phenomenon by which anyone can easily reach and interrogate the most informed experts in each area of the Church's national responsibilities, and that is a quality and immediacy of access to specialist help and advice that far exceeds the possibilities of postal or telephone communications. The corollary of this access is that the conversation develops sometimes beyond the control of the staff member, with pressure – from those who do not like the original response – to justify or explain the policy or law behind the advice. So a new form of communication has directly facilitated the questioning of policy, law, practice and the very polity of the Church itself.[2]

The layered structure of the Church breaks down here in healthy ways, as the central administration keen to be seen as serving and not controlling the Church suddenly finds itself a point of first contact and not just of last resort. By this unplanned democratisation of dialogue, the Church is changed by its own communication system: ecclesiology is driven by information technology.

The Loss of Local Conversation – a Question about Theological Diversity

The ministry of the Church of Scotland, however, is still based in theory upon a territorial ministry exercised through a parish system in all but the most experimental of places. Traditionally the first point of contact for any individual needing the ministrations of the Church was the parish minister or Kirk Session, and the answer received from those sources carried an authority that was normally treated as if it was final.

The preceding section of this chapter describes an innovation that loses that traditional, local starting point. The individual member or enquirer short-circuits the normal, local channels and approaches the institutional Church without the local minister knowing what is happening. It is difficult, therefore, for the officials at the Church offices to maintain the *locus* and involvement of the parish minister, especially when the queries that come obviously imply criticism of a local decision (e.g., not to baptise a child or conduct a marriage ceremony). Often it is appropriate to refer the enquirer back to the local minister or Presbytery Clerk; but if the answer is to be provided centrally, it is obligatory to respect the possibility that the minister might take a different view, or exercise discretion in a different direction, or start with a different theological premise. The answers have to be the one-size-fits-all answers of a diverse, broad Church. The territorial ministry as the shop-front of the Church of Scotland is therefore compromised by technological developments, though we have no option but to keep up with them.

Email in the Institutional Church – a Question in Ecclesiology

A few years ago the General Assembly decided to connect all Presbytery Clerks together, and to the Church offices, by email; this was intended to give the Church better cohesion between the central administration and its regional authorities. In addition to the obvious benefits of quick and cheap contact – and for material of bulk these advantages are not to be sneezed at – it has been possible to share with clerks useful resources in the most flexible form for their use, keep even the most fluid of written resources up-to-date (especially the law of the Church and the civil law affecting our practices) and make quick consultations where the view of the wider Church administration is useful.

One side-effect of the facility was not anticipated by the initiating Board: the clerks have realised it is possible at no cost to copy each other in on correspondence with the centre, and there has developed the habit among some of copying (or for all we know blind-copying) all clerks in on messages, most especially – for some reason – if the message is one of criticism or complaint. Unkindly likened to the wildfire effect of one child in an infant class asking to go to the toilet, discontent expressed by one clerk can spawn a multiplicity of complaints that would never have come under any older system.

Various psychological points are demonstrated by paying attention to this phenomenon, among which is the truth, very important for any institutional officer to grasp, that those who are content have no motivation to take the trouble to express themselves, and so the relative quantities of positive and negative feedback should not be taken as indicators of the level of contentment within the whole body. Put more positively, the clerks have developed in these last couple of years a more strongly collegial sense of themselves as a group, and found the means of asserting their needs and expectations of those who try to equip them.

Does email and the internet enable some parts of the Body of Christ to relate who have not related before? Is that always positive? Does it engender a sense of mutual dependence, or mutual benefit? In a corporeal model of ecclesiological thought, do we find ourselves with newly-discovered nerve-systems we did not consider before?

Email: the New Grammar of Debate –
a Question of Theological Engagement

Email conversations do not just facilitate unexpected and unprecedented conversation-partners; they also constitute a wholly new kind of conversation, and one with theological and missiological implications.

While planning the conference that generated this book, the organisers were struck by a suggestion from the United States that the shift from conventional conversation to email dialogue had caused the loss for most people of 'the grammar of debate'; that computer-based forums and engagement had separated people from churches as nurturing grounds for the debating of issues in formalised settings. Email has its protocols, but they are not the same as the Standing Orders of the courts of the Church or the conventions of academic debate, and perhaps the increase of the new will spell the doom of the old. While that may be true it is not necessarily disastrous, because the new dynamics of conversation enabled by email have strengths of their own and possible applications in theological discourse.

It is the pace of an email conversation that is its great merit over any other kind of dialogue. In a postal exchange the elements of the conversation are too far apart for the protagonists to feel they are truly taking part in a single dialogue event, and so the contributions to the debate tend to be almost self-standing statements. In an oral exchange the elements of the conversation are immediately close together and so the quality of the contributions depends entirely on the speed of thought of the conversation-partners, with little that is polished or refined flowing in either direction in the heat of the discussion.

In an email dialogue, however, there are several factors in favour of a high-quality flowing conversation. First and foremost, the speed of the exchanges is entirely under the parties' control, which means that each contribution can be thought out properly in advance and, if necessary, supported by research. The conversation becomes measured, and a degree of consideration can be given to each response, far beyond an initial, instinctive reaction. Responding is not the same thing as reacting, as most people find out the hard way. Second, the text of the whole conversation is often available on-screen, depending on the set-up of the software, and it can even be possible to respond to a previous message with indented sentences interspersed through your interlocutor's original. This gives an assurance that the subject is being engaged with on the terms in which it was intended, and the response is direct and relevant. Third, it often happens that new conversation-partners are drawn in for conference or reference by extending the recipient-list, and new expertise or a different point of view can quickly and easily be introduced and brought up-to-speed. Though all these techniques are possible in more traditional forms of communication, they are more easily available, and so more routinely used, in the medium of email. Finally, the hybrid quality of email correspondence, neither conventional written exchange nor immediate oral dialogue, gives it a characteristic feel, being informal in tone whilst keeping the possibility of significance of content.

The literature of media studies must be full of amplifications of these comments, but it is the particular implications for Church life and community that matter here. The substantial content of the Church's mandate to communicate is the gospel and its implications, which in practice means the Church has things to say that are profound, personal, thought-provoking, persuasive, challenging, prophetic, deeply comforting and so on endlessly. The appearance of a form of communicative art that promotes a pause for thought before each utterance, consultation mid-conversation, point-by-point engagement with another's view and a relaxed but articulate expression of priorities, is a resource and instrument for the work of the Church that may contribute more than it destroys.

At a practical level too, the benefit of all this is that an initial query, perhaps containing a hint of defensiveness or criticism, can often be dealt with by a couple of emails in each direction over the course of a single day. Misunderstandings are often caught and corrected before there is a chance for a sense of grievance to build up to problem-proportions; or an office-bearer can be fully equipped for a tricky situation and affirmed by the result of a careful but expedited consultation with a specialist.

Theological Spam – a Question for Missiology

The phenomenon of spam is expanding at great speed, and most email users have to weed out their inboxes, or get their server or a piece of software to do so for them, before reaching the genuine messages waiting for them Why is evangelical spam so much more depressing than any other? Is it because of the vague feeling of uneasy guilt you get when deleting unread something you're supposed to agree with? Is it irritation that the writers really think they can convey so much in so little compass? Is it irritation that some writers seem to convey so little in so great compass?!

There is probably something missiologically important to be pursued and researched here: if one's understanding of mission is linked to service and personal relationship, evangelical email spam will appear to be even less personal and intimate than TV evangelism, and so objectionable on that count. If one's view is rather that the gospel message is self-evident and effective even beyond any particular community of faith, spam will appear to be a legitimate tool that can only do more good than harm. But if its capacity to irritate means that it might do more harm than good (and all explicit evangelism begs this question, since the good it does in attracting people is measurable while the harm it does in putting people off religion is normally invisible and unmeasured), the Church may have to decide whether its strategy for mission properly includes email outreach.

The Church of Scotland Website – a Question in Hermeneutics

The World Wide Web serves the Church of Scotland in two ways: it provides us with a platform to give information about the work and service of the Church of Scotland, and it provides an enormous quarry from which we can mine resources for our work, in all sorts of disciplines including the homiletic, liturgical, educational and academic. The former of these functions is primarily served by our central website, into which the Church has put major financial sources and serious editorial control.

The use of the site is only as impressive as the understanding of its users, both contributors and casual readers alike. Its management constantly complains that the departments of the Church tend to present their pages as if the site were an 'intranet' (i.e., a device for the exchange of information within a limited community) with the effect that the content can be rather esoteric and the language impenetrable from the outside: it is interesting that the supervision of the web editor lies in the Media Relations Unit, demonstrating presumably that the task is a journalistic one of making text interesting and readable to real outsiders. However, those genuine outsiders do not laboriously work their way through the site layer by layer, picking up the helpful definitions and general information available: they use search-engines to focus tightly on a small item, and unwittingly fail to understand it because they had not first read the bit about our not having priests, or not having bishops, or being able to marry divorcees, or whatever.

This is another reason why it is regrettable, perhaps, that the gatekeeper to information that once was the parish minister, is now circumvented – through no-one's mischievous intent – in the flow of information. The principle, hinted at above, that the engagement of Church and potential Church member must be personal and direct makes the internet a tool of mixed blessing, very well suited to selling redundant properties or publishing attractive photographs of Church leaders perhaps, but a risky strategy for communicating the things that are most important and least tangible. The concept of a hermeneutics of the Net sounds artificial in some ways, but the challenge of this paper is perhaps to take it into consideration as branch of mission studies, and certainly of studies in Church polity.

Notes

1. H. Campbell, 'An Investigation of the Nature of Church Thought Through an Analysis of Christian E-mail-based Online Communities, 2001 (University of Edinburgh: New College, unpublished).

2. A common misapprehension, for example, is the exact nature of the democratic polity of the Church. A disappointed enquirer may often express the belief that the congregation as a whole should have made a particular decision, quite unaware of the difference between Presbyterian government in the hands of spiritual leaders and the routine use of plebiscite through congregational meetings in other kinds of polity. When the original query has short-circuited local consultation, where the methods of decision-making are visible and can be explained, there is more scope for unhappiness and objection when the answer from 'Edinburgh' is not the one hoped for.

The Kirk and the Internet

Brian McGlynn

I recently attended a truly twenty-first-century party. Every song we danced to was downloaded on the spot from the Internet and played directly on a PC. Instead of a DJ we had a group of teenagers tapping into a virtual jukebox with a play list as big as our collective musical memory. The soundtrack of all our lives is now available online.

There is a disconcerting tension in this: availability on this scale unveils the mystery while at the same time creating a sense of new and unfathomable possibilities. Here be a new culture. This unveiling perhaps offers part of the explanation of why the Church of Scotland (in common with almost all western European churches) has seemed to lose so much ground over recent decades. Knowledge is power and the growing immensity of available knowledge has demystified much of our traditional culture including our religious heritage. Knowing so much, people seem to be increasingly unwilling to accept received wisdom without question. Deference culture is being dismantled. And yet the old, haunting questions remain and I believe deeply that an unparalleled moment of possibility for a new sharing of the old, old story could open up before the Church. As with every opportunity of this kind throughout the Church's history, the only way to forge the key is the willingness to take the risk of love and humility – to embody the message of peace.

In many ways the development of the Kirk's website is a tiny microcosm of the opportunities and deep challenges that the Church faces at the beginning of the twenty-first century. As the Church strives to find new ways to embody and communicate faith in the midst of ancient structures and forms, we are largely used to the often-painful process of pouring new wine into old wineskins. But this is different. This is more a matter of pouring old wine into new wineskins.

In some ways this makes things easier. Unlike almost every other area of church life there is no need to invent new approaches – they have already come into being with what seems like stunning rapidity. Or perhaps it only seems that way to someone of my generation or older. I left secondary school and had never so much as seen a computer in the flesh far less used one. All my essays at university were hand written. It is difficult for my teenage children to relate to this idea. For as long as they can remember there has been a computer at school and at home and they made the transition to the virtual world with enviable ease. It may have been a giant step for mankind but it has been just one small step for them and millions like them.

Underlying the emergence of these new forms of communication there seems to me to be a large and important cultural fault line. The casual techno-grace with which those who grew up with the technology have slipped into the virtual world is at sharp odds with the techno-fear still displayed by many. Although it would not be true or fair to suggest that age is the only factor at work here given the impact of silver surfers, the grey pound and techno-poverty. However, the Internet, instant messaging, email, and – certainly in the UK – texting are established tropes of youth culture, however you care to define youth.

There have been drivers ensuring that people like me have largely kept up with this revolution. The most obvious of these is work. Over the past twenty years in Scotland there has been a well-publicised shift away from traditional heavy industries to service-based industries, meaning that the new technology is an entirely commonplace feature of the workplace for most of us. There has been an additional incentive for parents and others caring for young people to get into cyberspace. Email and text are the premier ways of keeping in touch with young people who, in many cases, have the confidence and the means to explore the world with an extraordinary degree of enterprise and élan. This is equally true whether it is the world on the doorstep or further abroad.

Connectedness is perhaps the most distinctive feature of early twenty-first-century society. Actual and virtual elements of relationships are fashioned into one seamless garment. Online friends are seen as just 'friends'; day-to-day friendships in the so-called real world now have a large and important virtual dimension. People do not seem to me to have any difficulty with the realness of the online part of this exchange. Even as some people continue to mourn the lost arts of conversation and letter writing others are immersed in the deeply social business of practising them in the new forms of email, instant messaging and text.

As we all know, the permeability that this creates comes with a price in terms of new levels of risk. Some of us – too few still – have more powerful communication tools in our hands than would have been thought possible a couple of generations back. There is little doubt that this is creating new social, cultural and economic patterns and perhaps equally little doubt that we are just at the beginning of this process. Along with everyone else, we are travelling in the unexplored edge of cyberspace, not yet seeing where all of this is leading us. But while much of the impact to date has been positive and welcome, there has been a darker side too. Children and younger adolescents are perhaps seen as being exposed to the darkest threat in the form of 'grooming' via the Internet.

This is where I think it gets thorny for the Church. Risk is entwined around the vine of faith; it is inseparable from it. I know of no other group of people down through the centuries who have taken greater risks than the Christian community – risks personal, social, intellectual, physical and moral; a truly humbling litany of risks in the search for truth and integrity of action. Across the world today this is still the case, and right here in Scotland one can see it at first hand. Yet at institutional level the Church often seems to be risk averse. But what is the Net if it no longer offers the rather risky, slightly unhinged thrill of surfing the big waves?

There is, of course, the understandable and proper desire to promote the Church's reputation as an organisation that seeks to protect all those who come into its orbit. The Church is not alone in this; witness the closure of web-based chat rooms by the Internet giant, Microsoft, for example. Initially, the Internet promised us its own brand of holy disorder and radical democratisation – a truly global power to the people. In reality, it has been a mixed bag not unlike television. There is no doubt that television has educated us and opened our minds to a bigger world but it has also led us into the wilderness of banal consumerism, celebrity culture, 'reality' shows and worse. We know it has changed us and yet it is curiously difficult to define just how or how much. As ever, the wheat and the tares are sown in the same field. Perhaps it is little wonder that those in positions of responsibility sometimes reach for the remote.

The struggle to find a balanced answer to questions like this has marked the early years of the Church of Scotland's website. The present site went online at the General Assembly of 2000. For a couple of years prior to that there had been a prototype site run by Iain Morrison, a minister who was one of the first to see the web's potential for the Church. In 2003 the hit rate had grown to twenty-five times its original size. Responses to the site from users around the world have been overwhelmingly positive and those responsible for the site, including myself, are proud of developments so far. Some of the more recent innovations like the devotional section with a prayer that changes every day or the message boards enabling comments on Church initiatives have opened the door to new online possibilities. The look, feel and accessibility of the site have all been comprehensively upgraded in a rolling programme of improvements.

I watched the site come online section by section over the course of a weekend in May 2000. It struck me very forcefully that, perhaps for the first time, it was possible to see the range and scale of the Church of Scotland in one integrated picture. It was impressive then and it still is. However, from the outset this integrated approach was under pressure from the possible development of a range of satellite sites. The proliferation of these sites would, in many ways, have mirrored the Church's rather loose, federal organisational structure. However, within a year of the site being launched, the Kirk's General Assembly agreed to a proposal from the Board of Communication that there should be one integrated site in order to promote an online experience that would be consistent in terms of quality, accessibility, user friendliness, security and safety.

To achieve this level of cooperation and integration the board offered a *quid pro quo*. In exchange for being entrusted with lead responsibility for developing an integrated site with a uniform house style, the board agreed to consult other boards and to draw them into the process of developing the protocols that would govern all aspects of the site and how it was used. An Internet Forum was set up to give flesh to this process and the guidelines for the website were drawn up in the context of an open consultation. Once these guidelines were written, all parties agreed to live under the rule of their own Internet law. To put the seal on this process, the board subsequently paid for the training of sixteen Internet 'coders' from across the Church organisation. Once trained, each of these was given the electronic key to their part of the site, which they can now update and develop within the agreed guidelines. I like to think of this as an authentically Presbyterian solution to the potential problem of disintegration – agreement being reached through including others in an open process of consultation. This form of power sharing seems to me to be close to the ethos of the Internet and, at the same time, an integral part of the Church of Scotland's culture at its best.

Of course, this has not been the end of the matter. I suspect – and sometimes even hope – that to this matter there will be no end. Pat Holdgate, head of media relations for the Kirk, has often remarked to me that the website is a journey, not a destination. There is a continuing exchange within the Church organisation on the subject of risk and where the lines should be drawn. How do we keep people safe without stifling the very thing that the web does so well – putting people right in the middle of the dialogue box? Here is the microcosm of opportunity and challenge, which I touched on earlier.

It seems to me to be significant that there are literally hundreds of pages of information on the Kirk's website and, at present, not one live dialogue box. However unfairly, this reinforces the impression – raised to almost mythological status by some critics – that the Church is much more at ease talking at people than talking with them, and that it is not very good at listening. What holds us back from having this dimension of live exchange is primarily a lack of moderators – that is Internet speak for the people who supervise the exchanges in live chat rooms, in line with Government guidelines aimed at ensuring online safety.

There seems to me to be a real irony in this, given that the courts of the Church – Kirk Sessions, Presbyteries and the Assembly itself – are all moderated. We have produced thousands of moderators over the course of our long history, yet for the want of a few more the Church has not so far been able to explore fully the interactive dimension of the Internet. There must be room here for us to stretch further and, at the very least, to recruit some virtual volunteers to be moderators in a new context. Old wine in new wineskins.

I am not suggesting that I understand fully all of the Internet's amazing potential to help the Church into a new form of connectedness. Nor am I suggesting that it is a communications panacea in this, or any other, context. What I am saying is that I believe it is worth the stretch. As Archbishop Oscar Romero of El Salvador said in his celebrated prayer:

> The kingdom of God is not only beyond our efforts, it is beyond our imagination ... Nothing we do is complete, which is another way of saying that the kingdom always lies beyond us ... We lay foundations that will need further development ... We are prophets of a future not our own.

The Role of Church of Scotland Congregations in Community Development

John Flint and Ade Kearns

Commentators have reported the declining significance of established religion within Scottish society, evident in terms of falling church membership and a reduced moral and political influence on the population. The churches' contribution to wider societal cohesiveness and inclusion is also subject to controversy, particularly in relation to the continuing debate about sectarianism in Scotland.

The Church of Scotland's recent strategic vision document *Church without Walls* both emphasises the importance of the 'local' and 'relational' processes which are the foundations of social capital, and acknowledges that building a 'church without walls' requires a renewal of the relevance of the Church within local communities and a strengthening of relations with other faiths. Pertaining to this aim, this chapter presents the findings from a national study of local Church of Scotland congregations. It assesses the extent to which the activities of congregations contribute to social capital in Scottish communities. The chapter identifies the challenges that congregations face in developing such a role and discusses the implications of the findings for the Church and policy-makers in Scotland.

Churches, Social Capital and Community Development

It is argued that Scottish churches now struggle to be relevant to the majority of the population (Reid 2002; Walker 2002) due to increasing disengagement from traditional religious participation, demonstrated in both declining church membership and attendance (Park 2002; Paterson 2002).

Within this context, the Church of Scotland published its *Church without Walls* report, setting out the Church's wider strategic vision (Church of Scotland 2001). The document explicitly argues that the Church works most effectively where congregations build relationships with the wider communities to which they belong, emphasising the importance of both *the local* and *the relational* in church work. This focus on local relations has a striking resonance with the Scottish Executive's recent policy emphasis upon achieving community renewal through ensuring that: 'Individuals and communities have the social capital – the skills, confidence and support networks to take advantage of, and increase the opportunities open to them' (Scottish Executive 2002).

The centrality of social capital to achieving governmental goals reflects a wider policy focus on strengthening local social processes as the central element of sustainable neighbourhood renewal, based on the understanding that successful policy outcomes are more likely to be achieved in civically engaged communities (SEU 2001; Putnam 1995: 19). This forms part of the 'Third Way' politics which seeks policy solutions located between the state and the market (Giddens 1998). Social capital refers to the value of cooperation and networking existent in social relations between residents and between organisations in local communities. Its most prominent advocate, the US scholar Robert Putnam (2000), defines social capital as: 'The features of social organisation such as networks, norms and trust that facilitate co-ordination and co-operation for mutual benefit.'

It is important to distinguish between two forms of social capital. *Bonding* social capital may be defined as thick social networks between like individuals (e.g., families), which enable people to 'get by', whereas *bridging* social capital comprises weaker, but wider linkages between heterogeneous individuals which provide opportunities to 'get on'. Thus strong internal social networks within deprived communities do not necessarily equate to the presence of beneficial linkages between local residents and wider social networks which embrace job markets or policy-making processes. The distinction between bonding and bridging social capital is also essential in studying the nature of relations *between* communities. This involves the recognition that strengthening social ties within groups can be a divisive process through which strong internal community bonds may be formed around perceived differences to, and the exclusion of, others (Portes and Landolt 1996). Such concerns are particularly relevant to discussions of the influence of religious sectarianism on community relations in parts of Scotland (Devine 2000; Walker 2002). In this context, the contribution, or otherwise, that churches make towards social cohesion and tolerance within a more diverse and multi-cultural society is under severe scrutiny. Distinguishing bonding from bridging social capital is also important in evaluating the extent to which the benefits of congregational activities are internalised or bring benefits to the wider community.

While social capital exists in relationships between individuals, it also defines the ability of people to work together more formally in groups and organisations (Fukuyama, 1995). Thus, the extent to which informal trust and cooperation in local communities is translated into strong institutional infrastructures, through organisations including churches, is crucial to the capacity of communities to generate both bonding and, particularly, bridging social capital (Temkin and Rohe 1998).

William Storrar has written about the potential for religious traditions in Scotland to be utilised in creating a democratic culture of active citizenship in civil society, reflecting a wider recognition that churches constitute a central element of many nations' civic orders (Storrar 1999; Ammerman 1996). The particular importance of churches as civic institutions is emphasised by Robert Putnam, who claims that congregations generate both what he terms *civically relevant values* such as public duty, compassion and concern for the excluded and *civic skills* such as those of association and organisation (Putnam 2000). Additionally, it is argued that churches provide a distinctive function in creating a sense of spiritual wellbeing, self-esteem and identity for individuals and communities (Ahmed 2001; Sweeney, Hannah and McMahon 2001).

The renewed interest in the role that faith communities may play in policy delivery and community development in the UK is illustrated in recent research identifying the importance of congregations within community regeneration strategies (Musgrove et al. 1999; Allen Hays 2001; Lewis and Randolph-Horn 2001; Sweeney, Hannah and McMahon 2001; Shaftesbury Society 2001). This interest is based upon a growing recognition of the synergy between faith groups' activities and government policy objectives relating to neighbourhood renewal, reinvigorating civic engagement and tackling social exclusion: 'Faith communities have a significant contribution to make to neighbourhood renewal and social inclusion' (DETR 1997).

This advocacy of a role for faith communities is based on their perceived strengths, including: the fact they are relatively well resourced; their strong links to their localities; their particular engagement in the most deprived and declining neighbourhoods; their ability to reach and support marginalised and excluded individuals; and their wider contribution to the cohesiveness and identity of local communities (CSM 2001; DETR 1997; Inner Cities Religious Council 2001; Ahmed 2001). The potential role of faith groups is seen as comprising both informal community activities as well as contributing to the delivery of local welfare services on a more formal basis.

However, there are concerns about the capacity of congregations to undertake a greater service delivery function. Churches have also raised concerns that, despite supportive political rhetoric, they continue to be discriminated against in community and voluntary sector funding mechanisms and excluded from partnership formation processes (Faithworks 2001; Shaftesbury Society 2001). There are also contrasts between the political support given to churches in England and Scotland. While south of the border policy documents contain explicit recognition of a distinct role for faith communities and provide mechanisms for facilitating their involvement (DETR 1997; SEU 2001), such supportive statements are less prevalent in Scotland. For example, the Scottish Executive's recent Community Regeneration Statement makes no explicit reference to churches.

The new devolutionary order in Scotland poses a challenge to the Church of Scotland (and other organised religions) to stake its claim to be heard (Walker 2002). Church of Scotland congregations' contribution to building social capital in Scottish communities represents one element in evaluating the basis on which such claims for ensuring a continuing role for the Church within local and national policy processes may be made. This chapter contributes to this debate by reporting findings from a national study of Church of Scotland congregations and discussing the implications of these findings for both the Church and policy-makers.

The Research

The study, funded by the Church of Scotland Board of Social Responsibility, was conducted between August 2001 and June 2002. It comprised a literature review, interviews with national church officers and policy-makers and a national questionnaire of ministerial charges, which achieved a 40 per cent response rate, representing 454 (one-third) of Church of Scotland congregations; including responses from every presbytery area in Scotland. In addition a series of nineteen case studies was conducted focusing on specific local church initiatives and individual congregations. A further four detailed congregation case studies involved focus groups with ministers and Church elders; postal surveys of congregation members and local residents who were not Church members (the total survey sample sizes for the four detailed case studies were 336 for congregation members and 148 for non-Church local residents). The full research findings are presented in Flint, Kearns and Atkinson (2002).

The Contexts of Congregational Activity

The survey findings affirm the concerns of commentators (Reid 2002) about the extent to which congregations reflect wider communities. While a quarter of ministers felt their congregations to be *very representative* of the local population, compared to 13 per cent who believed they were *not very representative*, the majority of ministers (61 per cent) were more ambiguous, suggesting only that their congregations were *fairly representative*. It could also be argued that congregations are to a degree primarily inward-looking, as six in ten congregations reported the main focus of their activities to be member-orientated, while 16 per cent had an evangelical emphasis. Only one in twenty congregations reported community activities to be their main focus (although a fifth of congregations reported all three of these activities as being equally important).

However, a half of surveyed ministers believed their congregation was a locally well-known and trusted organisation, with the other half of ministers believing their congregation to be partially known and trusted. The case studies found little evidence of intolerance or antagonism to the presence of churches in communities, with non-church residents having positive or neutral perceptions. However, many residents were also unaware of the involvement of churches in wider community development roles.

Congregations' Contribution to Social Capital

The survey asked a range of questions about various activities that congregations may undertake which potentially contribute to stocks of social capital within their local communities. Using responses to these questions, we generated a social capital score ranging from 1–26, signifying the extent of congregations' involvement in these activities, with twenty-six indicating the highest involvement levels (for a full account of the social capital measurement instruments see Flint, Kearns and Atkinson 2002). These specific activities were collated into four categories:

> *Local Activities*: including provision of services and facilities, disseminating information, assisting integration and resolving conflicts within local communities
>
> *Community Development*: including advocacy, involvement in local campaigns and empowering local people
>
> *Community Relations*: including relationships with other organisations, facilitating partnerships, building networks and establishing new community groups
>
> *Pride, Safety and Belonging*: the extent of the congregation's involvement in activities that generate any of these elements of social capital in local communities.

TABLE 1   *Average Social Capital Scores (All Congregations, N = 454)*

	Max. Pos.	Average
Local Activities	8	3.6
Community Development	6	1.8
Community Relations	8	3.8
Pride, Safety and Belonging	4	1.7
Social Capital Score	26	10.9

The results shown in Table 1 indicate that on average, congregations were engaged in just under half of the identified social capital generating activities, although they are relatively less likely to be involved in community development processes. This indicates the scope for congregations to be more heavily involved in these activities. Alternatively, given the institutional size of the Church of Scotland, it can be claimed that these levels of involvement represent a very substantial contribution to social capital in Scottish communities.

The findings reveal that congregations in urban and deprived areas were, on average, involved in a greater number of social capital-generating activities than congre-gations in rural or affluent communities. These findings are consistent with previous research and support the current policy focus upon churches as crucial institutions in regenerating deprived communities. Neither the size of a congregation, nor the presbytery it was located in, were found to be significant factors in levels of community involvement.

Congregations and Community Institutional Infrastructure

A key finding of the research was that much of the contribution that congregations make to local social capital is generated through their members participating in other (non-church) community organisations. A central issue here is whether members of congregations have a greater propensity for involvement in community organisations, and the extent to which the Church itself contributes to such involvement. Our survey of congregation members in three case studies (N = 296) found that 30 per cent were members of other local organisations (most commonly charitable or voluntary groups). These figures reflect the estimates given by ministers in the national postal survey.

Comparing these results to recent estimates of levels of volunteering in Scotland (Paterson 2002) suggests that congregation members appear to be proportionately more likely to be involved in volunteering than the general population. Coupled with the fact that four in ten congregation members reported being office bearers in community groups, this indicates that members of congregations play a prominent role in the institutional infrastructure of their local communities.

How far is this involvement facilitated by membership of a congregation? Seven in ten congregations indicated that individuals in the church had gone on to be involved in other community organisations. These individuals may have joined the church because they were already predisposed to participation in community groups. However, the congregation membership surveys indicated that an individual's faith and the encouragement of the Church were important factors in their wider community involvement, suggesting that congregations do make a specific contribution here.

Table 2 shows that a significant number of congregations provide support to a range of other local organisations, and voluntary sector organisations in particular. The most common form of support was the provision of meeting places (64 per cent of congregations), providing staff or volunteers (44 per cent) and offering financial assistance (39 per cent).

TABLE 2   *Local Organisations Supported by Congregations*

Types of organisation	Number	Per cent
Voluntary sector organisation	268	59.0
Religious organisation	193	42.5
Community council/forum	187	41.2
Other community group	155	34.1
Residents or tenants association	70	15.4
Other	45	9.9
(N = 454)		

The degree to which congregations are involved with local political and policy networks appears limited. Table 3 shows that congregations were most likely to be involved in partnerships with other churches or with charities and care organisations. Only a small proportion of congregations were involved in partnerships with community councils and even fewer with local authorities. Political and policy issues such as political campaigning and local regeneration are not commonly the focus of partnerships in which congregations are involved.

TABLE 3   *Congregation's Involvement in Local Partnerships*

Partner organisation	Number	Per cent
Other church	195	43.0
Local charities	108	23.8
Local care organisations	86	18.9
Community council	76	16.7
Local authorities	47	10.4
Other organisation	28	6.2

Purpose of the partnership

Community events	126	27.8
Community development	115	25.3
Local care services	111	24.4
Regeneration	56	12.3
Campaigning activity	36	7.9
Other	52	11.5
(N = 454)		

A Direct Provision Role for Congregations

Much of the recent debate about the role of congregations in community development has focused upon them providing direct services and facilities to local people. The extent to which congregations are engaged in this is illustrated in Table 4. Two-thirds (65 per cent) of congregations directly provided educational, cultural or health services to local people, with children's clubs being the most frequent service, followed by creches, cultural events, transport services and day care clubs for the elderly. However, only a quarter (27 per cent) of congregations provided self-help and personal growth services. The most common services were pre-school clubs, followed by addiction and parent support groups. Very few congregations provided employment or training services. A similar proportion of congregations (26 per cent) provided direct services to local people in immediate need, most frequently support to the homeless, with smaller numbers providing food, housing or shelter to local people.

Although these findings suggest a modest role for congregations in direct service provision they also reveal an important finding in the context of the earlier discussion about bonding or bridging social capital. One criticism of

TABLE 4   *Congregations Directly Providing Services and Facilities*

Congregations (N = 454)	N	Per cent	More than 50% of users are non-members (%)	More than 80% of users are non-members (%)
Providing educational, cultural or health services to local people	290	65.3	72	36
Providing self-help and personal growth services to local people	118	26.9	84	64
Providing direct services to local people in immediate need	117	26.0	81	65

congregations is that the gains from their activities accrue to their membership, but may not generate external benefits for wider local communities. However, the fact that over seven in ten service-providing congregations reported providing these services to a majority of non-church members suggests that this is not the case.

Reflecting the earlier findings about congregations' institutional networks, congregations have established very limited access routes to funding sources for these and other activities. While one in five congregations received funding from the Church of Scotland for a specific initiative, only 13 per cent received grants from local or national government, and less than one in ten received support from a religious or secular charity.

Table 5 shows that congregations are in general supportive of a greater role for the church in providing local services, and that a third would be interested in applying for government funding to facilitate this. Similarly, surveys

COMMUNITY DEVELOPMENT 261

TABLE 5   *Congregation's Attitudes to Funding and Service Provision*

Partner organisation	Number	Per cent
Would congregation be interested in applying for government funding to provide services to local people?		
Yes	156	34.8
No	80	17.9
Not sure	212	47.3
Should the church be seeking a greater role in the provisions of services to local people?		
Yes	229	51.7
No	74	16.7
Not sure	140	31.6

of the membership of case study congregations showed that a majority (53 per cent) across the four case studies (N = 355) wished to see more involvement in community development activities, with the remaining 47 per cent wishing to maintain their present levels of engagement. Some of the local (non-church member) residents in these areas provided indicative evidence that non-church members were receptive to a greater role for congregations in service provision. Other local community organisations in the main were also positive about the actual and potential contribution that congregations make.

It should also be noted, however, that there was a great deal of uncertainty about this issue. This is related to concerns about the capacity of congregations to undertake such activities, the appropriateness of local congregations undertaking this role rather than the national Church and disparate views about the respective roles and responsibilities of the Church and government (local and national).

The research also indicated that in many instances, congregations see their contribution as more usefully being that of enabling and supporting other local organisations already engaged in these services, as described earlier.

Congregations and Social Cohesion

A key element of the recent debate about the role for churches and other faith groups is the extent to which they are a socially cohesive or divisive presence in local communities, particularly in relation to sectarianism in some areas of Scotland. This study reveals a very strong commitment among Church of Scotland congregations to working in partnership with other faith organisations. Of congregations, 88 per cent were involved in work with other faith groups in their local area, most frequently through joint services and worship and informal meetings, but in some instances through more formal partnerships.

This collaboration is often on an ecumenical basis, with many congregations reporting attempts to reduce religious divisions in local communities through working closely with Roman Catholic congregations in joint services, public solidarity events and anti-sectarian education in local schools. The picture that emerges is of a strong ethos of inter-faith working, rather than isolated and divisive local institutions. Sectarianism, where it exists, appears to be largely perpetuated outwith congregations.

The case studies revealed that congregations often have strong links with other non-Christian faiths. In areas of Glasgow and Edinburgh, local congregations have been heavily involved in partnership working with Islamic and Sikh groups and assisting asylum seekers, including facilitating the religious practices of other faiths. Many congregations also play a role in seeking to support and integrate marginalised groups within local communities. A third (34 per cent) of congregations reported supporting young people, while a quarter of congregations reported supporting vulnerable older people, people with physical and mental disabilities, and homeless individuals. One in ten congregations had actively attempted to resolve conflicts between sections of their local community.

Beyond this, many congregations also play a role in building a sense of community identity, through involvement in community events, gala days, history projects, etc. Church premises themselves serve an important function here. Symbolically, they may represent a sign of community and continuity (particularly in declining communities); in times of community conflict church premises are viewed as neutral sites of arbitration, but also practically they offer a site for associational activity which is essential in generating interaction (both formal and informal) within communities. A majority of congregations reported making a hall or meeting rooms available to local people, suggesting that church premises are far more than 'street furniture'.

Congregations and Community Development

This paper indicates that congregations make important contributions to the institutional infrastructure and social cohesion of many Scottish communities. However, their contribution to wider community development appears more tenuous and fragile.

Table 6 shows that less than half of congregations had been approached to become involved in a local issue, and only a third had acted as advocates for the community or been involved in local community campaigns.

A number of factors appear to explain this. First, as we have already identified, many congregations do not envisage such activities as being central to their role and function and this perception is also shared by many non-church organisations and individuals so that a church congregation may be 'off-radar' locally in relation to these issues. Second, these activities are inherently controversial or divisive. Congregations, attempting to appeal to all sections of their

TABLE 6   *Congregation's Involvement in Community
Development Activities*

In the last two years has your church ...	Congregations	
	Number	Per cent
Been involved in activities that help local people define their needs?	79	17.7
Helped local people to find a solution to a local problem?	95	21.6
Been involved in any local community campaigns?	135	35.6
Represented or spoken on behalf of the community to external bodies?	144	32.5
Been approached to become involved in any local issues?	206	46.5

local community, find it difficult to simultaneously become involved in issues such as new housing developments which may divide local residents. Third, the issue of human, financial and knowledge resources is central. Many congregations expressed a desire to be more fully engaged in such community development issues, but did not believe they had the capacity to do so against competing priorities. Finally, such involvement may require both a redefining of the congregations' remit and the development of partnership working with new organisations, many of which will have little understanding of Church priorities and working processes.

However, widening and deepening congregations' engagement in community development may be crucial to the realignment of the Church's role within local communities. Involvement in community development activities often provides the most visible indication to non-church members of a congregation's secular as well as spiritual local importance. In a dynamic process, this is likely to lead to other organisations perceiving a role for congregations in local networks. Involvement in community development can also enable congregations to evolve into new areas of activity that reflect the changing needs of their local communities. This research found congregations involved in local economic development, promoting tourism and establishing credit unions. Engagement in these 'non-traditional' activities renews congregations' wider relevance to local communities.

Conclusions

Potentially the activities of congregations can be more effectively aligned with policy aims of strengthening local communities. However, facilitating a greater role for congregations in governance processes involves reconceptualising their role, in which diversity and religious priorities need to be regarded as integral to, rather than in opposition to, wider policy aims of fostering social inclusion and cohesion. This requires an understanding that the spiritual and secular dimensions of congregational activity are inherently complimentary components of the ability of congregations to contribute to local stocks of social capital. In other words, it is not possible to harness the benefits of congregational activities without recognising that these cannot be divorced from the religious priorities and practices of the Church.

For both policy-makers and congregations, this involves retaining the unique identity of the Church while recognising that it represents one voice among many. This plurality suggests a reconfiguration of how the roles of congregations are conceived within policy processes. First, it needs to be accepted that congregations pursuing greater levels of engagement within communities are generally viewed positively by both church members and non-church organisations and residents. Thus fears among policy-makers about a widespread hostility to faith groups' involvement in community development may be unfounded. Related to this issue, this research found that congregations acted as forces of social cohesion rather than exclusion, including facilitating the integration of the most marginalised groups in society. This finding indicates that the reluctance of policy-makers to engage with congregations because of their potentially divisive impact within local communities should also be reassessed.

We would recommend that churches be identified as potential partners or significant actors in a wider range of local and national policy initiatives than is presently the case. Practically, policy-makers should support the maintenance and renovation of church buildings as important sites of community interaction and activity for church and non-church residents. Further, they could facilitate funding mechanisms that enable congregations to access more readily funds to support community development activities, recognising that the centrality of faith to congregations' activities should not present insurmountable barriers to applications. The Church can provide organisational support to such activities by ensuring that there is sufficient flexibility and autonomy among congregations to engage in innovative (therefore risky) initiatives, combined with mechanisms to enable resources to be shared between congregations.

It is clear that the limited resources of local congregations necessitate their involvement in partnerships with others to secure the most effective contribution to local social capital. While partnership inevitably involves compromise, successful partnerships can be entered into without a diminution of the Church's strengths, identity and priorities. In fact, our research found that the most successful partnerships had involved an explicit declaration and understanding of the priorities and values of the partner organisations at the outset.

A related issue for the Church and policy-makers is whether congregations should become more firmly embedded in the wider voluntary sector or continue to be regarded as a unique form of organisation. We would argue that a closer alignment with the voluntary sector would enable congregations to plug into existing circuits of support, funding mechanisms and communication channels to policy-makers, from which congregations are presently relatively isolated.

Congregations' contribution to social capital is more often likely to be through the activities of individual members, and informally supporting other community organisations, rather than through formal 'church-labelled' activities. Congregations should be supported in this facilitating and enabling role as well as in any involvement in direct service delivery.

However, we would also argue that the Church itself should be aware that more formal partnerships should not be neglected. Similarly the continuing involvement of congregations in traditional community support activities should be coupled with a willingness to widen the engagement of congregations to other areas of community development such as community campaigning and advocacy. Such engagement is most likely both to empower local people and to provide the most visible demonstration of the commitment and relevance of congregations to local communities. This is crucial because a current lack of awareness of congregations' activities, among both policy-makers and local communities contributes, more than anything else, to limiting the engagement of congregations in local community development strategies.

Churches face the task of redefining their identity in ways compatible with a highly diverse and unpredictable society (Walker 2002). Similarly policy-makers face the challenge of reassessing some of the assumptions about congregations that have limited the full recognition and understanding of their contributions to social capital in Scottish communities.

In the words of one interviewee, the Church of Scotland needs to 'move from being the heart of the community to being at the heart of the community'. The implications of such a change need to be more fully thought through if the contribution of congregations to social capital and wider community development is to be maximised.

References

Ahmed, R. (2001), 'Foreword', in J. Lewis and E. Randolph-Horn, *Faiths, Hope and Participation: Celebrating Faith Groups' Role in Neighbourhood Renewal*, London: New Economics Foundation and Church Urban Fund p. 3.

Allen Hays, R. (2001), 'Habitat for Humanity: Building Social Capital through Faith Based Service', revised version of a paper presented at the 2001 Annual Meeting of the Urban Affairs Association (Detroit, MI), April 2001.

Ammerman, N. T. (1996), 'Bowling Together: Congregations and the American Civic Order', Arizona State University Department of Religious Studies Seventeenth Annual University Lecture in Religion, 26 February 1996.

Christian Socialist Movement (CSM) (2001), *Faith in Politics* (London: Christian Socialist Movement).

Church of Scotland (2001), *A Church without Walls: The Report of the Special Commission anent Review and Reform* (Edinburgh: Saint Andrew Press).

Department of the Environment, Transport and the Regions (DETR) (1997), *Involving Communities in Urban and Rural Regeneration: A Guide for Practitioners* (London: HMSO).

Devine, T. M. (ed.) (2000), *Scotland's Shame: Bigotry and Sectarianism in Modern Scotland* (Edinburgh: Mainstream).

Faithworks (2001), *Political Endorsement for the Role of Faith Groups in Community Regeneration* (Faithworks Press Release).

Flint, J., A. Kearns and R. Atkinson (2002), *The Role of Church of Scotland Congregations in Contributing to Social Capital and Community Development in Scotland* (Edinburgh: Church of Scotland).

Fukuyama, F. (1995), *Trust: The Social Virtues and the Creation of Prosperity* (London: Hamish Hamilton).

Giddens, A. (1998), *The Third Way: The Renewal of Social Democracy* (Cambridge: Polity Press).

Inner Cities Religious Council (2001), *A New Commitment to Neighbourhood Renewal* (Press Release).

Lewis, J. and E. Randolph-Horn (2001), *Faiths, Hope and Participation: Celebrating Faith Groups' Role in Neighbourhood Renewal* (London: New Economics Foundation and Church Urban Fund).

Musgrove, P., M. Chester, M. Farrands, D. Finneron and E. Venning (1999), *Flourishing Communities: Engaging Church Communities with Government in New Deal for Communities* (London: Church Action on Poverty, Churches' Community Work Alliance and the Church Urban Fund).

Park, A. (2002), 'Scotland's Morals', in J. Curtice, D. McCrone, A. Park and L. Paterson (eds), *New Scotland, New Society: Are Social and Political Ties Fragmenting?* (Edinburgh: Polygon).

Paterson, L. (2002), 'Social Capital and Constitutional Reform', in J. Curtice, D. McCrone, A. Park and L. Paterson (eds), *New Scotland, New Society: Are Social and Political Ties Fragmenting?* (Edinburgh: Polygon).

Portes, A. and P. Landolt (1996), 'The Downside of Social Capital', *The American Prospect*, 26, pp. 18–21.

Putnam, R. (1995), 'Bowling Alone: America's Declining Social Capital', *Journal of Democracy*, 6, pp. 65–78.

Putnam, R. (2000), *Bowling Alone: The Collapse and Revival of American Community* (New York: Simon & Schuster).

Reid, H. (2002), *Outside Verdict: An Old Kirk in a New Scotland* (Edinburgh: Saint Andrew Press).

Scottish Executive (2002), *Better Communities in Scotland: Closing the Gap. The Scottish Executive's Community Regeneration Statement* (Edinburgh: Scottish Executive).

Shaftesbury Society (2001), *Faith Makes Community Work* (available at www.faithandcommunity.org.uk).

Social Exclusion Unit (SEU) (2001), *The New Commitment to Neighbourhood Renewal: A National Strategy Action Plan* (London: Social Exclusion Unit).

Storrar, W. (1999), 'Three Portraits of Scottish Calvinism', in R. D. Kernohan (ed.), *Realm of Reform* (Edinburgh: Handsel Press).

Sweeney, J., D. Hannah and K. McMahon (2001), *From Story to Policy: Social Exclusion, Empowerment and the Churches* (Cambridge: Von Hugel Institute).

Temkin, K. and W. Rohe (1998), 'Social Capital and Neighbourhood Stability: An Empirical Investigation', *Housing Policy Debate*, 9(1), pp. 61–88.

Walker, G. (2002), 'The Role of Religion and the Church', in G. Hassan and C. Warhurst (eds), *Anatomy of the New Scotland: Power, Influence and Change* (Edinburgh: Mainstream).